Geography

Key Stage 2

Scotland P4-P7

Stephen Scoffham

Colin Bridge

Terry Jewson

First published in 1996 by:
Stanley Thornes (Publishers) Ltd

Reprinted in 2001 by:
Nelson Thornes Ltd
Delta Place
27 Bath Road
CHELTENHAM
GL53 7TH
United Kingdom

05 / 10 9 8 7 6

A catalogue record of this book is available from the British Library

ISBN 0 7487 3595 X

Printed and bound in Great Britain by Ashford Colour Press Ltd, Gosport, Hants

CONTENTS

Welcome to Learning Targets iv

Introduction vi

Links to the National Curriculum viii

The weather 2

UNIT 1 Types of weather 4

UNIT 2 Seasons 8

UNIT 3 Weather worldwide 12

Rivers 16

UNIT 4 River systems 18

UNIT 5 Shaping the land 22

UNIT 6 The River Rhine 26

UNIT 7 The River Nile 30

Settlement 34

UNIT 8 Finding shelter 36

UNIT 9 Villages 40

UNIT 10 Towns 44

UNIT 11 Cities 48

Work 52

UNIT 12 Farming 54

UNIT 13 Making things 58

UNIT 14 Services 62

Transport 66

UNIT 15 Routes and journeys 68

UNIT 16 Types of transport 72

UNIT 17 Transport problems 76

UNIT 18 Links around the world 80

Environment 84

UNIT 19 Caring for the countryside 86

UNIT 20 Caring for towns 90

UNIT 21 Water 94

UNIT 22 Rainforests 98

School buildings 102

UNIT 23 Exploring your school 104

UNIT 24 Areas in school 108

UNIT 25 School improvements 112

Local area 116

UNIT 26 Your local area 118

UNIT 27 Special character 122

UNIT 28 Change 126

UNIT 29 Local issues 130

United Kingdom 134

UNIT 30 All about the UK 136

UNIT 31 Weymouth 140

UNIT 32 Llandrindod Wells 144

UNIT 33 Elgin 148

Europe 152

UNIT 34 All about Europe 154

UNIT 35 European tour 158

UNIT 36 Four European countries 162

Our world 166

UNIT 37 Planet Earth 168

UNIT 38 Africa 172

UNIT 39 Asia 176

UNIT 40 South America 180

Bibliography 184

Welcome to
LEARNING TARGETS

Learning Targets is a series of practical teacher's resource books written to help you to plan and deliver well-structured, professional lessons in line with all the relevant curriculum documents.

Each Learning Target book provides exceptionally clear lesson plans that cover the whole of its stated curriculum plus a large bank of carefully structured copymasters. Links to the key curriculum documents are provided throughout to enable you to plan effectively.

The Learning Targets series has been written in response to the challenge confronting teachers not just to come up with teaching ideas that cover the curriculum but to ensure that they deliver high quality lessons every lesson with the emphasis on raising standards of pupil achievement.

The recent thinking from OFSTED, and the National Literacy and Numeracy Strategies on the key factors in effective teaching has been built into the structure of Learning Targets. These might be briefly summarised as follows:

➤→ that effective teaching is active teaching directed to very clear objectives
➤→ that good lessons are delivered with pace, rigour and purpose
➤→ that good teaching requires a range of strategies – including interactive whole class sessions
➤→ that ongoing formative assessment is essential to plan children's learning
➤→ that differentiation is necessary but that it must be realistic.

The emphasis in Learning Targets is on absolute clarity. We have written and designed the books to enable you to access and deliver effective lessons as easily as possible, with the following aims:

➤→ to plan and deliver rigorous, well-structured lessons
➤→ to set explicit targets for achievement in every lesson that you teach
➤→ to make the children aware of what they are going to learn
➤→ to put the emphasis on direct, active teaching every time
➤→ to make effective use of time and resources
➤→ to employ the full range of recommended strategies whole-class, group and individual work
➤→ to differentiate for ability groups realistically
➤→ to use ongoing formative assessment to plan your next step
➤→ to have ready access to usable pupil copymasters to support your teaching.

The page opposite provides an at-a-glance guide to the key features of the Learning Targets lessons and explains how they will enable you deliver effective lessons. The key to symbols on the lesson plans is set out here. ➤→

How to deliver structured lessons with pace, rigour and purpose

Explicit targets for achievement in every lesson

The concise subject knowledge you need

Crystal clear lesson plan layouts

Homework suggestions

Rigorous and practical activities

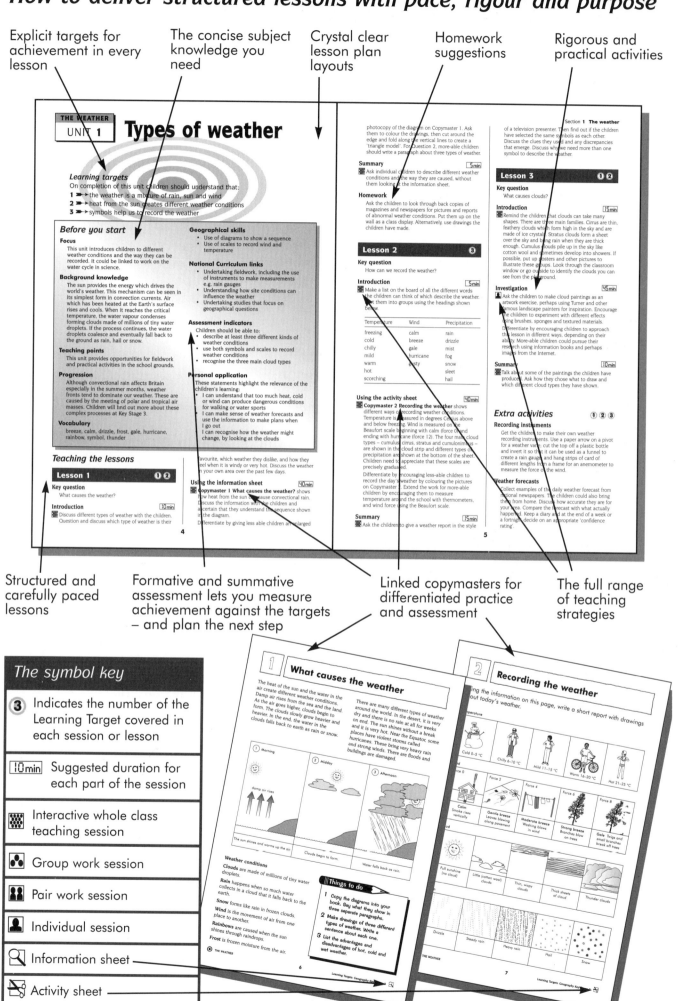

Structured and carefully paced lessons

Formative and summative assessment lets you measure achievement against the targets – and plan the next step

Linked copymasters for differentiated practice and assessment

The full range of teaching strategies

The symbol key

③	Indicates the number of the Learning Target covered in each session or lesson
10 min	Suggested duration for each part of the session
⚫	Interactive whole class teaching session
⚫⚫	Group work session
👥	Pair work session
👤	Individual session
🔍	Information sheet
✂	Activity sheet

INTRODUCTION

Geography is the study of people and places. It introduces children to the world with all its variety and contrasts, as part of a broad and balanced curriculum. Children are naturally curious about their immediate surroundings. They also want to learn about places beyond their direct experience. Geography satisfies these demands and teaches children a variety of skills including mapwork, fieldwork and how to record and analyse information.

Geography in the National Curriculum

The aims of geographical education (DES 1990) are to:

(a) stimulate pupils' interest in their surroundings and in the variety of physical and human conditions on the Earth's surface
(b) foster their sense of wonder at the beauty of the world around them
(c) help them to develop an informed concern about the quality of the environment and the future of the human habitat
(d) thereby enhance their sense of responsibility for the care of the Earth and its peoples

Geography in the twenty-first century

Geography can contribute unique elements to the curriculum for the next century. As well as developing essential thinking and learning skills, geography makes an important contribution to pupils' emotional and spiritual development. Research shows that children as young as three and four years old are able to complete basic route finding and mapwork exercises. Ideas about different peoples and cultures also appear to reach back to early childhood. The foundations of geographical thinking need to be laid down in primary school so that pupils are not disadvantaged in later life. Positive ideas about different peoples and places are best developed at this stage. (*See* Figure 1)

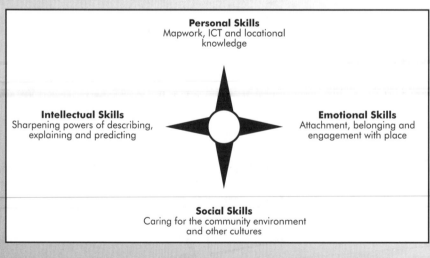

Personal Skills
Mapwork, ICT and locational knowledge

Intellectual Skills
Sharpening powers of describing, explaining and predicting

Emotional Skills
Attachment, belonging and engagement with place

Social Skills
Caring for the community environment and other cultures

Figure 1
How geography can contribute to a curriculum of the future
(after Bridge 1998)

Learning Targets Geography

Learning Targets Geography covers eleven topics each of which is divided into three or four units. These provide full coverage of the National Curriculum requirements and include extensive opportunities for fieldwork and practical investigations. Links to the current expectations and standards are identified throughout the book and are also summarised in the tables on page viii.

The lessons and ideas in *Learning Targets Geography* have been devised in the light of current experience and research into successful geography teaching. Effective teaching needs to take account of children's misconceptions. For example, even upper juniors often offer highly confused explanations of physical processes such as landscape formation and changes in weather. Considerable care has been taken to ensure that the material is conceptually appropriate to the child's level of ability.

Technical vocabulary also presents difficulties for many pupils. For this reason, the lesson plans have been designed to encourage children to reflect upon their learning. Specific word lists are also included in the notes for each lesson.

Figure 2   Geography seen from the child's perspective

We believe that geography offers children, whatever their ability, a raft of skills and understanding that will be of relevance to them as they grow into adulthood (See Figure 2). It also provides them with a unique vision of the world. These are essential ingredients in an effective education for the future.

Links to the National Curriculum

The guidance issued by the Secretary of State for Education states that from September 1988 to September 2000 all schools providing for Key Stages 1 and 2 will be required to teach a broad and balanced curriculum including the ten National Curriculum subjects and religious education.

A brief statement summarises the nature of geography at Key Stage 2 in the following terms:

At Key Stage 2, children investigate and learn about people, places and environments at different scales, in the United Kingdom and overseas. They learn how places are linked to one another and to the wider world. Studying geography involves fieldwork, and developing and using a range of geographical enquiry skills. (QCA 1998)

Expectations in geography at Key Stage 2

	Character of places	Location of key places	Patterns	Change	Environment	Investigations
The weather	●		●			●
Rivers			●			
Settlement	●	●				●
Work	●					●
Transport		●	●		●	●
Environment	●				●	●
School buildings			●		●	●
Local area				●		●
United Kingdom	●	●		●		
Europe	●	●				
Our world	●	●				

Links to the programme of study

	England and Wales								Scotland (Social Studies P4–P6)						Northern Ireland			
	Local area	Contrasting UK localities	Distant localities	Weather	Rivers	Settlement	Environment	Skills	Comparative study in Britain	Comparative study in Europe	Physical and built environment	Interaction between people and places	Location, linkages and networks	Making and using maps	Weather	People	Environment	Skills
The weather	●			●			●	●				●	●		●			●
Rivers			●	●				●		●				●		●		●
Settlement	●	●				●		●	●			●	●			●		●
Work	●					●		●					●			●		●
Transport	●		●				●	●					●	●	●	●	●	●
Environment		●					●	●			●	●					●	●
School buildings	●					●	●	●				●		●		●	●	●
Local area	●					●	●	●	●			●				●	●	●
United Kingdom		●						●	●							●	●	●
Europe				●				●		●			●			●		●
Our world			●	●				●			●			●	●			●

viii

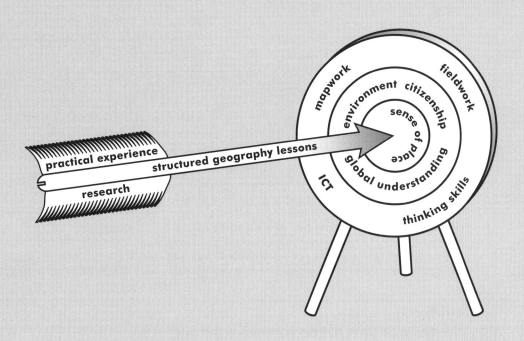

Learning Targets Geography provides structured lessons based on practical
experience and research, giving full coverage of the elements, skills and
understanding specified in the National Curriculum and highlighting links to
other subjects and ways of thinking

THE WEATHER

Focus

The energy which drives the world's weather all comes from the sun. The sun's rays heat the Earth's surface and warms the surrounding air. As the air gets hotter, it expands, becomes less dense and rises. Cold air then flows in to take its place. On a global scale, this process accounts for different weather systems.

Generally, the atmosphere is hottest at the Equator and coldest at the Poles. This difference in air pressure creates winds. It also causes rain as hot and cold air mix.

In the UK, we have a temperate climate which is influenced by different types of air. The weather changes as we move from one air mass to another.

North-west winds bring cold, damp air from Greenland

North-east winds bring cold, dry air from Russia

South-east winds bring hot, dry air from Africa

South-west winds bring hot, damp air from the Caribbean

Brainstorm

Use this brainstorm to help you develop a medium-term plan.

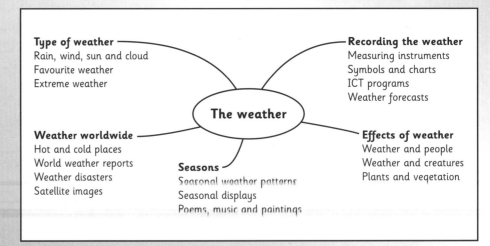

Type of weather
Rain, wind, sun and cloud
Favourite weather
Extreme weather

Recording the weather
Measuring instruments
Symbols and charts
ICT programs
Weather forecasts

The weather

Weather worldwide
Hot and cold places
World weather reports
Weather disasters
Satellite images

Seasons
Seasonal weather patterns
Seasonal displays
Poems, music and paintings

Effects of weather
Weather and people
Weather and creatures
Plants and vegetation

Research findings

Many junior school children find it difficult to explain weather processes. They think that rain is caused by clouds 'bursting', 'disintegrating' or 'colliding' (Moyle 1980). They are confused by the wind which they sometimes suggest is caused by 'aeroplanes going past'. Other children invoke the moon and the stars to explain weather phenomena (Wiegand 1993). For these reasons, it is valuable to start by getting children to observe, experience and record the weather. This is something which can best be pursued through work in the school grounds. There are also good reasons for focusing on day to day conditions. Many children find it difficult to generalise and so are unable to appreciate the notion of climate. They can, however, understand extremes of weather experienced in deserts, rainforests and polar regions.

Content

Unit 1   Introduces children to different weather conditions and descriptive vocabulary.

Unit 2   Considers seasons which involves the notion of long-term pattern.

Unit 3   Looks at weather around the world by focusing on very hot and very cold places.

National Curriculum expectations

By the end of Key Stage 2, it is expected that most children will be able to:
- explain the physical and human characteristics of places, and their similarities and differences
- explain patterns of physical and human features

Literacy links

Year 3   Collect new words: Unit 1 *Types of weather*, Lesson 2. Write notes: Unit 3 *Weather worldwide*, Lesson 1.

Year 4   Collect poems based on common themes: Unit 2 *Seasons*, Extra activities, Season poems. Collect and collate information from a variety of sources: Unit 3 *Weather worldwide*, Lesson 3.

Year 5   Write reports e.g. news reports, weather forecasts, weather disasters: Unit 3 *Weather worldwide*, Lesson 3. Use content from other subjects: Unit 3 *Weather worldwide*, Extra activities, Weather reports.

Story

Our House on the Hill by Philippe Dupasquier (Andersen Press 1988) uses pictures to show how the weather changes month by month throughout the year.

ICT links

CD-ROM   *Weather Mapper* (TAG 1994) allows children to make their own weather forecasts by moving symbols across a map of the UK. It also has a section for recording and storing weather data.

Internet   A great deal of weather data from places around the world is available on the Internet along with reports of weather events.

Satellite images   Many children will see satellite images on television weather forecasts and it makes sense to build on this experience.

UNIT 1   Types of weather

Learning targets

On completion of this unit children should understand that:

1 ➡➤ the weather is a mixture of rain, sun and wind
2 ➡➤ heat from the sun creates different weather conditions
3 ➡➤ symbols help us to record the weather

Before you start

Focus

This unit introduces children to different weather conditions and the way they can be recorded. It could be linked to work on the water cycle in science.

Background knowledge

The sun provides the energy which drives the world's weather. This mechanism can be seen in its simplest form in convection currents. Air which has been heated at the Earth's surface rises and cools. When it reaches the critical temperature, the water vapour condenses forming clouds made of millions of tiny water droplets. If the process continues, the water droplets coalesce and eventually fall back to the ground as rain, hail or snow.

Teaching points

This unit provides opportunities for fieldwork and practical activities in the school grounds.

Progression

Although convectional rain affects Britain especially in the summer months, weather fronts tend to dominate our weather. These are caused by the meeting of polar and tropical air masses. Children will find out more about these complex processes at Key Stage 3.

Vocabulary

breeze, calm, drizzle, frost, gale, hurricane, rainbow, symbol, thunder

Geographical skills

- Use of diagrams to show a sequence
- Use of scales to record wind and temperature

National Curriculum links

- Undertaking fieldwork, including the use of instruments to make measurements e.g. rain gauges
- Understanding how site conditions can influence the weather
- Undertaking studies that focus on geographical questions

Assessment indicators

Children should be able to:
- describe at least three different kinds of weather conditions
- use both symbols and scales to record weather conditions
- recognise the three main cloud types

Personal application

These statements highlight the relevance of the children's learning:
- I can understand that too much heat, cold or wind can produce dangerous conditions for walking or water sports
- I can make sense of weather forecasts and use the information to make plans when I go out
- I can recognise how the weather might change, by looking at the clouds

Teaching the lessons

Lesson 1   ① ②

Key question

What causes the weather?

Introduction   10min

▨ Discuss different types of weather with the children. Question and discuss which type of weather is their favourite, which weather they dislike, and how they feel when it is windy or very hot. Discuss the weather in your own area over the past few days.

Using the information sheet   40min

▨ **Copymaster I What causes the weather?** shows how heat from the sun can cause convectional rain. Discuss the information with the children and ascertain that they understand the sequence shown in the diagram.

Differentiate by giving less-able children an enlarged

photocopy of the diagram on Copymaster 1. Ask them to colour the drawings, then cut around the edge and fold along the vertical lines to create a 'triangle model'. For Question 2, more-able children should write a paragraph about three types of weather.

Summary

5 min

▓ Ask individual children to describe different weather conditions and the way they are caused, without them looking at the information sheet.

Homework

Ask the children to look through back copies of magazines and newspapers for pictures and reports of abnormal weather conditions. Put them up on the wall as a class display. Alternatively, use drawings the children have made.

Lesson 2 ③

Key question

How can we record the weather?

Introduction

5 min

▓ Make a list on the board of all the different words the children can think of which describe the weather. Sort them into groups using the headings shown below.

Temperature	Wind	Precipitation
freezing	calm	rain
cold	breeze	drizzle
chilly	gale	mist
mild	hurricane	fog
warm	gusty	snow
hot		sleet
scorching		hail

Using the activity sheet

40 min

▓ **Copymaster 2 Recording the weather** shows different ways of recording weather conditions. Temperature is measured in degrees Celsius above and below freezing. Wind is measured on the Beaufort scale beginning with calm (force 0) and ending with hurricane (force 12). The four main cloud types – cumulus, cirrus, stratus and cumulonimbus – are shown in the cloud strip and different types of precipitation are shown at the bottom of the copymaster. Children need to appreciate that these scales are precisely graduated.

Differentiate by encouraging less-able children to record the day's weather by colouring the pictures on Copymaster 2. Extend the work for more-able children by encouraging them to measure temperature around the school with thermometers, and wind force using the Beaufort scale.

Summary

15 min

▓ Ask the children to give a weather report in the style

of a television presenter. Then find out if the children have selected the same symbols as each other. Discuss the clues they used and any discrepancies that emerge. Discuss why we need more than one symbol to describe the weather.

Lesson 3 ① ②

Key question

What causes clouds?

Introduction

15 min

▓ Remind the children that clouds can take many shapes. There are three main families. Cirrus are thin, feathery clouds which form high in the sky and are made of ice crystals. Stratus clouds form sheets over the sky and bring rain when they are thick enough. Cumulus clouds pile up in the sky like cotton wool and sometimes develop into showers. If possible, put up posters and other pictures to illustrate these groups. Look through the classroom window or go outside to identify the clouds you can see from the playground.

Investigation

45 min

👤 Ask the children to make cloud paintings as an artwork exercise, perhaps using Turner and other famous landscape painters for inspiration. Encourage the children to experiment with different effects using brushes, sponges and textured materials.

Differentiate by encouraging children to approach this lesson in different ways, depending on their ability. More-able children could pursue their research using reference books and perhaps images from the Internet.

Summary

10 min

▓ Talk about some of the paintings the children have produced. Ask how they chose what to draw and which different cloud types they have shown.

Extra activities

Recording instruments

Get the children to make their own weather recording instruments. Use a paper arrow on a pivot for a weather vane; cut the top off a plastic bottle and invert it so that it can be used as a funnel to create a rain gauge; and hang strips of card of different lengths from a frame for an anemometer to measure the force of the wind.

Weather forecasts

Collect examples of the daily weather forecast from national newspapers. The children could also bring them from home. Discuss how accurate they are for your area. Compare the forecast with what actually happened. Keep a diary and at the end of a week or a fortnight decide on an appropriate 'confidence rating'.

What causes the weather?

The heat of the sun and the water in the air create different weather conditions. Damp air rises from the sea and the land. As the air goes higher, clouds begin to form. The clouds slowly grow heavier and heavier. In the end, the water in the clouds falls back to earth as rain or snow.

There are many different types of weather around the world. In the desert, it is very dry and there is no rain at all for weeks on end. The sun shines without a break and it is very hot. Near the Equator, some places have violent storms called hurricanes. These bring very heavy rain and strong winds. There are floods and buildings are damaged.

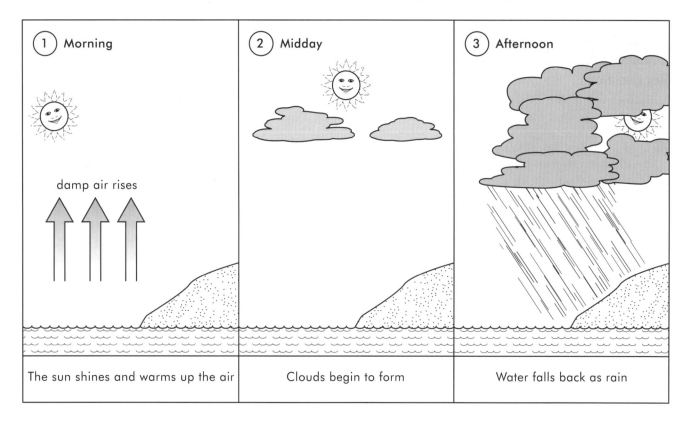

1 Morning — damp air rises — The sun shines and warms up the air

2 Midday — Clouds begin to form

3 Afternoon — Water falls back as rain

Weather conditions

Clouds are made of millions of tiny water droplets.

Rain happens when so much water collects in a cloud that it falls back to the earth.

Snow forms like rain in frozen clouds.

Wind is the movement of air from one place to another.

Rainbows are caused when the sun shines through raindrops.

Frost is frozen moisture from the air.

Things to do

1 Copy the diagrams into your book. Say what they show in three separate paragraphs.

2 Make drawings of three different types of weather. Write a sentence about each one.

3 List the advantages and disadvantages of hot, cold and wet weather.

Recording the weather

Using the information on this page, write a short report with drawings about today's weather.

Temperature

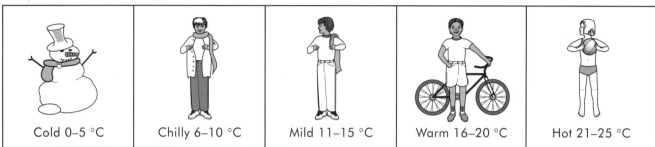

| Cold 0–5 °C | Chilly 6–10 °C | Mild 11–15 °C | Warm 16–20 °C | Hot 21–25 °C |

Wind

Force 0	Force 2	Force 4	Force 6	Force 8
Calm Smoke rises vertically	**Gentle breeze** Leaves blowing along pavement	**Moderate breeze** Washing blows in wind	**Strong breeze** Branches blow on trees	**Gale** Twigs and small branches break off trees

Cloud

| Full sunshine (no cloud) | Little (cotton wool) clouds | Thin, wispy clouds | Thick sheets of cloud | Thunder clouds |

Rain

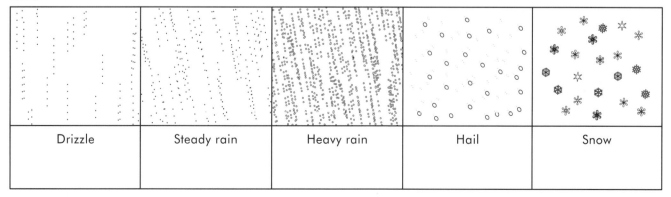

| Drizzle | Steady rain | Heavy rain | Hail | Snow |

Seasons

Learning targets

On completion of this unit children should understand that:

1 ➤➤ there is a pattern to the seasons throughout the year
2 ➤➤ the changing seasons affect people, plants and creatures

Before you start

Focus

The interaction between the seasons (physical environment) and natural life is considered in this unit. The descriptions and examples only apply to the UK and other mid-latitude locations which have four seasons of roughly equal length.

Background knowledge

The seasons are caused by the tilt of the Earth's axis. In June, in the northern hemisphere, the sun appears high in the sky. This results in long hours of daylight and warm temperatures. In December, in the northern hemisphere, the sun appears low in the sky. This results in long hours of darkness and low temperatures. The sequence of seasons lasts a year because it takes a year for the Earth to orbit the sun.

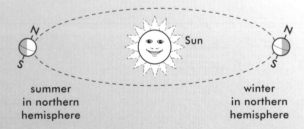

summer
in northern
hemisphere

Sun

winter
in northern
hemisphere

Teaching points

This unit considers seasons only in the UK. Other parts of the world have different patterns e.g. monsoon in SE Asia and wet and dry seasons in the tropics.

Progression

Children will learn more about what causes the seasons at Key Stage 3. It is sufficient for juniors to know that the seasons change in a regular manner and how this affects us.

Vocabulary

autumn, change, festivals, life cycle, pattern, season, spring, summer, winter

Geographical skills

- Recognition of patterns
- Identification of change
- Ability to make a sequence diagram
- Use of a season dial

National Curriculum links

- Recognising seasonal weather patterns
- Developing the ability to recognise patterns
- Analysing evidence, drawing conclusions and communicating findings

Assessment indicators

Children should be able to:
- describe the characteristics of each season
- explain how the seasons affect us

Personal application

These statements highlight the relevance of the children's learning:
- I understand that some activities are better suited to one season than another
- I understand how gardens and the countryside change with the seasons
- I understand that the seasons affect food production

Teaching the lessons

Lesson 1   ① ②

Key question

In what ways do the seasons change?

Introduction   10 min

▨ Talk about the seasons with the children to find out

what they already know and to focus their attention. The following questions and answers are appropriate.

What are the four seasons? (Winter, spring, summer, autumn.)

Which is the current season and what are its characteristics? (Get the children to consider the weather, temperature, daylight, people, plants and natural life and leisure activities in their answers.)

How long does each season last? (There are different ways of defining the seasons. It is simplest to think of each one lasting three months with winter starting in December and finishing at the end of February.)

Using the information sheet [40 min]

Copymaster 3 Seasons reinforces the notion of seasonal change by considering the way people respond to the weather. This cycle is particularly apparent in the natural world where plants and creatures follow the same pattern year in, year out.

Differentiate by encouraging less-able children to concentrate on Question 1, writing a sentence about each season and making a drawing to go with it. More-able children might find out about the life cycles of other creatures. Swallows and other migratory birds are particularly interesting examples.

Summary [10 min]

Ask the children to say one thing about the weather, about natural life and about human activities for each of the four seasons. Record their answers in a grid on the board.

Homework

Set up a seasonal display. Ask the children to contribute items which are characteristic of the season.

Lesson 2

Key question

How can we record the seasons?

Introduction [5 min]

Remind the children of work they did in the previous lesson. Questions to ask:

Why do the seasons matter to people? (The seasons affect the clothes we wear, how we spend our spare time and the festivals we celebrate.)

How do the seasons affect plants? (Most plants follow a seasonal sequence of growing, flowering and making seeds.)

How do the seasons affect animals? (Many animals rear their young in the spring and summer.)

Using the activity sheet [40 min]

Give each child **Copymaster 4 Season dial**. Check that the children understand how to complete the dial by discussing how they might complete one of the sectors such as winter.

Differentiate by encouraging children to complete the dial according to their varying levels of ability. Drawings will feature strongly in the work of less-able children while more-able children will make greater use of notes and labels.

Summary [15 min]

Ask the children to cut out their dials from Copymaster 4 and mount them as a class display. Emphasise high-quality work and significant achievements by getting individual children to describe their work to the rest of the class.

Lesson 3

Key question

How do the seasons affect the farmer's year?

Introduction [10 min]

Farmers are particularly affected by the seasons because they work with plants and animals.

Farm study [60 min]

Make a study of a farm. The children could either work from books or you could arrange a visit to a farm in your area. Make separate charts to show the seasonal cycles for animal husbandry, grain crops and fruit crops. Find out about the different jobs the farmer does and how these vary during the year.

Differentiate by allowing this lesson to be tackled at different levels according to the ability of the children.

Summary [10 min]

Ask the children to write down the three most interesting things they have learnt. Compare the things they have selected.

Extra activities

Season snap

Get the children to devise a pack of cards with labelled drawings of different seasonal clues to use in snap. You might divide the children into groups for this exercise. Remember, they will need to make at least two copies of each image in order to play the game.

Season poems

Look in poetry anthologies and other sources for seasonal poems. Discuss the main features of the poems then ask the children to write their own versions. Completed poems can be displayed alongside geography information. Ask the children to copy them out in their best handwriting for a class booklet.

Season music

Get the children to listen to different pieces of music that celebrate the seasons. Vivaldi's *Four Seasons* is an obvious example but less well-known works include Vaughan William's *English Folk Song Suite* and Tchaikovsky's 'Waltz of the Flowers' from the *Nutcracker Suite*. There are also plenty of seasonal songs which feature prominently in popular anthologies.

Seasons

Although the weather changes from day to day, a season lasts for several months.

In winter, the days are short and dark and the weather is cold.

In spring, plants begin to grow and birds build their nests as the days get longer.

Summer brings long, sunny days and higher temperatures.

In autumn, the days get darker and leaves on trees turn yellow, red and brown, and die.

These changes give a pattern to the year. In winter, we celebrate Christmas. In the summer, people go away on long holidays. Harvest festival is one of the events of the autumn. Easter is linked with the spring.

The seasons also affect our lives in other ways. The games that we play, the clothes that we wear and the food that we eat change through the year. The seasons even affect how we feel.

Frog life cycle

Animals and insects have life cycles which are linked to the weather in each season.

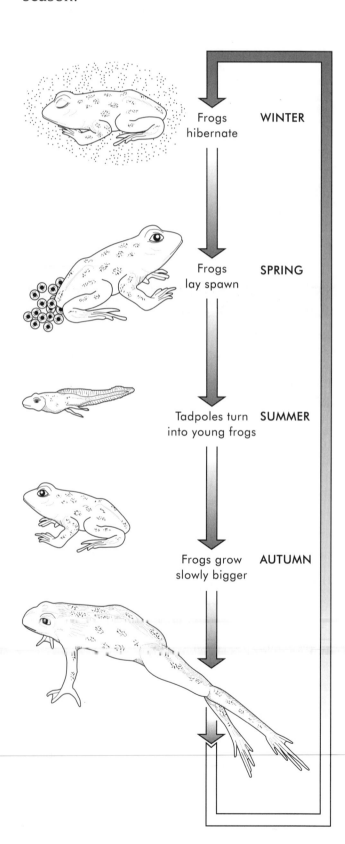

Frogs hibernate   WINTER

Frogs lay spawn   SPRING

Tadpoles turn into young frogs   SUMMER

Frogs grow slowly bigger   AUTUMN

Things to do

1 Write a sentence about each different season.

2 Name one food you like to eat in each season.

3 Copy the diagram of the frog's life cycle into your book.

4 Which is your favourite season? Say why.

Season dial

1. Write the name of the seasons in the centre of the dial.

2. Describe the weather in the first empty ring.

3. Make labelled drawings of plants and creatures to match each season in the second empty ring.

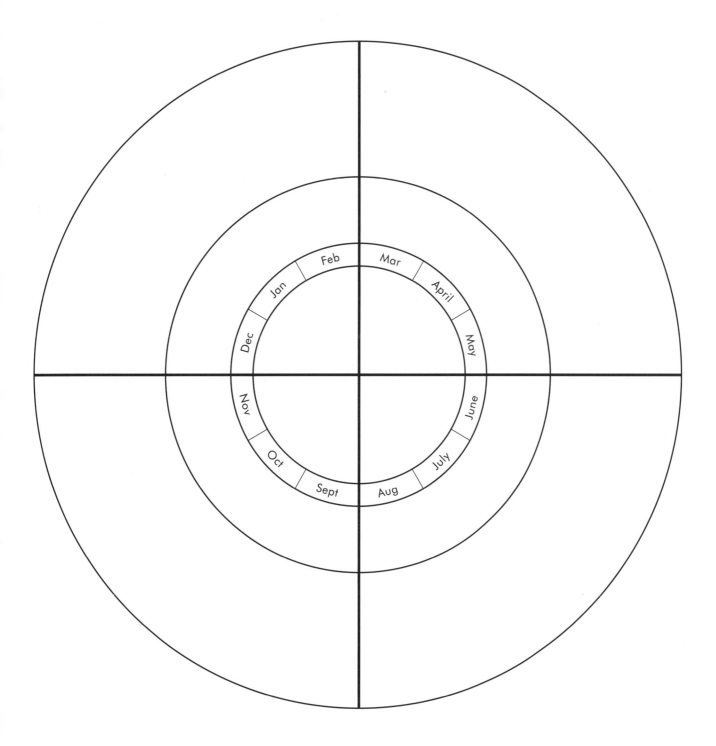

Weather worldwide

Learning targets

On completion of this unit children should understand that:

1 ➡➡ long-term weather patterns make a climate
2 ➡➡ there are different climates around the world

Before you start

Focus

This unit introduces a global dimension by looking at polar, desert and rainforest climates.

Background knowledge

In the United Kingdom, the climate is relatively moderate. Many other parts of the world have harsher conditions. In general terms, the weather is hottest at the Equator and coldest at the poles. This pattern is disrupted by three important factors. Firstly, equatorial regions are often covered with cloud which moderates the temperature. Secondly, large blocks of land heat up faster and cool down faster than the surrounding ocean. Thirdly, temperature drops with altitude (approximately 1 °C every hundred metres) so the highest mountains are covered in snow and ice throughout the year.

Teaching points

The impact of a climate is most readily demonstrated through flora and fauna. If possible, set up a display of photographs to help establish the variety of habitats in different climate regions.

Progression

Some children will have studied hot and cold places at Key Stage 1. In this unit, they find out more about key climate types around the world.

Vocabulary

climate, coastal, desert, Equator, polar, rainfall, rainforest, temperature, wind

Geographical skills

*   Ability to interpret a bar chart
*   Identification of places on a world map
*   Use of an atlas

National Curriculum links

*   Recognising weather conditions in different parts of the world
*   Using ICT to gain access to additional information sources and to assist in handling, classifying and presenting evidence

Assessment indicators

Children should be able to:
*   explain the difference between weather and climate
*   describe some major climate types
*   identify, on a map, places with different climates

Personal application

These statements highlight the relevance of the children's learning:
*   I can imagine living in places where there are extremes of weather
*   I appreciate that places a long way from the UK may have different weather conditions
*   I understand that creatures are very adaptable and can survive harsh weather conditions

Teaching the lessons

Lesson 1 ① ②

Key question

What different patterns of weather are there around the world?

Introduction   10 min

▦ Ascertain what the children already know about

different weather patterns around the world. You may find it helpful to show the children the Equator on a globe by way of preparation. The following questions and answers are appropriate.

Where are the coldest places in the world? (The North and South Poles.)

Where are the hottest places? (The Sahara, Middle East and other desert areas.)

Where are the wettest places? (The African and Amazonian rainforests and the eastern Himalayas.)

Using the information sheet `40min`

 Using **Copymaster 5 World climate**, ascertain that the children understand the bar charts and pictograms at the bottom. The pictograms indicate typical weather conditions; the line graphs show average temperatures; and the bar charts show rainfall figures.

Differentiate by encouraging less-able children to colour the charts at the bottom of the copymaster instead of completing Question 4. More-able children could add information from reference sources to their notes on the different climates.

Summary `10min`

Discuss with the children which of the three climates would present the most problems for travellers and explorers and the reasons why.

Homework

Ask the children to collect three photographs from magazines showing different weather conditions around the world and to write a description of each one.

Lesson 2 ②

Key question

How can climate zones be shown on a map?

Introduction `5min`

Remind the class that climate is a description of the weather patterns in an area measured over a long period of time and that this varies around the world. Different parts of the world have different climates.

Using the activity sheet `35min`

On **Copymaster 6 World climates**, ensure that the children understand the map. Begin by locating the UK and areas of land and sea. Then talk about the climate zones. The rainforest areas are distributed almost equally around the Equator with bands of desert on either side. The polar climate occurs in northern Canada and Russia. It is also found in Antarctica but this is not shown on the map.

Differentiate by enlarging the map on a photocopier and asking less-able children to complete only the first activity. Ask more-able children to draw pictures of people dressed for each of the three climates with notes explaining the need for different items of clothing.

Summary `5min`

Ask the children some questions to reinforce their understanding. Which three continents have significant areas of rainforest? Which continent is almost all desert? What climate type seems to occupy the largest area?

Lesson 3 ① ②

Key question

How do different climates affect animals?

Introduction `10min`

Make a list on the board of all the creatures the children can think of from each of the different climate zones.

Investigation `30min`

 Ask each child to choose one of the creatures and to make a drawing of it and write a short description. They could use magazines and reference books to help them find out more. Put their work into a class dictionary with a different creature for each letter of the alphabet or display it round the walls as a frieze.

Differentiate by encouraging less-able children to concentrate on drawing their creature, naming it and describing the climate it prefers. More-able children can give details of food, habitat and life cycle. They should also find out about any environmental threats and conservation initiatives.

Summary `10min`

Ask individual children to show their work and report on their findings to the rest of the class.

Extra activities ②

Famous explorers

Divide the children into groups and ask them to find out about different explorers such as Columbus, Magellan, Drake, Cook, Burton and Marco Polo. They should find out where they went, what different climates they encountered and how they coped. Younger children could write brief notes, older children could prepare simple biographies.

Weather reports

Get the children to write their own accounts of weather disasters in different parts of the world, using media reports (radio or television news) as sources of information. Encourage them to include maps and drawings if possible.

World climate

The hottest places on Earth are around the Equator. Here, the sun is almost directly overhead. The rays fall straight on to the surface and heat it up. Away from the Equator, the sun is lower in the sky. The rays are weaker so the air does not get so warm. The coldest places are around the North and South Poles.

Some places are much wetter than others. The wind brings rain from the sea to places near the coast. Mountains also have a lot of rain. Here, winds blow over the peaks and the air sheds water as it rises. The driest places are deserts. In some parts of Chile in South America, there has been no rain for several hundred years.

The pattern of weather over many years is called the climate. In the UK, we have a coastal climate. This means it never gets very hot or cold and we have a fair amount of rain. The polar, rainforest and desert climates are very different.

Things to do

1 Why are the hottest places near the Equator?

2 Why are some places wetter than others?

3 What is a climate?

4 Write notes on polar, desert and rainforest climates.

Polar climate

Dry and cold. Snow and ice last all the year. Very few plants and creatures survive.

Desert climate

Very dry and hot. Storms cause floods once every few years.

Rainforest climate

Wet and hot. Great numbers of plants and animals live here.

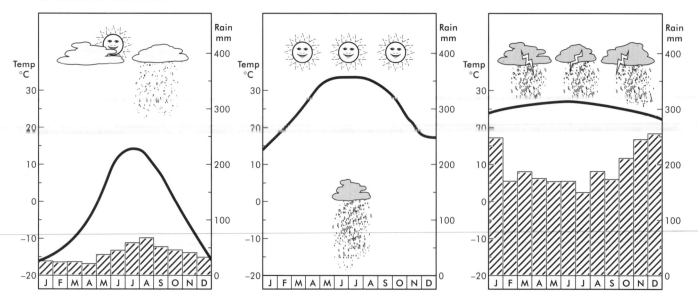

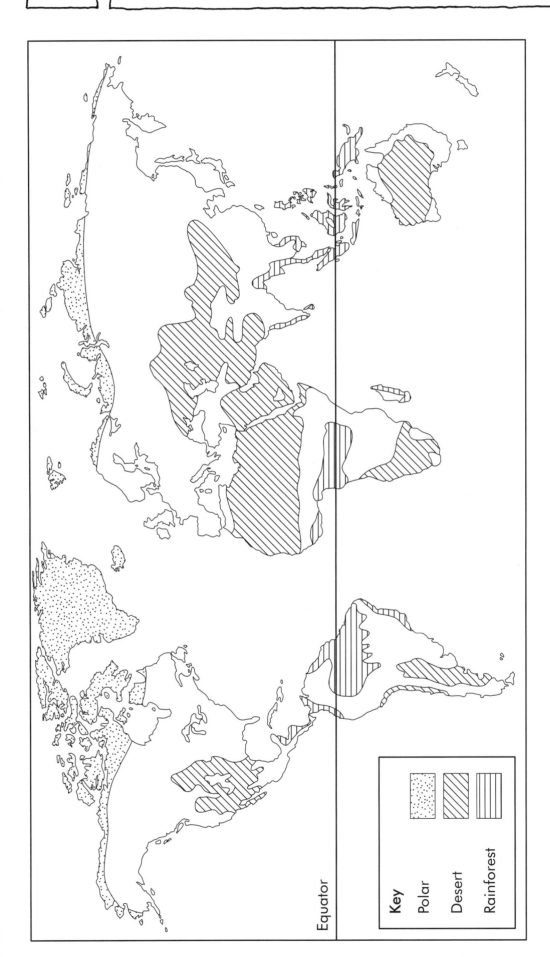

Equator

Key

Polar

Desert

Rainforest

	Polar climate	Desert climate	Rainforest climate

1. Colour the key and the map.

2. Using an atlas to help you,
   name three countries with polar,
   desert and rainforest climates.

RIVERS

Focus

Rivers have an immense effect on the landscape. Along with the sea, sun, wind, frost and ice, they are the main agents shaping the Earth. Rivers often start as small streams in hills and mountains. As they flow downhill, they gather more water and cut deep valleys, transporting material downstream. When the river flows into a lake or sea, it loses energy and deposits its load. In this way, rivers gradually smooth and flatten the landscape and can make it almost completely flat over millions of years.

From the earliest times, people have settled on river banks taking advantage of not only good communications afforded by rivers but also the supply of water and the fertile soil in the river valley. However, living on rivers has disadvantages. As cities and industries have grown larger, water pollution has become an increasing problem. Also, floods caused by heavy rain can cause serious damage. Today, most large rivers are controlled by embankments, dams and reservoirs. In Western Europe and North America, new laws and better management have helped to reduce pollution levels.

Some of the world's main rivers			Main rivers in the UK	
Nile	Africa	6,695 km	Severn	354 km
Amazon	South America	6,570 km	Thames	346 km
Mississippi-Missouri	North America	6,020 km	Trent	300 km
Chang Jiang	Asia	5,471 km	Great Ouse	230 km
Volga	Europe	3,688 km	Wye	209 km

Brainstorm

Use this brainstorm to help you develop a medium-term plan.

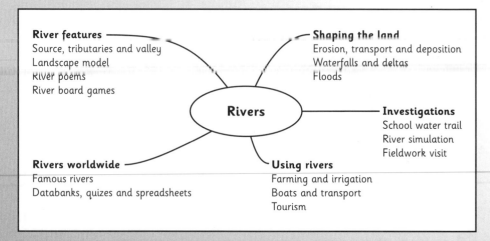

River features
Source, tributaries and valley
Landscape model
River poems
River board games

Shaping the land
Erosion, transport and deposition
Waterfalls and deltas
Floods

Rivers

Investigations
School water trail
River simulation
Fieldwork visit

Rivers worldwide
Famous rivers
Databanks, quizzes and spreadsheets

Using rivers
Farming and irrigation
Boats and transport
Tourism

Research findings

Many children appear to believe that the physical landscape has been created by people. Piaget (1929) described how children initially go through a stage of artificialism in which they attribute all natural events to human activity. Only as they grow older do they begin to recognise the effect of physical processes. More recent research largely upholds these findings. Children's understanding of rivers is also complicated by other factors. Milburn (1974) investigated children's understanding of geographical terms. Words like 'spring', 'channel' and 'mouth' which have a variety of meanings presented particular problems and were poorly understood even by upper juniors. In addition, a significant number of children appear to be confused about the direction in which river water flows. May (1996) interviewed a class of year 5 children in Devon and asked them where a river starts. The results showed five children thought it began in the sea, four suggested a pond or lake and another four mentioned walls and sewers. These studies suggest that it is important not to take anything for granted.

Content

Unit 4	Sets the scene by introducing children to the structure of a river and key vocabulary.
Unit 5	Considers how rivers shape the land.
Units 6, 7	Provide case studies in European and developing world contexts.

For related material on the Amazon *see* Unit 40 *South America*, Lesson 2 and the South America model on Copymaster 80.

National Curriculum expectations

At the end of Key Stage 2 it is expected that most children will be able to:
- explain patterns of physical and human features

Literacy links

Year 3	Collect new words from work in other subjects: Unit 4 *River systems*, Lesson 1.
Year 4	Design an advertisement: Unit 6 *The River Rhine*, Lesson 3.
Year 5	Write accounts based on personal experiences: Unit 5 *Shaping the land*, Lessons 2 and 3. Convey feelings, reflections or moods in a poem: Unit 4 *River systems*, Lesson 1. Fillet passages for relevant information: Unit 4 *River systems*, Extra activities, Floods. Traditional stories, myths, legends and fables from a variety of cultures: Unit 7 *The River Nile*, Extra activities, Nile myths and legends.
Year 6	Explanations linked to work from other subjects: Unit 5 *Shaping the land*, Lesson 3.

Story

Rivers feature strongly in many children's classics including *The Wind in the Willows* by Kenneth Graeme, Arthur Ransome's *Swallows and Amazons* and the stories of C.S. Lewis and A.A. Milne.

ICT links

CD-ROM	Compile information about rivers from an encyclopedia CD-ROM such as *Encarta*.
Word processing	Get the children to type up their work for a class display using a word processing package on the computer.

UNIT 4 | River systems

Learning targets

On completion of this unit children should understand that:
1 ➤➤ a river system is made up of different parts
2 ➤➤ there are many great rivers in the world

Before you start

Focus

This unit focuses on rivers as an aspect of physical geography.

Background knowledge

When it rains, some of the water soaks into the ground, some of it evaporates and some of it runs off the surface. The streams that are formed in this way gradually grow bigger as they flow downhill and make a river. All rivers have the same basic structure. They begin at a source, flow down a valley gathering tributaries and reach the sea at an estuary or mouth. The channel is rarely straight but usually bends or meanders. Typical features include rock pools, waterfalls, lakes and marshes.

Teaching points

Even top juniors are often confused about rivers, being uncertain which way they flow and how they were created. It is important not to take anything for granted.

Progression

This unit introduces specialist terms which will help pupils with case studies and subsequent lessons. It also develops map reading and atlas skills.

Vocabulary

landscape, marsh, mouth, ocean, slope, source, tributary, valley, waterfall

Geographical skills

* Use of specialist vocabulary
* Ability to interpret a local map
* Ability to read an atlas

National Curriculum links

* Rivers have sources, channels, tributaries and mouths
* Rivers shown on Map C (world map)
* How to use an atlas

Assessment indicators

Children should be able to:
* name the different parts of a river
* know about different rivers around the world

Personal application

These statements highlight the relevance of the children's learning:
* I can describe some of the features of a river from source to mouth
* I appreciate how rivers affect people in my area
* I realise that rivers are an important part of the landscape in many parts of the world

Teaching the lessons

Lesson 1 ①

Key question

What are the parts of a river?

Introduction 10 min

▓ The children will have observed how rain runs into drains next to the school building and in the playground. Use this in an introductory session about rivers and water. The following questions and answers are appropriate.

What happens to water when it falls on the school roof? (Rainwater collects in the gutter, flows into downpipes and disappears into drains.)

Where do drains lead to? (Drains lead to sewer works where the water is cleaned before being released into rivers or the sea.)

How do rivers begin? (Rivers begin as streams fed by rainwater in hills and mountains.)

Where do rivers flow? (Rivers flow downhill into lakes or seas.)

Using the information sheet 45min

Read **Copymaster 7 All about rivers** with the children and ask them to complete the activities.

Differentiate by encouraging more-able children to make poems which meander across the page in a river shape. Less-able children should only complete the first two questions.

Summary 5min

Ask some of the children to read out their descriptions and poems.

Homework

Give the children photocopies of a river poem such at 'The Brook' by Tennyson and ask them to learn it off by heart.

Lesson 2 ❶

Key question

What do you know about a local river?

Introduction 5min

Remind the children that rivers flow downhill and revise the specialist terms from the previous lesson – source, stream, valley, waterfall, tributary, mouth.

Using the activity sheet 40min

 Make a study of a stream or river near your school. You will need to give the children a map to work from. The 1:25,000, 1:50,000 or 1:250,000 scale Ordnance Survey maps are particularly suitable. Trace the course of the river as a class exercise so that the children are clear what they are looking for. Then give them **Copymaster 8 A local river** to complete.

Differentiate by encouraging more-able children to collect detailed information about the features shown on the map such as weirs, lakes, ditches and waterworks. Less-able children could draw a picture rather than a sketch map in the last part of the exercise.

Summary 5min

Before you collect the work, get the children to say how they answered each question. Compare their results and add any extra information you may know about the river, such as how long it is, where drinking water is extracted or how people used it in the past.

Lesson 3 ❷

Key question

What can we find out about rivers around the world?

Introduction 10min

Make a list on the board of all the rivers the children can name. See if they can locate some of them in an atlas.

Investigation 40min

Ask the children to compile a fact file about different rivers around the world. They will need to make a table to record the name of the river, the mountains where it rises, the sea or ocean it flows into and the towns and cities along its banks. See if they can find at least two rivers in each continent apart, of course, from Antarctica.

Differentiate by helping slow-learning children to name the rivers you want them to research. More-able children could enter the information they obtain in a computer spreadsheet.

Summary 5min

Compare the results from different groups. Which continent appears to have the most rivers? Which ocean (and neighbouring seas) receive the most water?

Extra activities

Landscape model

Get the children to make a model of a river and landscape in a cardboard box. Begin by cutting away the lid and front to create a frame on three sides. Build up the landscape using egg cartons and pieces of screwed-up paper. Cover with layers of papier mâché. Then paint and add labels and other features.

Floods

Ask the children to find out about floods either in your own area or another part of the world. Newspaper articles and eyewitness accounts will bring the events to life. You may also be able to obtain television reports or video clips which show the water in full spate.

All about rivers

The place where a river begins is called its source. Most rivers have their source in hills and mountains. Sometimes, the water comes from melting snow and ice. In other places, water bubbles out of the ground from wet rocks.

As the water flows downhill, it cuts away the land to make a valley. Often this has steep slopes on both sides. There may also be waterfalls and rock pools.

Eventually, the river reaches flatter ground. It forms loops and wide bends. Other smaller rivers known as tributaries join up with it and make it bigger.

The river ends when it enters the sea. This is known as the mouth. There can be marshes, mudflats and sandbanks here. Also the water is often so deep that ships can sail into the mouth and some way up the river.

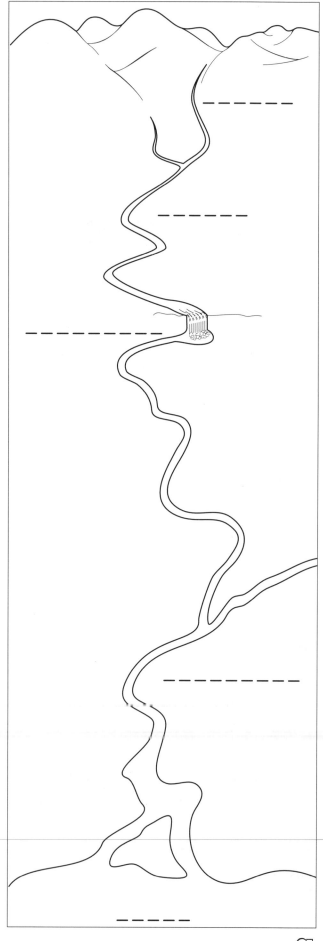

Things to do

1 Write these words in the correct place on the drawing:

   source   valley   waterfall
   tributary   mouth

2 Write the words in your book together with a drawing and the correct description from below:

   a) where a river flows over a cliff

   b) where a river reaches the sea

   c) where a river begins

   d) the gap between hills or mountains

   e) other, smaller rivers

3 Using the picture to help you, write your own river poem.

A local river

Using a map, answer these questions about a stream or river near you.

Name of stream or river	
Source (nearest place/village)	
Mouth (nearest place/town)	
Names of any tributaries	
Names of any marshes	
Villages, towns and other features along valley	

Your own map

Shaping the land

Learning targets

On completion of this unit children should understand that:

1 ➡➤ rivers gradually wear away the land

2 ➡➤ water flows downhill

Before you start

Focus

This unit introduces pupils to the ways rivers and water shape the landscape over geological time.

Background knowledge

Rivers and water have a powerful effect on the landscape. They wear away upland areas and transport material downstream depositing it as silt and sand. If all other conditions remained stable, rivers would eventually reduce the land to a low plain just above sea level. However, subterranean movements ensure that their effects are countered by periods of mountain building and uplift.

Teaching points

Many children find it hard to appreciate landscape processes because they happen over very long periods of time. Fieldwork, practical experience and first-hand observations can help to develop their ideas.

Progression

Having been introduced to the parts of a river in the previous unit, pupils learn about how rivers affect the physical landscape in this one.

Vocabulary

bank, delta, deposition, flood, flow, erosion, slope, transportation

Geographical skills

- Use of specialist vocabulary
- Ability to understand processes
- Ability to make a trail
- Observation of a simulation

National Curriculum links

- Rivers erode, transport and deposit materials
- Rivers affect the landscape
- Use appropriate geographical vocabulary

Assessment indicators

Children should be able to:
- identify erosion in the local environment
- describe how rivers affect the landscape

Personal application

These statements highlight the relevance of the children's learning:
- I can understand that water very gradually wears away the land
- I know what happens to rainwater when it runs across the ground
- I understand how rivers affect the landscape

Teaching the lessons

Lesson 1 ①

Key question

How do rivers shape the land?

Introduction 10 min

▦ Explain to the children that rivers wear away the land over long periods of time. This is a difficult concept. You can illustrate the effects of erosion by asking the children to think about the school building. Discuss whether any steps or floor areas have been worn away by people walking over them and whether there are any bricks or patches of stonework on the outside that are crumbling or flaking. Introduce the idea of water erosion by discussing how the sea makes stones round and smooth on the seashore.

Using the information sheet 30 min

▦ Read **Copymaster 9 Shaping the land** with the children. Ask them to apply the terms 'erosion', 'transportation' and 'deposition' to the diagram at the bottom of the page before they begin the exercises.

Differentiate by providing less-able children with pictures to copy in Question 2.

Summary 5 min

▦ Ascertain whether the children can say what erosion, transport and deposition are, without them looking at their work.

Homework

Ask the children to make a drawing of a river and its surroundings, working from a postcard or their imagination. Get them to add labels or write notes explaining how the river has shaped the land.

Lesson 2 ②

Key question

Where does water flow in our school?

Introduction 10min

Discuss with the children the different places where they can see water in and around the school building. They might mention downpipes, drains and drinking fountains, wash basins, taps and lavatories. Stress the way the water flows from higher to lower levels in each example.

Using the activity sheet 60min

Divide the children into groups and ask them to make a short trail around your school linking different places where they can find flowing water. They will need to observe and record the examples they select on **Copymaster 10 Water trail**. They should also add notes, saying where they think the water has come from and where it is going.

Differentiate by encouraging less-able children to concentrate on collecting evidence rather than making a trail. More-able children might arrange their drawings around a plan of the school for a wall display. They might also take photographs of the things they discover.

Summary 10min

Discuss the work done by different groups and whether they have chosen different examples. Ask some children if they can explain what makes water flow downhill.

Lesson 3 ① ②

Key question

What are the effects of water erosion?

Introduction 10min

Ask the children if they can think of an experiment or simulation which will show the effects of water erosion. Consider their ideas, then tell them what you have planned. Write the aim of the experiment on the board together with the things you want them to look for.

Investigation 30min

Pour water from a watering can over a sand tray or hose water over a pile of sand or gravel. Discuss and record what happens. Streams of water will begin to cut channels carrying the sand downhill and spreading it out at the bottom. Even on a very small scale the typical fan or delta shape is usually apparent.

Discuss the results with the children. Get them to record what happens as they would in a science experiment using the headings 'Equipment used', 'What we wanted to find out' and 'What happened'.

Differentiate by getting less-able children to draw a picture of the simulation and write about what happened. Challenge more-able children to explain the processes involved stressing the three separate stages of erosion, transportation and deposition.

Summary 5min

Discuss how the experiment matches real rivers that the children have seen. Ask the children to identify the source, valley, tributary and mouth and whether the simulation is realistic. You might also consider ways of extending the simulation. For example, ask how much each full watering can reduces the height of the sand, and how far the sand spreads outwards.

Extra activities

Waterfalls

Waterfalls are one of the most dramatic river features. Famous examples include the Niagara Falls on the River Niagara between Lake Ontario and Lake Erie, the Victoria Falls on the Zambezi and the Kabalega Falls on the Nile. Ask the children to find out about waterfalls around the world as a research exercise, perhaps using information from a CD-ROM or the Internet.

Deltas

Many rivers form a delta where they enter the sea. Some deltas such as the Camargue at the mouth of the Rhône have been set aside for wildlife. Others like the Nile, Mekong and Ganges are heavily populated. Make a detailed study of one example with the children using maps and reference books.

Shaping the land

Over long periods of time, rivers wear away the hills and mountains where they begin. Tiny pieces of rock and earth are carried off by the water. These scrape along the river bed cutting it wider and deeper.

If there is a lot of rain, the water rises and flows faster. Sometimes, the flood waters are so strong they can move rocks and boulders.

Further downstream, the water gets muddier. It can no longer hold so much material. Banks of sand and mud build up, especially at the mouth where the river enters the sea. These can fan out into the sea making small islands. This is known as a delta.

Over millions and millions of years, rivers shape the landscape. They wear down hills and build up the coast. This happens so slowly that people do not notice the changes.

Special words

Erosion means the wearing away of the land. Valleys are caused by erosion.

Transportation means moving things about. Rivers can transport trees downstream and dump boulders in fields.

Deposition means dropping something. Rivers deposit sand and mud to make islands.

Things to do

1 Make a list of all the movement words you can find on this page.

2 Draw pictures to show:

a) erosion

b) transportation

c) deposition

How rivers shape the land

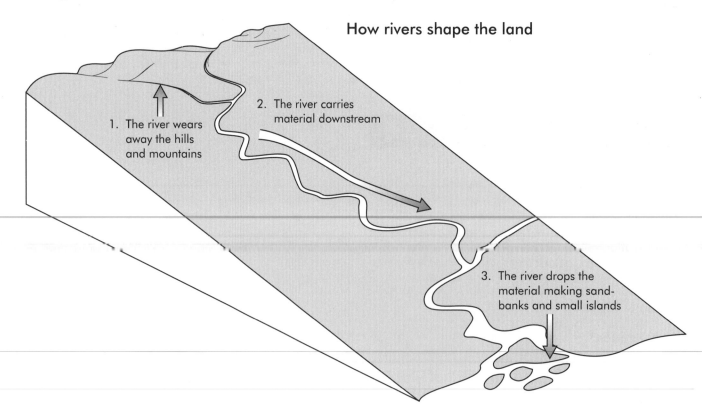

1. The river wears away the hills and mountains

2. The river carries material downstream

3. The river drops the material making sand-banks and small islands

Visit four places in and around your school where you can find flowing water. Record what you see on the chart below.

Drawing	Place
	How does the water flow?

Drawing	Place
	How does the water flow?

Drawing	Place
	How does the water flow?

Drawing	Place
	How does the water flow?

The River Rhine

Learning targets

On completion of this unit children should understand that:

1 ➤➤ the Rhine is a great European river
2 ➤➤ people use the Rhine for industry, agriculture and leisure

Before you start

Focus

This unit considers the physical and human geography of a river using the Rhine as an example.

Background knowledge

The Rhine is one of the longest and most important rivers in Europe. It rises in the Alps and flows 1,320 kilometres across Switzerland, Germany and the Netherlands, reaching the sea in a delta. There are many ancient towns and industrial cities on the banks of the river and a vast, modern port, Europort, at the mouth. Barges and small ships carry goods inland from here as far as Switzerland. Although some parts of the Rhine are popular holiday destinations, pollution is a serious problem. Chemical spills and other accidents pollute the water killing fish, and heavy metals are carried downstream and discharged into the North Sea.

Teaching points

If possible, find the Rhine on a map of Europe so that the children see how it relates to the United Kingdom before they begin the work.

Progression

This unit reinforces previous work on the physical structure of rivers and shows how people use the Rhine in different ways.

Vocabulary

barge, country, environment, flood, flow, mouth, slope, source, tributary

Geographical skills

• Ability to read a map
• Play a geographical game
• Devise a leaflet

National Curriculum links

• Rivers receive water from a wide area
• Points of reference specified on Map B (Europe)
• The European Union

Assessment indicators

Children should be able to:
• locate the Rhine on a map of Europe
• name the main physical and human features of the Rhine
• explain why the Rhine is an important river

Personal application

These statements highlight the relevance of the children's learning:
• I can extract information from a map or plan
• I understand why rivers are important to daily life
• I understand the difference between a holiday brochure and a reference book

Teaching the lessons

Lesson 1 ❶

Key question

What do you know about the River Rhine?

Introduction 5min

▓ Find out what the pupils know about the River Rhine through a class discussion. Write down all the things they mention, whether they are true or false. Keep this list until the end of the lesson.

Using the information sheet 35min

▓ Ensure that the children understand the map on **Copymaster 11 The River Rhine** and ask them to answer the questions in their books.

To differentiate, you may wish to discuss each question with less-able children and put the answers on the board for them to copy. More-able children can use the information from the exercise to create a simple fact file about the Rhine.

Summary `10min`

Look back at the ideas you wrote on the board at the start of the lesson. Consider each one in turn and decide if it is true or false. Is there anything else the children want to add now they have done the work?

Homework

Ask the children to find out some more things about the Rhine from an encyclopedia, atlas or other books.

Lesson 2 ②

Key question

In what ways do people use the River Rhine?

Introduction `10min`

Remind the children what they learnt about the Rhine in the last lesson and talk about some of the ways people use the river.

Transport	Roads and railways follow the valley Barges and small ships carry goods from Europort to Basel
Settlement	There are many towns and cities along the river
Tourism	People take their holidays in towns and villages along the Rhine
Farming	Vines grow on the sheltered, sunny slopes
Industry	Power stations use the water for cooling turbines Factories use the water to help make their goods
Environment	Millions of people depend on the Rhine for drinking water

Using the activity sheet `30min`

Divide the children into two groups and give each group the River Rhine board game on **Copymaster 12 The River Rhine game**, a dice and two counters.

Develop and differentiate the work by asking less-able children to make a table listing the good and bad things that happened in the game. Ask the more-able children to make up their own River Rhine board game based on a 'track' of their own.

Summary `5min`

Discuss the importance of the Rhine to the people of north-west Europe, and who would suffer most if it suddenly dried up.

Lesson 3 ②

Key question

How do people use the River Rhine for leisure?

Introduction `5min`

Trace the route of the Rhine on a map or a copy of **Copymaster 11 The River Rhine**.

Investigation `45min`

Get the children to devise a leaflet advertising a three-day cruise on the Rhine. They should include costs and details of the itinerary and overnight stops if possible. Provide travel brochures and reference books to help give the children extra ideas. For example, they might want to include weather statistics and journey times.

Depending on their ability, the children could make their brochures as realistic as possible. Material which is word-processed looks particularly professional.

Summary `20min`

Invite another member of staff or a small panel from another class to come and listen to the various proposals. Ask them to choose one of the holidays from the range presented, giving reasons for their choice.

Extra activities ① ②

Word picture

Ask the children to make a picture of the Rhine by simply repeatedly writing out the words that describe the different parts of the scene they want to show. For example, they might write the word 'river' several times in blue, snaking across the middle of the page. They could then write 'slope' many times around it and 'hill' on both sides.

Wall display

Get the children to create a large collage of the River Rhine as a class display. Begin by making an outline of the landscape from sugar paper, starting with the Alps on one side and leading to the North Sea on the other. Then add waterfalls, lakes, hills, bridges, towns, docks, boats and other features. Name the places along the river with the help of a map of Europe. Ask the children to add notes about different topics (e.g. tourism, pollution) round the edges.

11 | The River Rhine

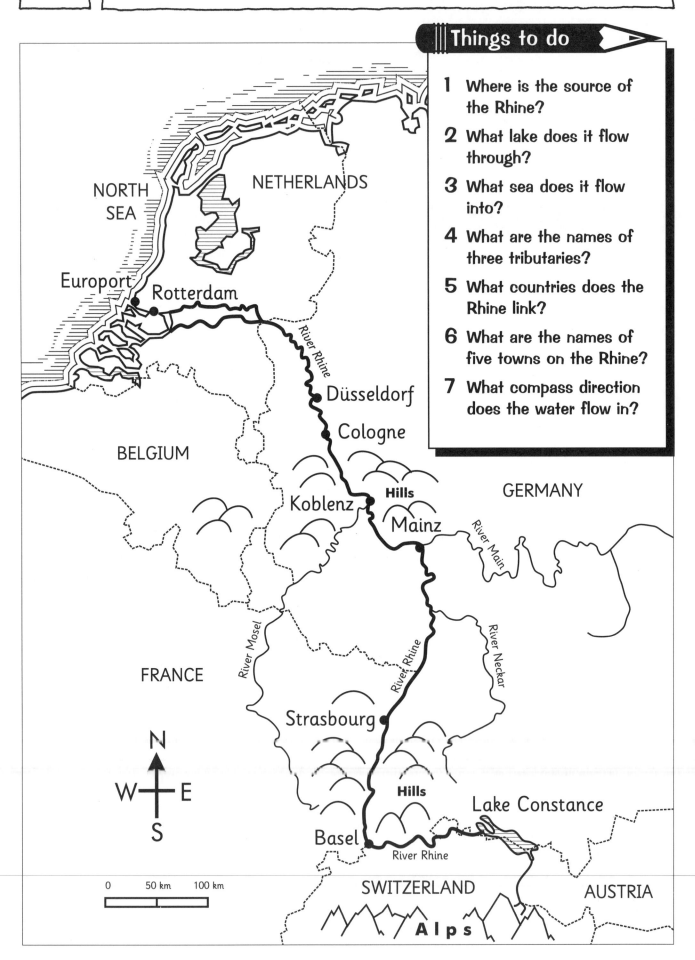

NORTH SEA

NETHERLANDS

Europort

Rotterdam

River Rhine

Düsseldorf

Cologne

BELGIUM

Hills

GERMANY

Koblenz

Mainz

River Main

River Mosel

River Neckar

FRANCE

River Rhine

Strasbourg

N

W E

S

Hills

Lake Constance

Basel

River Rhine

0   50 km   100 km

SWITZERLAND

AUSTRIA

Alps

Things to do

1 Where is the source of the Rhine?

2 What lake does it flow through?

3 What sea does it flow into?

4 What are the names of three tributaries?

5 What countries does the Rhine link?

6 What are the names of five towns on the Rhine?

7 What compass direction does the water flow in?

The River Rhine game

Play the game with a partner or in a group. You will need a dice and a counter for each player.

START 1 Alps	**2** Streams flow fast down steep slopes. Move on 1 space.	**3**	**4** Warm weather melts ice on mountains. Move on 3 spaces.	**5**
10	**9**	**8** Go sailing on Lake Constance. Miss a turn.	**7**	**6**
11 Plunge over Schaffhausen Falls. Have another go.	**12**	**13**	**14** Chemical spill from factory. Go back 4 spaces.	**15**
20	**19** River Neckar joins Rhine. Move on 3 spaces.	**18**	**17**	**16** Water races through Rhine Gorge. Go to 24.
21 Drinking water pumped from river. Miss a turn.	**22**	**23** Rhine slows on flatter land. Miss a turn.	**24**	**25**
FINISH North Sea	**29** Incoming tide slows flow. Miss a turn.	**28**	**27**	**26** Lock gates closed on canal. Throw a 3 or a 6 to continue.

The River Nile

Learning targets

On completion of this unit children should understand that:

1 ➤➤ the Nile is one of the world's great rivers
2 ➤➤ the Nile brings water to Egypt
3 ➤➤ people, plants and creatures depend on the Nile

Before you start

Focus

This unit explores some of the human and environmental issues to do with the River Nile.

Background knowledge

Not only is the Nile the longest river in the world, it also nurtured one of the ancient civilizations. Six thousand years ago, surplus crops from the Lower Nile valley permitted the development of city life and a centralised state. The culture which resulted became a powerful influence in the region for several thousand years. None of this would have been possible without water. Today, the effective use of the Nile remains just as important as it was in the past. Egypt sustains its industries and agriculture by using virtually 100 per cent of the Nile's flow.

Teaching points

You could use this unit in conjunction with the study of a locality in the Nile valley as well as work on Egyptian history and art.

Progression

Pupils who have learnt about the physical characteristics of rivers in previous lessons are introduced to a case study in this unit.

Vocabulary

crops, dam, delta, desert, marsh, pyramids, source, tourism, tributaries

Geographical skills

* Ability to draw a map
* Use of secondary sources of information

National Curriculum links

* Points of reference specified on Map C (world map)
* Rivers erode, transport and deposit materials
* How and why people seek to manage and sustain their environment

Assessment indicators

Children should be able to:
* locate the Nile on a map of Africa
* name the main physical and human features of the Nile
* explain why the Nile is an important river

Personal application

These statements highlight the relevance of the children's learning:
* I understand how the Nile is both similar to and different from other rivers
* I know that the world's first civilisations grew up on river banks
* I understand that people, plants and creatures share the same environment

Teaching the lessons

Lesson 1 ①

Key question

What is the Nile like?

Introduction 15min

▨ Ask the children to find the Nile in an atlas or wall map of Africa. Use the discussion to reinforce the terms for different parts of a river from previous lessons and talk about the different things shown on the map. The following questions and answers are appropriate.

Where is the source of the Nile? (The main river, the white Nile, rises in streams around Lake Victoria.)

What sea does the Nile flow into? (It flows into the Mediterranean Sea.)

Does the Nile have any important tributaries? (The Blue Nile and Atbara flow into the Nile from the Ethiopian highlands.)

What countries does the Nile flow through? (The Nile flows through Uganda, Sudan and Egypt.)

What cities are built on the Nile? (Cairo, Khartoum and Alexandria are the largest cities.)

Using the information sheet 45min

Read the information on **Copymaster 13 The River Nile** with the class. Discuss the different features in turn before the children complete the activities.

Differentiate by encouraging less-able children to colour the map on Copymaster 13. More-able children could write a description of a journey down the Nile.

Summary 5min

Make a list on the board of ten things the children have learnt about the Nile.

Homework

Ask the children to make up a quiz about the Nile using the information they have gained from the lesson. Not only is this a valuable exercise in its own right, but it could also serve as an assessment activity.

Lesson 2 ② ③

Key question

How is the Nile important to Egypt?

Introduction 5min

Discuss with the children how the Nile brings water to the desert. This is particularly important in Egypt where almost the entire population lives in a narrow thread of fertile land along the river valley. Until recently, farmers depended on summer flood waters to irrigate their fields. Now the Aswan High Dam has helped to provide them with water and electricity all year round. While this brings benefits, silt from the Nile no longer revitalises the soil and people have to buy artificial fertilisers.

Using the activity sheet 45min

 Give each pupil a strip of light card 60 cm long and 10 cm deep. Ask them to fold the card into six panels to form a concertina. Now get them to cut out the pictures on **Copymaster 14 The Nile in Egypt**, stick them on the concertina of card and colour them.

Differentiate by helping less-able children, if necessary, to fold the card beforehand. More-able children can be given copies of Copymaster 14 in which the captions have been blanked out. The captions can be written on the board in no particular order for the children to copy into the space under the appropriate drawing.

Summary 10min

Discuss how Egypt would be affected if the Nile was to run dry. Make a brainstorm list on the blackboard of all the possible consequences.

Lesson 3

Key question

What can you find out about the River Nile?

Introduction 5min

Remind the children about the main features of the River Nile and its importance to the people who live on its banks.

Wall display 45min

 Collect some reference books, leaflets, photographs, postcards and other material about the Nile. Divide the children into groups and ask them to work on one these topics – historic sites, farming, wildlife, tourism and environmental problems. Display their writing and drawings as a wall display around a map of the River Nile.

Differentiate by allocating topics to less-able children, if necessary. More-able children should make their own choices and use a wider range of presentation techniques such as charts and graphs and an explanatory text word-processed on a computer.

Summary 10min

 Ask each group to report briefly to the rest of the class about the things they have discovered.

Extra activities ① ③

Exploring the Nile

Get the children to write a diary about a journey up the Nile as a creative writing exercise. The Victorian explorers have left us with accounts of their journeys into the heart of Africa. You could use one of these to support the work.

Nile myths and legends

Ask the children to find out about some of the legends and traditional stories to do with the Nile. These could include links to the Bible with the story of Moses in the bulrushes as well as myths from ancient Egypt.

The River Nile

The River Nile is the longest river in the world. It flows from the middle of Africa to the Mediterranean Sea. It is nearly 7,000 kilometres long and links nine different countries.

The Nile rises in snowy mountains around Lake Victoria. From here, the river tumbles over some high waterfalls. When the water reaches lower ground, it makes a vast marsh.

Tributaries from East Africa join the Nile. The river then flows north across the Sahara desert for thousands of kilometres. A lot of the water disappears in the sand. Finally, the river fans out to make a delta and reaches the sea.

Many different creatures live in the Nile. There are crocodiles and tiger fish, and Nile perch which can grow to over 100 kilograms in weight. Millions of waterbirds also use the Nile as a stopping place as they fly across the desert.

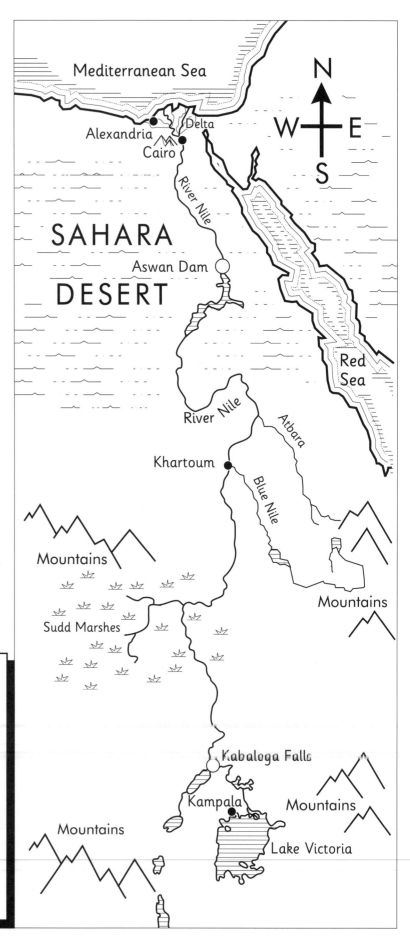

Things to do

1 Copy the map into your book.

2 Make drawings to show four of the features marked on the map. Add labels to say what they are.

3 Make up three questions of your own and write out the answers.

Boats sail up and down the Nile carrying goods and tourists.

The Aswan Dam stops floods and makes electricity.

Cairo is built where desert routes cross the Nile.

Water from the Nile is used to water fields.

Tourists visit temples and pyramids on the banks of the Nile.

People eat fish from the Nile.

SETTLEMENT

Focus

Settlement is an important geographical theme. It involves the study of the places where people live, the features which make places different and the way that places are changing. There are links to many familiar primary school topics such as houses and homes, shops, jobs and transport. There will also be opportunities for studying new developments and local issues. This is a key element of any work on democracy and citizenship education.

Most modern towns and cities have developed from smaller settlements. River crossings, gaps in hills and defensive sites have tended to flourish. Today, as in the past, cities dominate trade routes. For example, most of the largest cities in Europe are found on the coast, rivers or estuaries where they can benefit from sea transport.

In Britain, many cities sprang up during the Industrial Revolution. Today, populations have stabilised. In other parts of the world, cities are still expanding rapidly, especially in Asia and South America. It is estimated that for the first time in history more people are now living in towns than in the countryside. Coping with these changes is a huge problem, which is likely to take up a lot of time and energy in the twenty-first century.

small village	100–500 people
large village	500–3,000 people
small town	3,000–20,000 people
large town	20,000–100,000 people
city	100,000–1,000,000 people or more

Settlements are arranged in a hierarchy according to size

Brainstorm

Use this brainstorm to help you develop a medium-term plan.

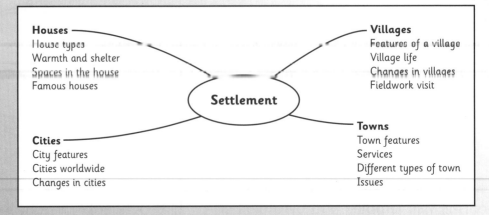

Houses
House types
Warmth and shelter
Spaces in the house
Famous houses

Villages
Features of a village
Village life
Changes in villages
Fieldwork visit

Settlement

Cities
City features
Cities worldwide
Changes in cities

Towns
Town features
Services
Different types of town
Issues

Research findings

Children come to understand their surroundings through complex processes. Piaget remarked how young children found it hard to grasp that places exist in a nested relationship (for example, a house is part of a street which is part of a town which belongs to a region). More recent research by Harwood and McShane (1996) indicates that this is an idea sometimes misunderstood even by upper juniors. Another interesting question concerns the images that children hold of different places. A small-scale study by Baldwin and Opie (1996) showed that children in rural Devon associated cities with pollution, overcrowding, crime and large buildings. They failed to appreciate that a wide range of people live in cities and tended to mention either 'rich people' or 'tramps'. Even more significantly, they denied that cities exist at all in poorer countries. It follows from this that we need to challenge children's stereotypes and enlarge their ideas.

Content

| Unit 8 | Introduces the idea of settlement by considering how people need shelter and protection. |
| Units 9, 10, 11 | Take a more detailed look at villages, towns and cities. |

See Local area section, Units 26, 27, 28 and 29, for linked material.

National Curriculum expectations

At the end of Key Stage 2, it is expected that most children will be able to:

- explain the physical and human characteristics of places, and their similarities and differences
- know the location of key places in the United Kingdom, Europe and the world

Literacy links

Year 3	Collect new words: Unit 8 *Finding shelter*, Lesson 1. Read information passages and identify main points: Unit 10 *Towns*, Lesson 1.
Year 4	Make short notes: Unit 9 *Villages*, Lesson 2.
Year 5	Locate information confidently and efficiently: Unit 8 *Finding shelter*, Extra activities, Houses from the past.
Year 6	Retrieve information from a text: Unit 9 *Villages*, Lesson 3. Select appropriate style and form: Unit 11 *Cities*, Homework.

Story

There are a number of classics such as *The Tale of Johnny Town Mouse* by Beatrix Potter (Warne 1987) which compare urban and rural life.

ICT links

| Aerial photographs | Use aerial photographs in conjunction with maps to find out about settlements. |
| CD-ROM | *Discover London* (NRSC 1996) and *Discover York* (NRSC 1994) are two innovative programs which allow viewers to find out about towns and cities using maps, aerial photographs, pictures and text. |

Finding shelter

Learning targets

On completion of this unit children should understand that:

1 ➤➤ people need shelter and protection

2 ➤➤ houses provide for the needs of individuals and families

3 ➤➤ houses are linked to water, gas, electricity and other services

Before you start

Focus

In this unit, children study the organisation of settlements through personal experience.

Background knowledge

People are social creatures who need shelter and protection. An individual living alone is isolated and vulnerable, so people gather in communities for mutual support. In a settlement, people can develop specialist skills and organise the provision of food, leisure and health services. Increasingly, too, better dist-ribution, transport and communication systems help to lift people above subsistence living.

Teaching points

The children may find it difficult to see their everyday experiences as part of wider systems and processes. Explore their understanding of key vocabulary and initial perceptions.

Progression

Children should understand the needs they share with others and the way in which homes are organised to meet these needs.

Vocabulary

area, bungalow, detached, flat, protection, semi-detached, services, settlement, space, survive, terrace, ventilation

Geographical skills

- Analysis of human needs
- Identification of different areas (land use)
- Ability to make an input–output diagram

National Curriculum links

- Understand main physical and human features that give a locality its character
- Undertake studies that focus on geographical questions
- Undertake fieldwork

Assessment indicators

Children should be able to:
- describe why human beings need shelter
- explain how a house helps us to survive
- say why houses differ

Personal application

These statements highlight the relevance of the children's learning:
- I know how houses provide the things I need
- I understand how spaces are used in my home
- I can describe how the things I need are provided

Teaching the lessons

Lesson 1 ①

Key question

What do we need to survive?

Introduction 10 min

▨ Discuss what people need in order to survive. The following questions and answers are appropriate.

What do we need for daily life? (We need air, food, water, shelter and companionship.)

What is the effect of the weather? (People cannot survive in extreme weather conditions.)

What other dangers are there? (Dangers are diseases and health problems; also people being unpleasant to each other.)

How can we meet all these needs? (Families look after each other and homes give protection.)

Using the information sheet 30 min

▨ The drawings on **Copymaster 15 A place to live**
⚬⚬ illustrate some common different types of house. The children should be able to think of other examples such as mobile homes, houseboats and maisonettes.

Differentiate by discussing the answers with slow-learning children. More-able children could identify different house types in their local area, working from a large-scale map or plan as an extra activity.

Summary
10 min

Make a class list of different types of homes. Discuss what basic things all these homes provide.

Homework

Ask the children to make a list (with drawings) of six different ways their own homes provide for their needs. For example, the taps provide water for drinking, washing and cooking; the roof provides shelter from the rain; and the garden is somewhere to play.

Lesson 2
②

Key question

What are houses for?

Introduction
10 min

Discuss how a house might be described to a visitor from another planet. The following questions and answers are appropriate.

How does a home keep out the weather? (The roof keeps out rain and snow; the heating system keeps the rooms warm; and windows provide light and ventilation.)

What jobs and tasks are done in a home? (Work in the home includes washing clothes, cooking, cleaning, tidying, mending and repairing things.)

What are the purposes of the spaces in a home? (The kitchen is a working area, the living room is for meeting and leisure, the bedrooms are for sleep and privacy.)

Using the activity sheet
30 min

Read the labels on the drawing on **Copymaster 16 Meeting our needs** with the children and ensure that they understand how to use the headings in the tables.

Differentiate by encouraging less-able children to complete the copymaster working in groups. Ask more-able children to write a report about how the house meets basic human needs.

Summary
5 min

Discuss which rooms in a home are vital and which are less important. Ask the children what rooms they would add to a home, if they could, and why.

Lesson 3
③

Key question

What are the essential services?

Introduction
10 min

Discuss the things that go into and out of a house (inputs and outputs). Make a list of the children's ideas on the board. The following questions and answers are appropriate.

What are the main inputs to a house? (Some of the main inputs are water, electricity, food and information (telephone, post, television).)

What are the main outputs? (Some of the main outputs are waste water, rubbish, smoke and fumes from chimneys.)

Investigation
15 min

Make a simple input–output diagram of a home using arrows to show the things that come into and go out of a home.

With less-able children, complete this exercise as a whole-class activity leading to a wall display. Challenge more-able children to think of ways that the outputs could be reduced in order to protect the environment.

Summary
5 min

Ask some of the children to display and discuss their diagrams with the rest of the class.

Extra activities
① ②

House survey

Help the children to make a study of the different house types in your area. Divide the children into small groups so they can 'adopt' a house and draw and photograph it for a class frieze.

Houses in the past

Get the children to find out about houses in the past (including Victorian, Georgian and Tudor buildings). Divide the children into groups and ask each group to study one example saying how it met basic human needs for shelter, warmth and protection.

Houses worldwide

Get the children to make a wall display of pictures and drawings of traditional houses from around the world, for example, flat-roofed desert houses and thatched huts from East Africa. Explain how each one is suitable for the local climate and draw attention to the building materials used to construct them.

A place to live

A settlement is a group of buildings where people live. It can be as small as a farm or as large as a city.

In a settlement people share the jobs of providing food, making things, caring for each other and even relaxing and having fun.

You can see how a settlement works by looking at your own home. It is much more than a collection of spaces. Each area has a purpose. These are used for cooking, washing, sleeping, storing goods, playing games and so on. In this way a home provides the things we need for daily life.

There are many different types of house. A house which stands on its own is detached. A house which is joined to another is semi-detached. When a house is joined in a row with several other houses, this is called a terrace.

Things to do

1 Write a sentence saying what a settlement is.

2 Why do people live in settlements?

3 How are homes part of a settlement?

4 List as many different types of house as you can.

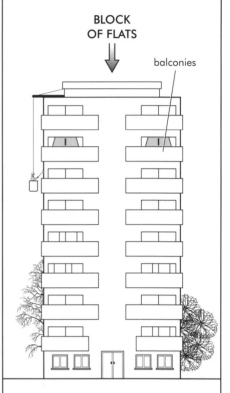

BLOCK OF FLATS

balconies

BUNGALOW

DETACHED

picture window   weather board

casement

SEMI-DETACHED

pebbledash   slates

TERRACED HOUSES

skylight   dormer window   bow window

Meeting our needs

Write each label in the most suitable part of the table.

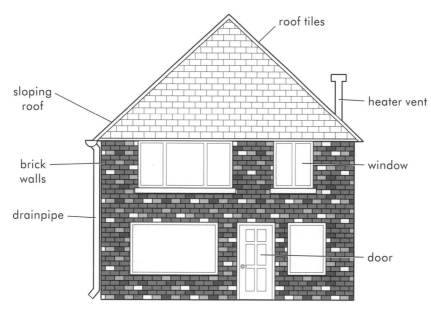

WEATHER PROTECTION	LIGHT AND VENTILATION	HEAT

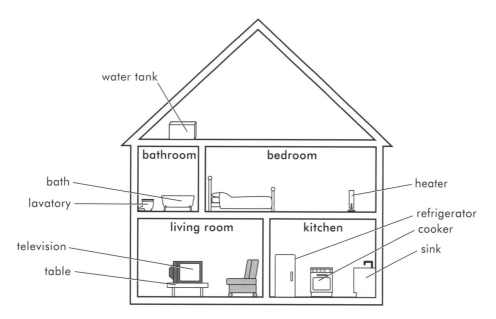

SUPPLIES FOOD AND WATER	FOR HEALTHY LIVING	RELAXING AND LEISURE

Villages

Learning targets

On completion of this unit children should understand that:

1 ➤➤ a village has a number of key buildings
2 ➤➤ the pattern of the roads gives a village its shape
3 ➤➤ village life is changing

Before you start

Focus

In this unit, children learn about different types of village. Pattern and change are the key geographical ideas.

Background knowledge

The village is one of the basic units of human settlement. Throughout history, people have lived together in rural communities. Until recently, villages were more or less self-sufficient as people earned their living from the sea or the land. Today, the character of villages is changing as people move into the countryside from towns and cities while villagers move to the towns and cities.

Villages are usually quite small places and vary in size from a few hundred to several thousand people. There are many different layouts or plans. Two of the most common are the nucleated village where all the buildings are gathered together and the linear village which is stretched out along a street.

Teaching points

The children need to appreciate that a village is a living community rather than a collection of buildings.

Progression

Children will be familiar with villages from

nursery rhymes, songs and folk tales. This unit extends their understanding by introducing them to the structure and character of a village.

Vocabulary

church, farm, inn, map, road, school, shop, street, village

Geographical skills

- Ability to make maps and plans
- Comparison of different places
- Ability to recognise pattern
- Identification of change

National Curriculum links

- Settlements, e.g. villages, towns, cities, vary in size
- Land in settlements is used in different ways

Assessment indicators

Children should be able to:
- name the features of a village
- draw a plan of a village
- say what a village might be like to live in

Personal application

These statements highlight the relevance of the children's learning:
- I can imagine what it is like to live in a village
- I can find clues which tell me about the past
- I can interpret the layout of a village

Teaching the lessons

Lesson 1 ❶ ❷

Key question

What is a village?

Introduction ⏱10min

▓ Discuss with the class what they think villages are like. Consider how they provide people with water, shelter and food (see Unit 8). The following questions and answers are appropriate.

Where do you find villages? (Villages are in the countryside and on the coast. Some villages are near mines.)

What buildings do the people who live in a village need? (A church, hall, shop, inn and school make a living community.)

What jobs do people do in villages? (In the past, people worked on farms and looked after animals.)

Are all villages the same? (All villages are small places but they vary a lot in character.)

Are there villages in other countries? (People live in villages all over the world because they are a basic unit of human settlement.)

Using the information sheet `40min`

 The maps on **Copymaster 17 Villages** show a linear village (Monkton in Kent) which has developed along a road and a nucleated village (Broadwindsor in Dorset) which is clustered around a church.

Differentiate by encouraging slow-learning children to make labelled drawings of four different village buildings. More-able children could write a report on what it is like to live in a village.

Summary `10min`

 Make a list on the board of the key features which make a village and discuss the advantages and disadvantages of village life.

Homework

Ask the children to use an atlas to find out the names of ten villages in your district, an area they have visited or from any part of the UK.

Lesson 2 ③

Key question

How are villages changing?

Introduction `10min`

 Even though our environment seems permanent, places are always changing. As an introduction to the concept, discuss with the children changes they have witnessed either at home or at school. The following questions and answers are appropriate.

Which are the oldest buildings in a village? (Usually the church, inn and houses in the centre.)

Which are the most recent buildings in a village? (New houses have been added to the edges of most villages.)

What jobs do people do in villages? (In the past, people worked on farms, looked after animals and practised country crafts such as thatching and hurdle-making. Now many people travel to towns for jobs.)

Using the activity sheet `30min`

 Copymaster 18 Changing villages begins by reinforcing the idea that villages have specific features. It then explores the changes that have happened over the last century.

Differentiation is provided by the questions on Copymaster 18 which are graded according to difficulty.

Summary `10min`

 Working around the class, make a list of some of the key changes on the board. Discuss the way these changes may have affected people's lives.

Lesson 3 ① ②

Key question

Can you design a village?

Introduction `10min`

 Read and discuss the description of Monkton in Kent with the children. You might also give them a copy of the map of Monkton in Kent on Copymaster 17.

Monkton

Monkton stretches out along a road. At one end there is medieval church with a tower. This is made of flints – lumps of hard stone found in the nearby fields. There are houses for about 350 people. Some of these houses are old farmhouses but many are modern. The school was built in Victorian times and has three classrooms and two mobile classrooms. Monkton has a post office and shop, a caravan park, a tractor sales site and a pub. One of the ancient farmhouses has been made into an old people's home. There is also a playing field.

Investigation `40min`

 Divide the children into groups and ask them to make a picture map of Monkton showing the key features. Get them to arrange their drawings around a street plan of the village, adding any notes or labels that might be needed.

Summary `10min`

 Discuss the different picture maps and the strengths and weaknesses of each. Which map seems the most accurate? Is Monkton similar to or different from villages in your area?

Extra activities ① ③

Village collage

Get the children to make a large collage picture of a village as a class display. Get them working in groups to make drawings and label the key buildings. Round the edge, add pictures of the people who live there and the jobs that they do.

Village visit

Arrange a visit to a nearby village. It will be best if you plan a route beforehand linking the things you want the children to study. Get them to use drawings, descriptions and photographs to record their observations.

17 Villages

Villages are small places where most people know each other. The church, post office, inn, school and shop form the heart of the village. Houses spread out along the roads in different directions. Sometimes there are small workshops where people make or repair things.

In the past, nearly all the people who lived in a village earned their living from farming or fishing. Nowadays, villages are growing bigger. New houses are put up for people who work in towns and for people who retire to the countryside.

You can find out more about villages by looking at maps and photographs. In some villages, the buildings are stretched out in a line along a street. In other places, the buildings are gathered around the church or village green at a crossing point.

Things to do

1 List all the buildings that are marked on the village maps.

2 Write down four buildings that are found in both villages.

3 Draw a map of one of the villages and label the different buildings.

4 Write down three sentences of your own about villages.

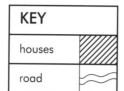

KEY	
houses	
road	

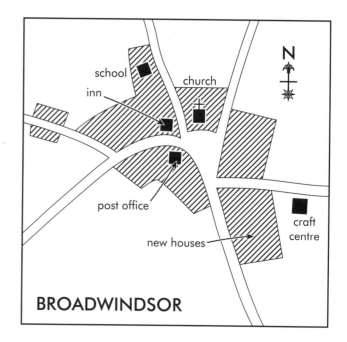

BROADWINDSOR

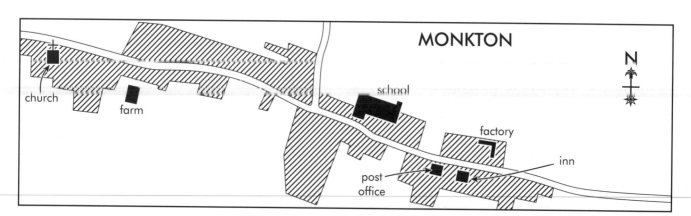

MONKTON

Changing villages

1. Make a list of the features shown on the map of the village.

2. Tick the features that would have been there a hundred years ago.

3. On a separate piece of paper, write notes about how the village has changed.

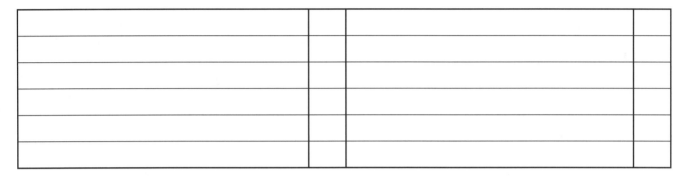

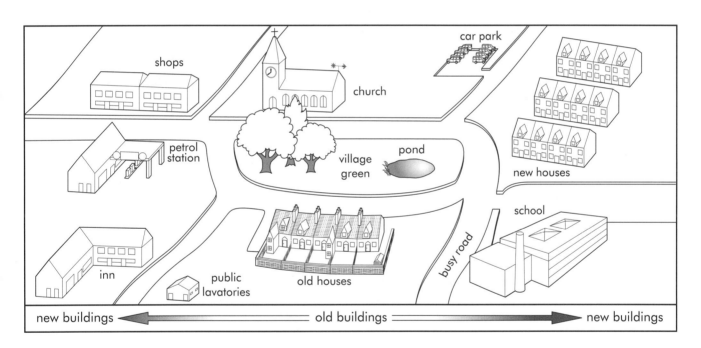

	100 YEARS AGO	NOWADAYS
PEOPLE	79 people	640 people
HOUSES	The houses belonged to a landlord Water supply from outdoor pumps Outside lavatories and no bathroom	Many people own their own house Hot and cold water in all houses Indoor lavatories and bathrooms in all houses
WORK	Main jobs: farmhand, labourer, maid, country craftsman, blacksmith	Main jobs: farmhand, office worker, shop worker, house maintenance
TRAVEL	People either walked or travelled by horse	People travel by car or use public transport

Towns

Learning targets

On completion of this unit children should understand that:

1 ➡️ all towns have common characteristics
2 ➡️ there are systems that support town life
3 ➡️ towns develop for different reasons

Before you start

Focus

In this unit, children learn about the development and structure of towns.

Background knowledge

The Industrial Revolution changed many settlements and lifestyles in Britain. Before 1850, most people lived in scattered villages. Now 90 per cent live in urban areas. Most towns grew larger because they held some advantage over the surrounding area. Significant factors included a market, road bridge, crossroads, industrial site or port.

Towns vary in size. In isolated rural areas, the population may be as little as 3,000. In densely settled regions, towns can be as large as 100,000. However, all towns have a range of basic amenities such as shops, council offices, secondary schools, health services, employment and leisure facilities.

Teaching points

In Britain, some towns are called cities because they have a cathedral and have been given a charter. From a geographical point of view, however, cities are major centres of population with a regional or national catchment and the historical title is misleading.

Progression

At Key Stage 1, children learn to recognise buildings in towns and ask simple questions about their use. This unit seeks to extend their understanding of the features of towns.

Geographical skills

- Ability to read a map
- Make a fieldwork survey
- Ability to give explanations

Vocabulary

bridge, crossing, council, grating, industry, market, office, port, resort, route centre, services

National Curriculum links

- Settlements, e.g. towns, vary in size
- Types of economic activity in a settlement
- How land is used in different ways

Assessment indicators

Children should be able to:
- compare and describe differences between towns and other settlements
- explain clues to town origins
- describe the workings of town systems and predict problems that arise

Personal application

These statements highlight the relevance of the children's learning:
- I know about some of the things I can get and places I can visit in a town
- I understand some of the ways I depend on other people
- I know why towns are not all the same

Teaching the lessons

Lesson 1 ❶

Key question

What is a town?

Introduction 15 min

▓ Ask the children to name any towns they know. Using questions, brainstorm the features that the class thinks a town should have. Note the children's ideas on the board. The following questions and answers are appropriate.

Which buildings in a town provide essential services?

(Schools, colleges, heath centres, fire stations, police stations and doctors' surgeries provide essential services.)

What other services does a town provide? (Shops, museums, libraries, cafés, restaurants, churches and leisure centres provide other services.)

What transport facilities does a town have? (Transport facilities include rail and bus stations, garages and car parks.)

Where do people work in towns? (In towns, people work in offices, factories and shops and provide services.)

Using the information sheet 30 min

▓ As well as providing a general description of towns,

Copymaster 19 Towns contains a case study of Lancaster.

Differentiate by encouraging less-able children to concentrate on the first three questions. Question 4 is more open-ended. The position of Lancaster at the lowest crossing point on the River Lune and the land use pattern (a dense central area, factories along the river and new schools and hospitals on the outskirts) could feature in the answers.

Summary [10 min]

Get the children to look back at the places and facilities they listed in the initial discussion. Ask them whether they want to make any changes.

Homework

Make up a puzzle or game using the names of towns in your area.

Lesson 2 ②

Key question

How do towns work?

Introduction [15 min]

Discuss the nature of town life. Few people grow their own food, supply their own water or keep a log fire. They depend upon essential services being supplied to them. The following questions and answers are appropriate.

How are shops supplied with goods? (Lorries bring goods to warehouses which act as distribution centres.)

How are gas, water and electricity provided? (Pipes and wires bring gas, water and electricity long distances.)

How do people communicate with each other? (Telephone and postal services keep people in touch. There are also local newspapers.)

Who keeps a town running? (The local council keeps roads repaired, looks after parks and gardens and helps a town to run smoothly.)

Using the activity sheet [45 min]

Organise a short walk in the streets near your school. Use **Copymaster 20 Reading the street** to help the children look for the evidence of the services which keep the town running. You may need to adapt the examples to suit your local circumstances.

Differentiate by keeping the walk short and simple for less-able children, if you wish to. As well as going further, older and more-able children could make rubbings of the different traps and gratings that they find. They may also discover historical clues such as boot scrapers and coal-hole covers.

Summary [10 min]

Ask the children to explain, from their surveys, which items they found most and least common? Can they explain this? Were there any other features they wanted to record and investigate? Check that they realise the fire hydrant markers mark the position of a high-pressure water system.

Lesson 3 ③

Key question

Why do towns develop?

Introduction [15 min]

Discuss that, although all towns have certain common features, they developed for a number of different reasons. The following questions and answers are appropriate.

In the past, why would people want to travel from their village to a town? (To sell their goods in the market or buy something for their homes.)

In what way was transport important to a town? (People needed to reach the town easily from the surrounding countryside. Many towns grew up at crossroads and bridges.

What else might cause a towns to grow? (Factories, mines and cotton mills, especially during the Industrial Revolution, caused towns to grow. Some towns developed as seaside resorts.)

What are the different types of town in your area? (Make a list on the board of local towns and classify them into these groups – market, industrial, resort, port and route centre.)

Investigation [30 min]

Divide the children into groups. Give each group a map of the region (1:250,000 scale is ideal). Ask the children to make their own map on a sheet of A3 paper marking local towns and adding short notes and simple drawings about what might have caused each place to develop.

Differentiate by grouping the children in mixed-ability groups. The more-able children should guide the group and write the notes. The less-able ones could concentrate on the drawings.

Summary [10 min]

Each group should present and explain their map to the rest of the class.

Extra activities ① ③

Good town guide

Get the children to make a 'good town' guide for their local area. This could list interesting places to visit and include plans, photographs, written descriptions and drawings. The children could work individually or in groups. They could also pursue the project as part of their homework.

Local issues

Get the children to find out about the growth and development of their town. Use old maps and plans along with written accounts and photographs to trace how it has grown. How is it changing nowadays? What new schemes are planned?
You will find that the local library, council planning department and local newspaper are useful sources of information.

19 | Towns

Towns are settlements where many people live. Most towns started off as villages and have grown larger. There are often old buildings near the centre. Newer buildings and ring roads are found around the edge.

Towns provide the things we need for daily life. These include homes where people can live, shops for food and clothes, and offices and factories where people work.

Towns also have parks, cinemas, sports centres and churches. Schools, colleges and hospitals provide other important services.

People travel to towns by car, train and bus. The railway station and bus station need to be within walking distance of the centre. The car parks also have to be near the middle.

Things to do

1 What is the difference between a village and a town?

2 Make a list of the buildings and places you would find in a town.

3 Colour the key and map of Lancaster.

4 Write a few sentences describing Lancaster.

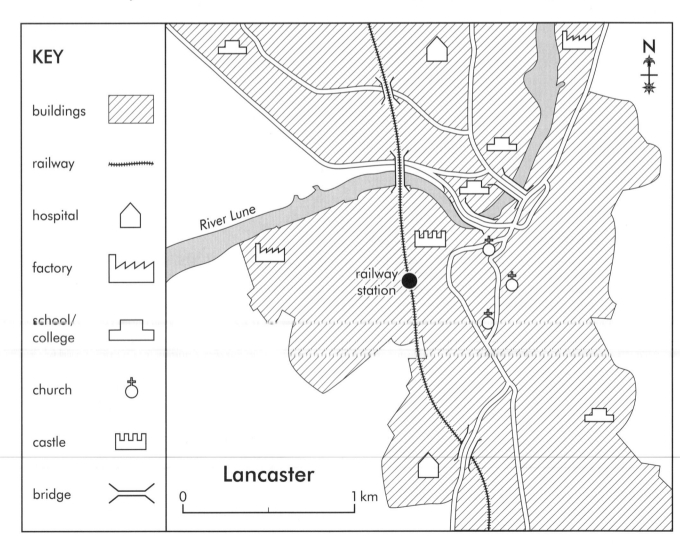

KEY

buildings

railway

hospital

factory

school/ college

church

castle

bridge

River Lune

railway station

Lancaster

0   1 km

Reading the street

1. Tick or colour a box each time you find one of the things shown on the drawings.

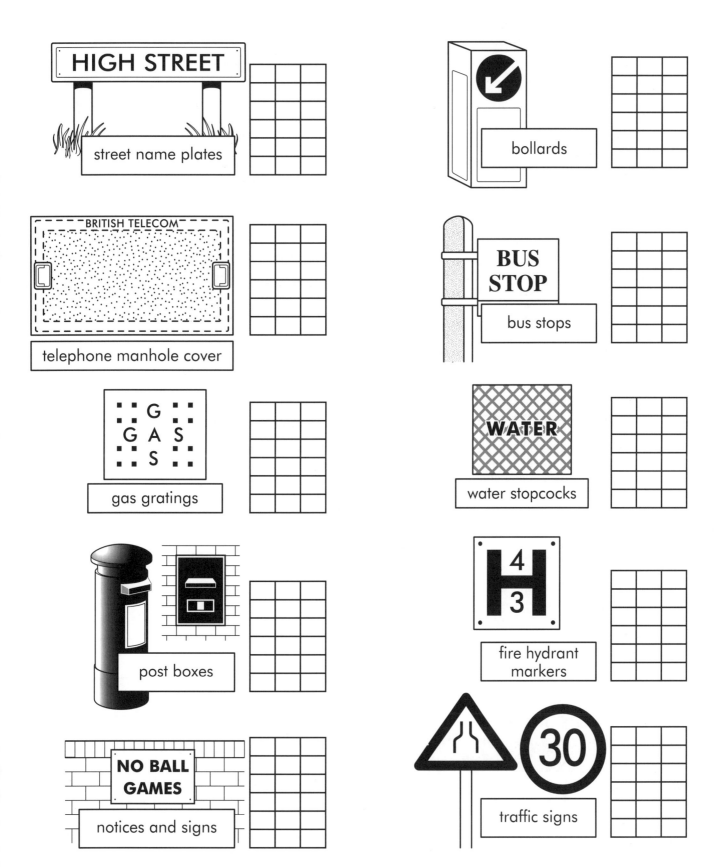

HIGH STREET

street name plates

bollards

BRITISH TELECOM

telephone manhole cover

BUS STOP

bus stops

G
GAS
S

gas gratings

WATER

water stopcocks

post boxes

H 4 3

fire hydrant markers

NO BALL GAMES

notices and signs

30

traffic signs

UNIT 11 | Cities

Learning targets

On completion of this unit children should understand that:

1 ➨➔ cities are very large settlements with wide influence

2 ➨➔ there are cities all over the world

Before you start

Focus

Unlike towns, cities do more than meet daily needs of the surrounding area. Through wealth and political authority, they have national and international influence.

Background knowledge

Cities first developed in India, China, Egypt, South America and the Middle East. They grew from towns which prospered and attracted rich and influential people. Once established, cities became the seats of government and so exerted political power. In turn, this encouraged their function as centres for trade and finance. At the same time, city dwellers set trends and influenced culture through universities and the arts.

Today, cities dominate world affairs. Every country has a capital city and by the year 2000 half of the world's population will be living in urban areas. Cities have always had a magnetic attraction. Their growth in Europe and America in the last century is reflected in economically developing countries today. However, cities are also beset by problems. These include shanty towns, homelessness and the decay of the historic core. Coping with these is one of the great challenges of the twenty-first century.

Teaching points

Children sometimes have difficulty appreciating the sheer size and scale of cities. In London, for example, the built-up area extends for over 50 kilometres.

Progression

By the time they complete Key Stage 1, children should know the names of some cities. As children progress through Key Stage 2, they learn that cities are complex places. This lays the foundations for a deeper understanding of urban issues at Key Stage 3.

Vocabulary

airport, cathedral, city, commute, emergency services, government, office, tourists, traffic, transport, underground railway, university

Geographical skills

- Location of places on a world map
- Ability to make judgements
- Use of secondary sources of information

National Curriculum links

- Settlements, e.g. cities, vary in size
- Localities are set within a broader geographical context
- Localities are linked with other places

Assessment indicators

Children should be able to:
- describe the character of a city
- identify and compare cities worldwide
- explain the attractions of city life

Personal application

These statements highlight the relevance of the children's learning:
- I know that some facilities can be found only in a city
- I know that large cities have famous buildings
- I understand why some people have to work at night

Teaching the lessons

Lesson 1 ❶

Key question

What makes a city?

Introduction [10 min]

▓ Remind the children what they have learnt about villages and towns in previous lessons. Discuss what makes cities different. The following questions and answers are appropriate.

What special buildings do cities have? (Airports, mainline railway stations, well-known museums, famous buildings, large hotels and shops, government offices, law courts and universities are special buildings.)

Why are cities so big? (Cities grow large because people want to live in them. They are attracted by the work, entertainment and other facilities.)

Using the information sheet 〔30min〕

▓ **Copymaster 21 Cities** describes the main features of cities and some of the issues which affect them.

Differentiate by encouraging less-able children to concentrate on listing city buildings. More-able children can consider the advantages and disadvantages of city life through a role-play or drama.

Summary 〔10min〕

▓ Make a class list of the features of a city. Ask the children to rank them in order depending on their importance.

Homework

Ask the children to write their own news report of an event which might happen in a city.

Lesson 2

Key question

What do you know about cities around the world?

Introduction 〔10min〕

▓ Make a list on the board of the cities from around the world which the children know.

Using the activity sheet 〔30min〕

▓▓ Read the instructions and the text boxes on **Copymaster 22 Cities worldwide** with the whole class, then divide the children into pairs. Question 1 (naming the continents) is a reinforcement exercise designed to revise their knowledge.

Differentiate by encouraging slow-learning children to colour and name the continents as a class exercise. Challenge more-able children to make up their own list of cities and descriptions on a separate sheet of paper.

Summary 〔10min〕

▓ Split the children into teams. Choose the cities at random from the map. The team which describes it accurately receives a point.

Lesson 3

Key question

How does a city function during 24 hours?

Introduction 〔10min〕

▓ Discuss the way a city functions night and day. The following questions and answers are appropriate.

Which places are used during normal working hours? (Offices, banks, factories, shops, schools and colleges.)

Which jobs do people do round the clock? (Radio and television news presentation, providing transportaton and emergency services.)

What activities happen at other times of day? (Cleaning buildings, delivering goods, providing meals and entertainment.)

Investigation 〔30min〕

▓▓ Divide the children into groups and ask them to make an hour-by-hour timetable covering 24 hours. Ask them to write down in each square the different jobs people might be doing.

Differentiate by providing slow-learning children with a prepared list from which they can select the relevant jobs.

Summary 〔15min〕

▓ Ask the children to use their timetables to talk about city life. Discuss which jobs are done day and night, perhaps as shift work, and why; which are the busiest times; and what effects these peaks of activity have.

Extra activities

Visiting London

Divide the children into groups and ask them to find out famous buildings and other places to visit in London. Get them to draw a map to show the locations. As well as guides and reference books, ICT packages such as the *Discover London* CD-ROM are valuable sources of information.

City timeline

Get the children to make a timeline for a class display showing how a city such as London, Edinburgh or Paris has changed over time. As well as identifying key dates, the display could include drawings, photographs and written accounts of specific buildings and events. Develop the links to work in history as appropriate.

Cities

Cities are the largest type of settlement. In the centre, office blocks and flats reach up into the sky. From here, roads and buildings stretch in all directions. Hundreds of thousands of people live in cities. This makes them busy, crowded places.

All cities have large and important buildings. There are government offices, universities, cathedrals, museums and art galleries. There are also parks, gardens and sculptures. Some cities have old palaces and castles.

Cities need good transport systems so that people can move around easily. Workers, shoppers and tourists travel to the centre during the day. In the evening, people come to theatres and cinemas or to eat in restaurants. Buses, trains and railways carry people from one place to another. Airports provide links to other cities and countries.

There is so much traffic in cities that the roads are often jammed. The fumes from cars, homes and factories gather in the air. Some people do not have proper homes. Noise and rubbish can also be a problem.

Things to do

1 Make a list of the buildings and places you would find in a city.

2 Why do cities need good transport systems?

3 What problems effect cities?

4 What would make you want to live in a city?

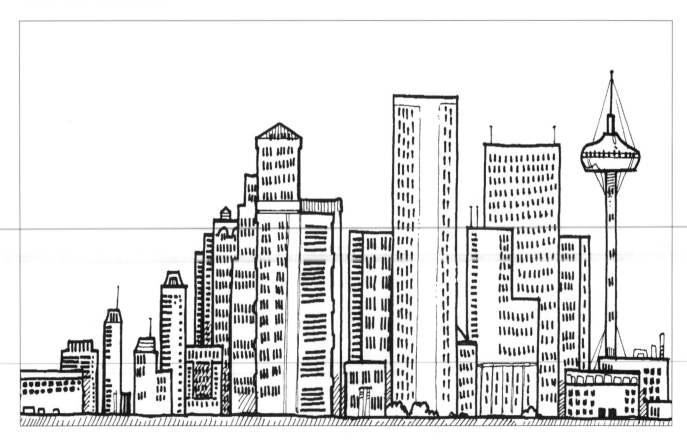

Cities worldwide

1. Write the name of each continent on the appropriate dotted line.
2. Join each clue, in the boxes below, to the correct city on the map.

A city in North America. The world's most important financial centre.	An ancient city in Europe. The centre of an empire 2000 years ago. The home of the Pope is within this city.	The capital city of the world's largest country. Famous for the Kremlin where the government is held.	The largest city in the world on an island off the coast of Asia.

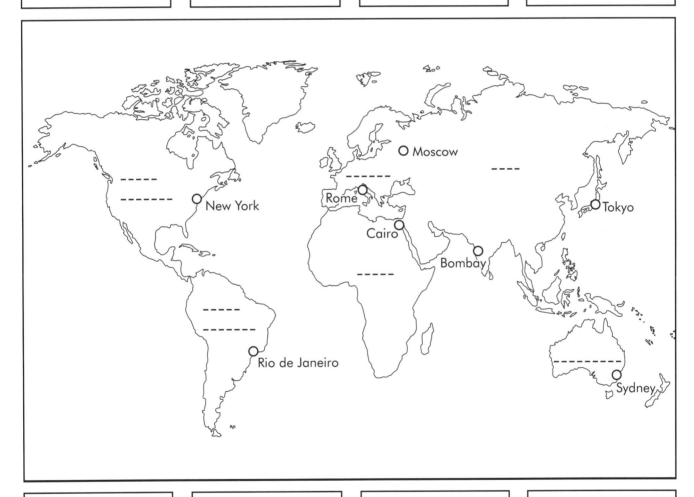

A great city in South America with a famous carnival.	An ancient city with pyramids on the edge of the Sahara desert.	The Victorian gateway to India. Now a great commercial centre.	The largest city in Australia with a large port and harbour.

WORK

Focus

Economic activity is one of the dynamics which underpins the modern world and is one of the keys to understanding the contemporary world. It is studied by geographers who are interested in the nature, distribution and classification of work.

Work can be divided into three main categories. Primary activities involve obtaining raw materials from the Earth's surface. Secondary activities consist chiefly of manufacturing but also include building and construction. Tertiary activities involve providing services which people use, such as healthcare, education or legal advice.

Within the UK, some regions focus on particular activities. In the mountains of Wales and Scotland, farming, forestry and mining predominate. The West Midlands, by contrast, has a particularly high concentration of manufacturing industry. South-east England, the Severn valley and the central valley of Scotland are noted for electronics and service industries. However, this pattern is constantly changing as new economic forces come to shape our working lives.

On a global scale, there are also clear patterns. Generally, developing countries in Africa, South America and Asia provide raw materials for the USA, Japan and the industrial nations of Europe. However, the prices they receive are often very low. This is one of the reasons for the massive inequalities of wealth.

Primary industry	Farming, fishing, forestry, mining
Secondary industry	Engineering, textiles, chemicals, construction
Tertiary industry	Education, healthcare, transport, finance, leisure, retail

Examples of different types of work

Brainstorm

Use this brainstorm to help you develop a medium-term plan.

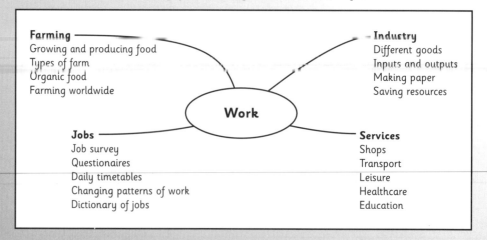

Farming
Growing and producing food
Types of farm
Organic food
Farming worldwide

Industry
Different goods
Inputs and outputs
Making paper
Saving resources

Work

Jobs
Job survey
Questionaires
Daily timetables
Changing patterns of work
Dictionary of jobs

Services
Shops
Transport
Leisure
Healthcare
Education

Research findings

Many children have very little idea of what people do when they go to work. Their parents disappear from home each day to perform largely unseen tasks. If they observe adults at work in school, children tend to form misleading impressions as most of the tasks involve some form of child care. However, the research indicates that if children observe their parents at work it helps to develop their concepts. Also, children appear able to sort jobs into basic categories from an early age (Wiegand 1993). One interesting question concerns sex roles. A small-scale study of five-year-olds by Green (1994) revealed that, although most children of this age already hold clear gender stereotypes, their ideas are also amenable to change. Green concluded that geography teaching 'should not simply be reflecting reality but should be constructing a new one, based on the possibilities open to both sexes in the workplace'.

Content

This section considers the three main types of economic activity, primary, secondary and tertiary, in turn.

Unit 12 Looks at farming.

Unit 13 Considers manufacturing and focuses on paper making.

Unit 14 Focuses on services.

For a portrait of a job in the service sector *see* Europe section, Copymaster 69 European tour.

National Curriculum expectations

At the end of Key Stage 2, it is expected that most children will be able to:

- explain the physical and human characteristics of places, and their similarities and differences
- undertake geographical invest-igations by asking and responding to questions and using a range of geographical enquiry skills, resources and their own observations

Literacy links

Year 3	Use dictionaries: Unit 14 *Services*, Extra activities, A dictionary of jobs. Ways of writing ideas in shortened forms: Unit 12 *Farming*, Lesson 1, Homework.
Year 4	Make short notes: Unit 12 *Farming*, Lesson 1. Identify main features of newspapers: Unit 14 *Services*, Lesson 1, Homework.
Year 5	Short explanatory texts: Unit 13 *Making things*, Lesson 1.
Year 6	Construct effective arguments: Unit 12 *Farming*, Lesson 3. Write a balanced report of a controversial issue: Unit 13 *Making things*, Extra activities, Scarce resources.

ICT links

Internet	Use the Internet to find out about natural resources around the world.
Word processing	Get the children to present their work using word processing and computer spread sheets.

Farming

Learning targets

On completion of this unit children should understand that:

1 ➤➤ we depend on farms for food
2 ➤➤ there are different types of farm
3 ➤➤ farming affects the environment

Before you start

Focus

These lessons examine the origins of foodstuffs, how farms are run and some of the issues affecting farming.

Background knowledge

Farming has gone through great changes in recent years. The UK now provides nearly three-quarters of its basic food needs. At the same time, the number of people employed in agriculture has dropped due to the greater use of machinery, pesticides and fertilisers. These economic achievements have to be balanced against their environmental cost. Today, the loss of hedgerows, the degradation of the soil and the build-up of chemicals in the food chain are all the cause of considerable concern.

Farms in the UK differ according to the shape of the landscape and the weather pattern. The lower-lying, more-sheltered eastern half of Britain supports most of the crop farming. The western uplands have most of the livestock, dairying and forestry.

Teaching points

Many urban children have little or no direct experience of farms and see them as remote places. They think of food as coming from supermarkets and are surprised to learn of its real origins.

Progression

At Key Stage 1, children study the foods they eat and learn about common farm animals. Here, they find out more about farming and the way it relates to landscape and weather.

Vocabulary

arable, cereals, chemicals, crop, fertiliser, insecticide, market garden, organic, wheat

Geographical skills

• Use of appropriate vocabulary
• Ability to write descriptions
• Comparison of arguments

National Curriculum links

• Develop the ability to recognise patterns
• Become aware of how places fit into a wider geographical context

Assessment indicators

Children should be able to:
• talk about origins of foods
• describe basic types of farm
• explain how farming affects the environment

Personal application

These statements highlight the relevance of the children's learning:
• I realise that most of the food we eat depends on the soil
• I understand that farmers make a living from using the land
• I understand why it is important to consider the ingredients in my food

Teaching the lessons

Lesson 1 ❶

Key question

Where does our food come from?

Introduction
15 min

▓ Make a list of the food the children eat. Discuss the different types of food and where they come from.

The following questions and answers are appropriate.

Which foods are vegetables? (Discuss common vegetables. Some grow below ground. The cabbage family is extensive and beans and peas are of great importance.)

Which foods are based on meat? (Children may not associate pork, beef, veal with the names of the animals they come from or even think of pâté as a meat.)

What foods are based on cereals? (As well as breakfast foods, the children should consider wheat, oats and barley.)

What does sugar come from? (Sugar cane grows in the tropics. Sugar beet grows in Britain and northern France.)

Where do fruits and salad vegetables grow? (Orchards, market gardens and special locations overseas.)

Using the information sheet `30min`

Read the information on **Copymaster 23 Food and farming** with the children and discuss how they will answer the questions.

Differentiate by encouraging slow-learning children to concentrate on Questions 1 and 4. More-able children can explore how farming affects the countryside.

Summary `15min`

Divide the class into teams for a challenge game. One team names a food. The other team has to reply with ingredients, say where the food comes from and how it is grown. Award points for each correct part of the answer.

Homework

Ask the children to list the food they eat for their dinner, to draw pictures of the items and to describe the places and farms where the main ingredients are grown.

Lesson 2 ②

Key question

Are all farms the same?

Introduction `15min`

Discuss with the children what they think a farm is and how farms differ. The following questions and answers are appropriate.

Why do some farms only grow crops? (Crop farms are found in eastern England. The good soil, flat landscape and sunny weather are suitable for wheat and oats.)

What type of farms keep animals? (Hill farms keep sheep for wool and meat, dairy farms keep cows for milk, livestock farms keep cattle and other animals for meat. They all depend on grass.)

Using the activity sheet `30min`

 The drawings on **Copymaster 24 Different farms** show a hill farm and an arable farm. When they have written their reports, the children should colour the pictures carefully to indicate their understanding of the nature of the landscape.

Differentiate by allowing slow-learning children to list the activities on each farm, instead of writing reports. With more-able children, discuss how the landscape and weather affect farming.

Summary `10min`

Talk to the children about what they would like and dislike about running or working on a farm.

Lesson 3 ③

Key question

What is organic food?

Introduction `10min`

In the past, people were not surprised if they found insects in the fruit or vegetables which they bought. Now, it is unusual. Discuss how farmers improve the quality and quantity of crops using fertilisers and insecticides. Consider the disadvantages. These include pollution of streams and rivers and damage to wildlife. Also, large machines are used to harvest and maintain the plants. This means hedges are removed to create huge fields which encourages soil erosion.

Investigation `20min`

Divide the children into groups. Ask them to list the arguments in favour of (a) modern intensive farming and (b) organic farming.

Differentiate by ensuring that the groups contain children of varying abilities. Supply leaflets and extra information so that more-able children can undertake their own research. Provide less-able children with a prepared information sheet.

Arguments for modern farming

Pests are killed with chemicals

Farmers get good crops

Machines can be used for many tasks

People get cheap food

Arguments for organic farming

Good for wildlife

Keeps soil in good condition

Prevents pollution of land and water

Food tastes better

Summary `30min`

Organise a debate for and against modern farming methods.

Extra activities ① ③

Regional food

Get the children to make a display of different dishes and recipes from other parts of the UK. Examples could include Lancashire hotpot, Yorkshire pudding and Cornish pasties.

Farming around the world

Get the children to research farming around the world. Different groups could find out about tea plantations in India and Sri Lanka, ranching in Australia, paddy fields in South-East Asia, vineyards in France and wheat farms on the prairies.

Food and farming

We need to eat every day in order to survive. Most of our food comes from farms in the UK. The rest is brought from other countries.

Most of us buy our food from shops. Much of it comes in tins and packages so we tend to forget where it is grown. If you look on the back, you can see a list of ingredients. These often come from different places.

There are many different types of farm in Britain. In places like Scotland and Wales where there are many rainy days, grass grows quickly and farmers keep a lot of sheep. Wheat and other cereals come from arable farms in dry, sunny places such as eastern England. Lettuces, tomatoes and salad vegetables are often grown in market gardens near towns.

Many farmers put fertilisers and insecticides on their land. This kills pests and increases the amount of food they can produce. However, it can also damage the soil and pollute rivers and streams.

Organic farmers do not use any chemicals. Their crops taste good but do not grow so well. This method of farming is also much better for wildlife. You can buy organic produce in most supermarkets.

Things to do

1 Write a sentence about each of these:
  a) hill farms
  b) arable farms
  c) market gardens

2 Why do farmers put chemicals on their land?

3 What is organic farming?

4 Which countries supply the fruit and vegetables in the drawing?

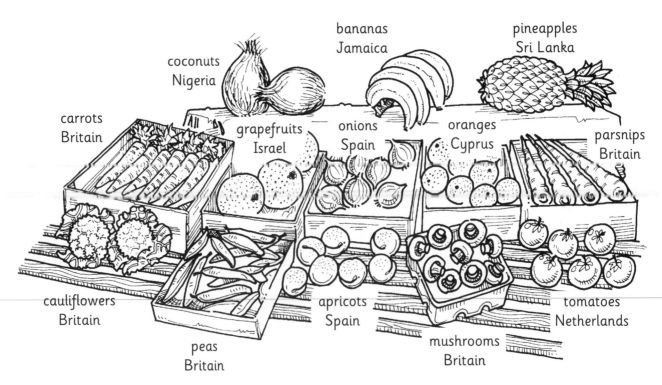

coconuts Nigeria · bananas Jamaica · pineapples Sri Lanka · carrots Britain · grapefruits Israel · onions Spain · oranges Cyprus · parsnips Britain · cauliflowers Britain · peas Britain · apricots Spain · mushrooms Britain · tomatoes Netherlands

Different farms

1. Look carefully at the pictures and decide what type of farm you can see.
2. Write a description of each farm and colour the pictures.

Type of farm

Type of farm

Making things

Learning targets

On completion of this unit children should understand that:

1 ➤➤ goods are made from raw materials
2 ➤➤ factories make goods in stages

Before you start

Focus

In this unit, children find out about how goods are manufactured.

Background knowledge

Factories manufacture the goods that people need from raw materials. They also assemble components which have been made elsewhere. These processes create jobs and attribute value to natural resources. Geographers identify several levels of economic activity. Primary industry is concerned with providing raw materials through farming, fishing, mining and quarrying. Secondary industry involves manufacturing goods and objects. Tertiary industry is the sale of goods and services. All work can be put into one of these three categories.

Teaching points

Children often do not recognise factory buildings and have very little idea of industrial processes. A visit to a factory is desirable but children can also examine the inputs and outputs of their homes and schools and set up their own simple production lines for cards and decorations.

Progression

At a basic level, children need to recognise that most of the objects around them have been made or manufactured. They should then proceed to find out what materials they are made from and how this is done.

Vocabulary

drilling platform, factory, goods, graphite, input, machine, output, production line, pulp, quarry, raw materials, resources

Geographical skills

- Identification of raw materials
- Recognition of sequences and processes
- Use of flow diagrams

National Curriculum links

- How localities are linked with other places e.g. through the supply of goods
- How land in settlements is used in different ways e.g. for industry

Assessment indicators

Children should be able to:
- name different raw materials
- say why factories are important
- explain how some goods are manufactured

Personal application

These statements highlight the relevance of the children's learning:
- I understand that the things I use affect people and places around the world
- I realise that most things I do involves working with other people
- I realise that people have found clever ways of using natural resources

Teaching the lessons

Lesson 1   ①

Key question

What are manufactured goods made from?

Introduction   10min

▓ Identify features or objects in the classroom made mostly of wood, metal, glass, plastics, stone or china. Ask the children to say what raw material they think each item is made of.

Using the information sheet   30min

▓ Read the information on **Copymaster 25 Making things** with the class and talk about the diagram. Discuss the inputs and outputs.

Differentiate by checking that slow-learning children understand the terms used in the text, such as raw materials, quarry and drilling platform. Question 5 is intended chiefly for fast-learning children who could copy the diagram into their books alongside their descriptions.

Summary 〔5min〕

Make a class list of all the different raw materials the children can think of.

Homework

Ask the children to find ten manufactured items in their homes and, by looking at the labels, to find out where each one was made.

Lesson 2

Key question

How is paper made?

Introduction 〔30min〕

This lesson uses a single case study on paper making to illustrate how manufacturing processes involve a number of stages. The following questions and answers are appropriate.

How is paper used in school? (Exercise books, printed books, watercolour paintings, record keeping, paper towels, packaging.)

What is paper made from? (Wood is cut into little pieces, turned into a pulp and pressed into sheets.)

Where does the wood come from? (In this country, most wood pulp comes from forests in Britain, northern Europe and north America.)

Using the activity sheet 〔30min〕

Give each child **Copymaster 26 Making paper**. Talk about the things the children might show in their drawings.

Differentiate by completing the drawings yourself before photocopying the copymaster for less-able children. They should cut out the pictures and arrange them on a separate sheet of paper as a flow diagram.

Summary 〔10min〕

Make a list of all the jobs people have to do when they make paper. These include cutting down trees, shifting logs, driving lorries and bulldozers, operating the pulp machine, running an office, and checking on health and safety risks.

Lesson 3

Key question

What are the inputs and outputs in a process?

Introduction 〔5min〕

Talk about inputs and outputs. Discuss what resources are necessary to create a picture in an art lesson. The inputs will include paint, brushes, paper and water. The output will be a picture and perhaps waste. A lot of work, effort, skills and ideas will also be needed in the process. Demonstrate how they can be shown in a diagram on the board.

Investigation 〔25min〕

Get the children to make a diagram to show the inputs and outputs in one or more of the following processes: making jam, making a woollen cardigan, making bread, making bricks, or making glass.

Differentiate by selecting one process and providing slow-learning children with a blank input–output diagram to complete. Ask more-able children to find out about more complex processes such as making electricity.

Summary 〔10min〕

Ask the children to describe the process they have studied to the rest of the class.

Extra activities

Made of wood and iron

Ask the children to make a survey of all the things which they can find in the classroom which are made from or contain (a) wood, (b) iron or steel. Use magnets to test metal objects.

Scarce resources

Around the world, people are using up resources faster than ever before. Using reference books, the Internet and other sources, get the children to find out how long resources such as timber, oil and iron ore are expected to last.

Making things

People use many different things in their daily lives. Some of these things are quite small, such as pens, books and clothes. Others are much larger such as buildings, buses and trains.

Most of the things we use are created from raw materials. Raw materials are dug out the earth in quarries and by drills on platforms. They are also produced by farmers and fishermen. Timber, stone, iron ore, oil, wool and cotton are some common raw materials. They can be used in lots of different ways.

Raw materials are turned into useful objects in factories. People work alongside machines to make things quickly and cheaply. By working in a team, they make the best use of their skills and abilities.

The raw materials and other things which a factory uses are known as the inputs. The things which it makes are known as the outputs. We can use diagrams to show inputs and outputs.

Making Pencils

INPUTS

Pencil Lead (graphite) comes from quarries in China.

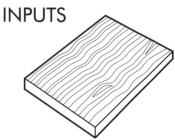

Thin blocks of wood come from the USA.

The graphite is pressed into strips.

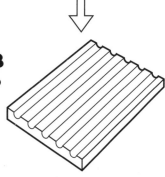

Grooves are cut into the wood.

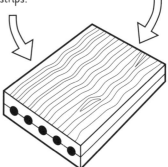

The graphite strips are put into the grooves and another grooved block is glued on top.

OUTPUTS

The pencils are cut, sharpened, painted and put into boxes.

Things to do

1 Make a list of ten objects you use in your daily life.

2 What are raw materials?

3 What is a factory?

4 Write down one thing which is made from each of these raw materials: timber, stone, iron ore, oil, wool, cotton.

5 Describe how pencils are made.

1. Make drawings in the empty boxes.
2. Colour the drawings.

1. Trees are cut down in the forest.	
2. The logs float down a river to the factory.	
3. Logs are stacked in a pile.	
4. The logs are ground into pieces to make a pulp.	
5. The pulp is rolled and dried to make rolls of paper.	

UNIT 14 | Services

Learning targets

On completion of this unit children should understand that:

1 ➤➤ many people earn their living providing services
2 ➤➤ we use a variety of services in our everyday lives

Before you start

Focus

In this unit, children learn about different services and how they effect their welfare.

Background knowledge

It is easy to appreciate jobs and work when the outcome is a finished product which can be handled and given a value. However, the service sector now provides more jobs than any other. Some services are readily identified by children as they include 'people who help us' such as doctors, nurses and teachers. Children find other services, such as office work, more abstract.

Teaching points

Children find it difficult to grasp that people in service jobs are actually earning a wage.

Progression

The study of services is a useful way of introducing children to the interdependence of modern society and its economic underpinning.

Vocabulary

education, entertainment, health, leisure, product, raw materials, repair, transport, vehicle

Geographical skills

- Ability to draw a timeline
- Use of a questionnaire
- Ability to draw conclusions

National Curriculum links

- Settlement characteristics and locations reflect the type of economic activity
- Using geographical vocabulary to describe surroundings
- Analysing information and communicating findings

Assessment indicators

Children should be able to:
- distinguish between jobs in services and the manufacturing industries
- identify some of the services which they use regularly
- explain how people who provide a service earn their living

Personal application

These statements highlight the relevance of the children's learning:
- I know that you cannot always see what work somebody has done
- I understand why people live in communities
- I understand that I depend on other people

Selling things	Transport	Welfare and learning	Entertaining people
Shops	Buses	Police Service	Cinemas
Supermarkets	Trains	Fire and Rescue Service	Leisure centres
Hotels	Aircraft	Ambulance Service	Libraries
Garden centres	Car parks	Doctors	Parks
Petrol stations		Teachers	

Teaching the lessons

Lesson 1 ❶

Key question

What are 'services'?

Introduction 15 min

▦ Make a list of all the jobs children can recall in five minutes. Circle all the jobs that produce a tangible product. The remaining jobs belong to the service sector. The following questions and answers are appropriate.

Which jobs are to do with selling things? (Shop assistant, pub landlord, hotel staff, hairdresser, bank staff.)

Which jobs are to do with leisure? (Cinema staff, leisure centre staff, librarian, park keeper.)

Which jobs are to do with transport? (Bus, train and lorry drivers, pilot.)

Which jobs are to do with repairing things? (Car mechanic, plumber, builder, painter, decorator.)

Which jobs are to do with health? (Doctor, dentist, nurse, surgeon.)

Which jobs are connected with education? (Teacher, secretary, caretaker, lecturer, school inspector.)

Which jobs are to do with emergencies? (Policeman, fireman, ambulance crew.)

Using the information sheet ⏱30min

The text on **Copymaster 27 Services** highlights the variety of jobs in the service sector. It also draws attention to the link between work and wages.

Differentiate by encouraging slow-learning children to concentrate on answering the first three questions and colouring the pictures. The timeline provides extension work for more-able pupils.

Summary ⏱10min

Write out a list of twenty jobs on the board. Ask the children to decide if each job involves providing a service with no tangible product or if it involves farming, mining or manufacturing.

Homework

Ask the children to make a list of ten jobs in the service sector from the vacancy section of the local newspaper.

Lesson 2 ②

Key question

What do you know about the different services?

Introduction ⏱10min

Make a class list of all the local services the children use apart from the school. This is likely to include shops of many kinds, play areas, libraries, churches and halls, clubs, swimming pools, leisure centres, parks, places of specialist tuition (e.g. music, dancing and sports centres), health services and post offices.

Using the activity sheet ⏱35min

Get the children to use **Copymaster 28 Different services** to find out how frequently each service is used. They could interview other children in the class or adults. Check that they know how to use the number scoring system.

Differentiate by encouraging less-able children to conduct the survey just for themselves by completing the first column and leaving the others blank. More-able children should analyse their results answering questions such as 'Which shops are used most/least?' 'Which leisure facilities seem most/least popular?' 'Which services seem underused?'. They could also draw block graphs of their findings.

Summary ⏱10min

Ask the children to talk about the results of their surveys. Discuss whether they all show a similar pattern, whether adults appear to use different services from children, and how the survey could be improved or developed.

Lesson 3 ②

Key question

What jobs are needed to run our school?

Introduction ⏱10min

Talk to the children about the different jobs needed to run a school. Discuss what work each person does. The following questions and answers are appropriate.

Who works in the school everyday? (Class teachers, head teacher, caretaker, cleaners, kitchen staff, crossing patrol.)

Who comes to the school occasionally? (Builders, painters, gardeners, heating engineers, postal workers, health visitors, the vicar, school inspectors.)

Investigation ⏱30min

Ask the children to make simple fact files about the different jobs done in school. Record each job on a separate card or chart using the following headings: 'Job', 'Name of person', 'Work they do', 'Hours they work' and 'Part of school they work in'.

Differentiate by completing the fact files as a class exercise with less-able children. Extend the work for faster-learning children to include an interview with different members of staff.

Summary ⏱10min

See if the children can decide which jobs are the most important and put them in order of priority.

Extra activities

A dictionary of jobs

With the children, make a class list of as many different jobs as possible, trying to find a job for every letter in the alphabet. Give each child a different letter and ask them to draw a picture and write a few sentences about the work for a wall display.

Changes in employment

The children could find out from a street directory about the jobs people used to do in Victorian times. Encourage them to note how many jobs have completely disappeared and to decide why. What new jobs do people do nowadays which were not done in the past?

Some people work at farming or mining. They sell food and raw materials. Others make things in factories or work outdoors building roads and houses. However, more and more people in Britain are now earning their living by providing a service. This means that they do a job which helps other people.

There are many different types of service. These include buying and selling goods, working in banks and offices, driving vehicles, providing entertainment and running schools and hospitals. The people who do these jobs do not make things you can see or touch. Their work involves keeping places running, caring for the sick and helping people enjoy their lives.

Most people are paid for what they do. The amount they are paid can depend on the number of hours they work. People who have special skills or take important decisions are also paid more.

Things to do

1 How are more and more people earning a living?

2 List six different jobs which provide services.

3 Why are people paid different amounts for their work?

4 Draw a timeline to show Joan Black's day at the bank.

Joan unlocks the door to the bank.

Joan writes letters to customers and answers telephone calls.

She meets a visitor who needs advice.

Joan discusses business over lunch.

She goes to a talk to learn new skills.

Joan puts money in the safe and locks up.

Different services

1. Ask six people in your class how often they use the services listed below. Record their answers using the correct number.

2. Add up the totals and write a few sentences about your findings.

3	**2**	**1**	**0**
nearly every day	about once a week	seldom	never

	Service	Person 1	Person 2	Person 3	Person 4	Person 5	Person 6	Total
Shops	Supermarket							
	Newsagent							
	Post office							
	Clothes shop							
	Café/restaurant							
	Garage							
Leisure	Church							
	Club							
	Library							
	Cinema							
	Swimming pool							
	Leisure centre							
	Play area							
Health	Doctor							
	Dentist							
	Optician							
Transport	Bus							
	Train							
	Taxi							
	Total							

TRANSPORT

Focus

The journeys that people make and the way that they travel have always been of interest to geographers. In the past, most people travelled on foot or by animal. Small boats often provided one of the best means of making longer journeys. Today cars, buses, trains and aeroplanes link many places. There is hardly a part of the globe that cannot be reached within 24 hours. The way that people have overcome natural barriers and obstacles makes a fascinating story.

Different methods of transport have their own strengths and weaknesses. For example, aircraft are very fast but cannot carry heavy goods. By contrast, trains and ships are slower but they can shift huge loads. Cars are very versatile. Each transport system needs a dedicated infrastructure such as airports, harbours or railway stations. In recent years, questions of pollution have come to the fore, particularly concerning fumes from cars which are damaging people's health. Finding more sustainable solutions is a high priority.

First Industrial Revolution 1770–1840	Second Industrial Revolution 1860–1910	Third Industrial Revolution 1950–present day
1769 Steam engine	1863 Underground railway	1948 Transistor
1802 Steam boat	1876 Telephone	1953 Electronic computer
1825 Railway	1885 Motor car	1957 Space probe
1838 Telegraph	1903 Aeroplane	1960s Mass air travel

Transport and communication have played key parts in industrial development

Brainstorm

Use this brainstorm to help you develop a medium-term plan.

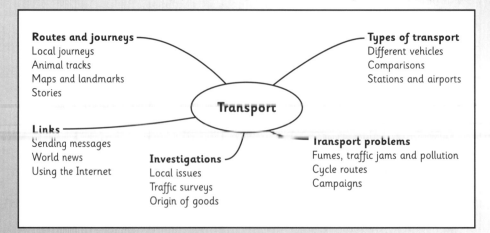

Routes and journeys
Local journeys
Animal tracks
Maps and landmarks
Stories

Links
Sending messages
World news
Using the Internet

Investigations
Local issues
Traffic surveys
Origin of goods

Types of transport
Different vehicles
Comparisons
Stations and airports

Transport problems
Fumes, traffic jams and pollution
Cycle routes
Campaigns

Transport

Research findings

It appears that children are able to read maps and find their way from place to place from an early age. Wiegand (1993) describes an experiment in which sixty children between the ages of three and five were asked to find a toy elephant hidden in a room. The results were impressive. Half the three-year-olds, three-quarters of the four-year-olds and all the five-year-olds completed the test successfully. Similar results were obtained with nursery school children who were asked to follow a route through a maze. Matthews (1984) found that girls tended to represent people and landmarks on their maps, whereas boys tended to show paths, cars and other forms of transport. In a further study, Matthews (1992) explored differences in wayfinding between boys and girls. He found that at junior school age, boys tended to perform better at spatial tasks than girls, perhaps because they are given more opportunities to explore the local area on their own. Whether this remains true today is a matter of some debate.

Content

Unit 15 Looks at routes and journeys.

Units 16, 17 Consider different types of transport and transport problems.

Unit 18 Focuses on international communications.

See also Unit 35, *European tour*.

National Curriculum expectations

At the end of Key Stage 2, it is expected that most children will be able to:
- know the location of key places in the United Kingdom, Europe and the world
- explain patterns of physical and human features
- describe how people can affect the environment and explain the different views held by people about an environmental change

Literacy links

Year 3 Stories with familiar settings: Unit 15 *Routes and journeys*, Lesson 3. Alphabetical texts: Unit 15 *Routes and journeys*, Extra activities, Vehicle dictionary.

Year 4 Make short notes: Unit 16 *Types of transport*, Lesson 3. Design an advertisement such as a poster: Unit 17 *Transport problems*, Homework.

Year 5 Read and evaluate letters e.g. from newspapers: Unit 17 *Transport problems*, Extra activities, Traffic schemes.

Year 6 Identify the features of balanced written arguments: Unit 18 *Links around the world*, Lesson 3.

ICT links

Satellite images — Show the children pictures of the Earth taken from space. These are ideal for showing variations in vegetation and land use, and illustrate the importance of modern communications.

CD-ROM — *Map Skills* (Pebbleshore 1993) uses routes and journeys as self-contained learning modules.

Routes and journeys

Learning targets

On completion of this unit children should understand that:

1 ➨➤ people plan their routes using maps
2 ➨➤ landmarks help us find our way from place to place
3 ➨➤ there are reasons for journeys

Before you start

Focus

This unit introduces children to the concept of routes and journeys.

Background knowledge

Most journeys, however short, are undertaken with a purpose. Each day, children and adults travel to work or school, visit the shops and make use of other services such as leisure facilities. People also sometimes go on longer trips for holidays and significant events. All these journeys involve following a route.

Roads and railways are permanent ways and usually make concessions to the landscape. In mountainous country, they follow valleys and avoid steep slopes. In other areas, they skirt marshes, lakes and forests. People select the route that suits them best either by referring to their personal experience or by using maps. Many organisations like the AA and the rail companies publish route maps to help people plan their journey.

Teaching points

Children need much practice in plotting and recording routes in their daily lives before using published material. They should be made aware of as great a variety of published material as possible.

Progression

At Key Stage 1, children use simple directions to orientate themselves in their immediate environment. Here they develop their wayfinding skills.

Vocabulary

direction, journey, landmark, obstacle, path, route, track

Geographical skills

- Description of routes using landmarks
- Recognition of order and sequence
- Ability to read route maps
- Interpretation of aerial photographs

National Curriculum links

- Use maps and plans, measure direction and distance, follow routes
- How land in settlements is used in different ways e.g. for housing, transport, industry
- Issues arising from how land is used e.g. conflicting views on the construction of a bypass across farmland

Assessment indicators

Children should be able to:
- say what a route is
- describe a familiar route using landmarks
- make a map to show a route

Personal application

These statements highlight the relevance of the children's learning:
- I can plan a route on a map
- I can give directions for a variety of journeys
- I realise that travel can enrich my life

Teaching the lessons

Lesson 1 ❶

Key question

How do maps help us plan routes?

Introduction |10min|

▓ Discuss why we move around from one place to another. There is usually a reason, even for short journeys. Classify the children's suggestions using these headings: 'Journeys to get things we need', 'Journeys which are part of our work' and 'Journeys we undertake for health and leisure'.

Using the information sheet |30min|

▓ As well as reading the information on **Copymaster 29 Routes and journeys** with the class, you could discuss the routes taken by local roads and railways, perhaps using an Ordnance Survey map.

Differentiation is provided by Question 4 which is

intended as an extension activity for more-able children.

Summary ☒ 10min
 Make a class list of all the obstacles which stop the children from taking a straight-line route to school.

Homework
Ask the children to contribute to a class display of maps showing the location of the school. This could include a world map, a map of the UK, bus and train maps, local Ordnance Survey maps, street plans and informal maps such as picture maps on postcards and tea towels.

Lesson 2 ②

Key question
Why are landmarks important?

Introduction 10min
 Discuss the routes the children take to school and the landmarks that they pass. Distinguish between fixed reference points and ephemeral clues such as roadworks and barking dogs. Explain that maps can show only permanent features.

Using the activity sheet 30min
👤 Using the map on **Copymaster 30 Landmarks**, the children compare the routes taken by three different children on their way to school. Peter travels by bus, Lisa goes by train and Tony walks.

Differentiate by encouraging slow-learning children to complete the details of Peter's journey as a class exercise. Ask more-able children to make their own map of their journey to school as an extension activity.

Summary 5min
 Ask the children which of the three routes they would prefer to make and why.

Lesson 3 ③

Key question
Can you draw a map of a journey in a story?

Introduction 15min
 Read the children a story involving a route or journey. Ask them to listen carefully and note down the landmarks that are mentioned.

Investigation 30min
👥 Ask the children to draw a map to go with a story of their choice. The stories could range from fictional journeys in picture books, novels and fairy tales, to historical journeys and accounts of contemporary travel. Some picture books about journeys are listed below.

Differentiate by encouraging slow-learning children to

make a map of the story you read to them as a class exercise.

Picture books about journeys

Author	Title	Publisher & date
Mitsumasa Anno	Anno's Journey	Bodley Head 1977
Michelle Cartlidge	Gerry's Seaside Journey	Heinemann 1981
Brian Patten	The Magic Bicycle	Walker 1995
Susie Jenkin Pearce	Percy Short and Cuthbert	Viking 1990
Sue Scullard	The Great Round the World Balloon Race	Macmillan 1993
Steve Skidmore	Fantastic Journey: All Around the World	Hodder & Stoughton 1992
Brian Wildsmith	The Hare and the Tortoise	Puffin 1990

Summary 5min
 Compare the maps the children have drawn, asking them to hold up their work and talk briefly about the route they have shown.

Extra activities ① ③

School directions
Get the children to write directions for visitors wanting to go from the front door to various important places in school, such as their classroom, the headteacher's room, the library or the caretaker's room.

Animal tracks
Get the children to find out about animal tracks using footprints and other clues. Ask the children to make drawings of the prints left by three different creatures. Can they think why each one would be making a journey?

Aerial photographs
Get the children to trace some of the routes they take using an aerial photograph of the local area. Ask them to describe one in detail, listing the key landmarks and changes in direction. Check if another child can follow the route from the description.

Routes and journeys

We spend a lot of time moving around. For example, at school you move around the classroom to find books, sharpen pencils, speak to the teacher and so on. After school, you make longer journeys to get home, visit the shops or see friends.

All these journeys follow routes. Sometimes, you take the same route each day. Your route to school is one example. At other times, you have to work out a new route for yourself.

Roads, paths and railway lines can be used as routes from one place to another.

Routes are important because when we set out on a journey we usually can't see the place we want to reach. Buildings, trees, hills and other obstacles make it difficult to travel in a straight line. This means we have to go around them.

On short journeys, we often remember the route by looking for landmarks. We plan longer journeys using maps. These tell us how to reach unfamiliar places and about the things we will pass on the way.

Things to do

1   Write down two short and two long journeys you have made recently. Say why you made them.

2   What can be used as routes from one place to another?

3   Why don't most routes go in a straight line?

4   Make a list of the places you pass through on a train journey:
    a) from Edinburgh to Penzance
    b) from Dover to Fort William

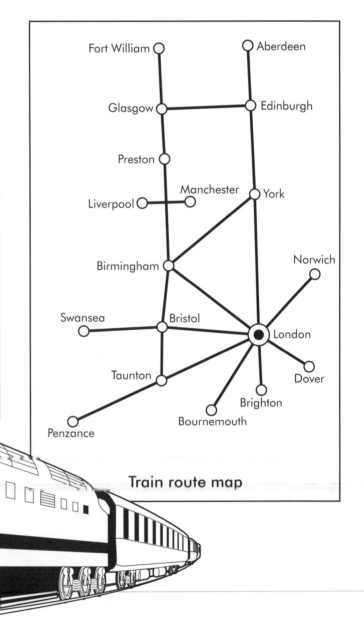

Train route map

Landmarks

1. Colour the houses where Peter, Lisa and Tony live.
2. Trace their routes to school on the map.
3. Complete the table at the bottom of the page.

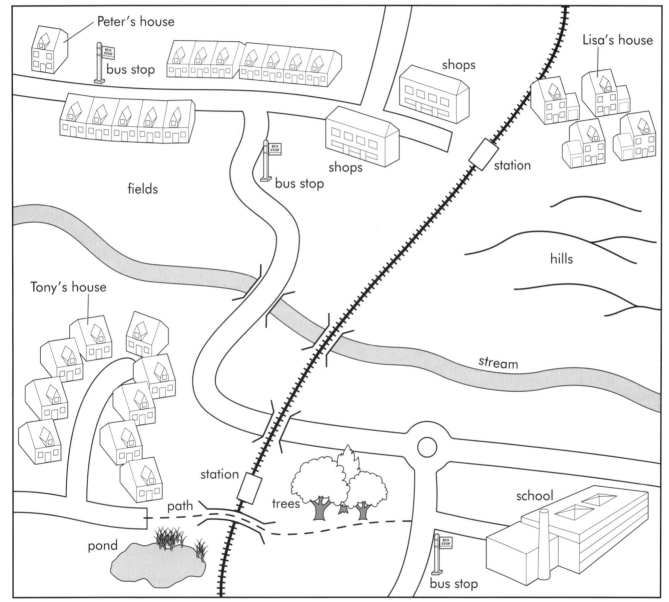

Name of child	Peter	Lisa	Tony
Method of travel			
Landmarks passed			

Types of transport

Learning targets

On completion of this unit children should understand that:

1 ➤➤ each type of transport has advantages and disadvantages
2 ➤➤ people and goods can travel by road, rail, sea or air

Before you start

Focus

The unit examines different types of transport and the reasons why they are needed.

Background information

Each type of transport has a particular advantage. Ships can carry bulky cargoes at low cost but are slow. Trains provide fast intercity links and are good for long-distance freight transport. Aircraft are ideal for international travel but are limited in the size and weight of what they carry. Road vehicles are versatile and can reach a wide variety of places.

Historically, networks of roads and railways developed through local use but today they must be considered on a national scale. Changes, improvements and neglect of one part of a system can create pressures many miles away. Governments are now seriously promoting integrated transport policies so that people and goods use a range of modes of transport depending on the type and the purpose of the journey. Transport has become a major human and environmental issue for the twenty-first century.

Teaching points

There are good opportunities for relating this unit to the children's personal experience and for developing it through traffic surveys and other fieldwork studies.

Progression

Children will be familiar with the different types of transport but may not have considered how they are suitable for different purposes or the impact that different vehicles have on the environment.

Vocabulary

Channel, ferry, goods, obstacle, SeaCat, system, transport, vehicle

Geographical skills

- Ability to make comparisons
- Ability to draw a bar chart
- Ability to read a UK map

National Curriculum links

- Identify points of reference on Map A (UK map)
- Use maps and plans, measure distance and direction, follow routes
- How localities are linked with other places e.g. through the supply of goods

Assessment indicators

Children should be able to:
- describe different modes of transport
- compare different modes of transport
- talk about the advantages and disadvantages of the modes

Personal application

These statements highlight the relevance of the children's learning:
- I know that there are different ways of making the same journey
- I know why different types of transport are needed
- I appreciate that the quickest method of transport is not always the best

Teaching the lessons

Lesson 1 ❶

Key question

What types of transport are there?

Introduction ⬜5min

▦ Talk to the children about the different types of transport that they use on a regular basis. Their answers will include walking, cycling and travelling by bus and car. Question and discuss what the advantages and disadvantages of these different methods are. Question and discuss why we need to travel in different ways.

Using the information sheet ⬜20min

▦ Read the text and information panels on **Copymaster 31 Types of transport** with the class. Discuss how many forms of transport use fossil fuels which lead to pollution and the steps being taken to protect the environment.

Differentiate by encouraging less-able children to make a class list of advantages and disadvantages of different forms of transport. The bar chart (Question 4) provides a link with mathematics and is designed for more-able children.

Summary
 Discuss which form of transport would be best for bringing the following to Britain: (a) oranges from Spain (lorry), (b) oil from Saudi Arabia (ship), (c) letters from Australia (aircraft), (d) people from Paris (train or aircraft).

Homework
Ask the children to collect photographs from magazines and other sources showing different forms of transport.

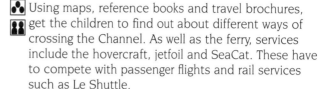

Key question
What ways of travelling are there?

Introduction
 Discuss with the children the journeys they or members of their family have made around the UK. How did they travel? Did any of them use a ferry, fly or travel by train? Was there a reason for using that particular method of transport?

Using the activity sheet
 Copymaster 32 Ways of travelling shows how different types of transport are best for specific journeys. The ferry from Lerwick is the only way of crossing the sea to Aberdeen; the coach is convenient for the fairly short journey from Aberdeen to Edinburgh; the aeroplane is the quickest way of reaching London from Edinburgh; and the train provides a frequent service to Bristol from London.

Differentiate by encouraging more-able children to calculate the distance of the whole journey and suggest alternative routes and methods of travel for the same journey.

Summary
 Talk to the class about why each type of transport is best for individual sections of the journey.

Key question
How can we cross the English Channel?

Introduction
 Find the English Channel and Straits of Dover on an atlas map. Discuss the way the sea provides an obstacle to land transport. What are the main ferry ports along the Channel coast? Can the children

trace the route of the Channel Tunnel from Folkestone to Dover?

Investigation
 Using maps, reference books and travel brochures, get the children to find out about different ways of crossing the Channel. As well as the ferry, services include the hovercraft, jetfoil and SeaCat. These have to compete with passenger flights and rail services such as Le Shuttle.

Differentiate by encouraging slow-learning children to make drawings and write short descriptions of the different forms of transport for a wall display. More-able children could draw maps showing the different routes and compare the fares and the speeds of travel.

Summary
 The Channel Tunnel is now taking increasing quantities of freight and passenger traffic. Speculate with the children on how services might change in five years' time.

Extra activities

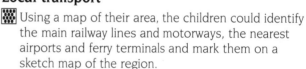

Local transport
Using a map of their area, the children could identify the main railway lines and motorways, the nearest airports and ferry terminals and mark them on a sketch map of the region.

Motorway quiz
Working from a road map or atlas, get the children to find out which motorways they would take from their area to different parts of the country. Divide the children up into pairs and see if they can devise some quiz questions for the rest of the class to follow.

Vehicle dictionary
Ask the children to make up a dictionary with different vehicles for each letter of the alphabet, starting with 'a' for aeroplane, 'b' for boat.

Types of transport

Day and night across the UK and the rest of the world, huge numbers of vehicles move from place to place. They travel along roads and railway lines or follow air routes and sea lanes.

In the modern age, everybody relies on good transport links. We expect to have food and other items delivered to the shops each day. We depend on speedy help in emergencies. Many people also travel to other countries for their work or holidays.

There are advantages to each type of transport. Find out more about these by looking at the pictures on this page.

Things to do

1 Why are transport links important?

2 Name four different types of transport.

3 Write down one advantage of each method of transport.

4 Draw a bar graph comparing the energy used by each type of transport.

Motor vehicles

Motor vehicles can go to lots of different places and move people and goods easily.

Trains

Trains link big towns and can carry lots of people and heavy goods.

Ships

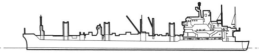

Ships and boats cross the oceans providing links between countries.

Aeroplanes

Aeroplanes are the fastest way of travelling and can cross mountains and seas as well as land.

Which vehicle uses energy best?

A double-decker bus with 70 people

A coach with 20 people

A car with 1 person   A car with 4 people

Some children travel to school by car, some by coach and others by bus. Many teachers drive to school. Look at the diagram and decide which is the best use of energy. What effects this?

Ways of travelling

When Tony Smith travelled from Lerwick to Bristol he used a boat, an aeroplane, a bus and a train.

1. Complete the table to show how he travelled.

2. Draw a picture of each vehicle on the correct part of the map.

Lerwick

Aberdeen

0   100   200   300 km

Edinburgh

JOURNEY	VEHICLE USED
Lerwick–Aberdeen	
Aberdeen–Edinburgh	
Edinburgh–London	
London–Bristol	

Bristol   London

Transport problems

Learning targets

On completion of this unit children should understand that:

1 ➤➤ road traffic is a major environmental problem
2 ➤➤ there are a variety of ways of tackling traffic problems

Before you start

Focus

Children will learn about different traffic problems and ways of solving them.

Background information

There are about 25 million vehicles in the UK – about one vehicle for every two people in our densely populated and relatively small country. If current trends continue, the number of cars and lorries will double by the middle of the next century. Each year, road vehicles travel billions of miles creating enormous quantities of exhaust fumes. These fumes are detrimental to the environment and our health because they contain greenhouse gases and toxic chemicals as well as harmful particulates. One child in seven now suffers from asthma and breathing difficulties.

Traffic congestion is a problem which also affects the quality of town life and damages buildings. For many years, governments have sought to ease the situation by building new roads, motorways and bypasses. However, this tends to increase traffic because better roads make journeys easier, so other strategies are being tried. Petrol tax is being increased, road building reduced, access to cities restricted and more thought being given to developing public transport. However, it is a complex issue and no strategy is a panacea.

Teaching points

Traffic problems are both abstract and adult in nature. The best approach with children is to make the issues more immediate by relating them to their own lives.

Progression

Young children are constantly warned about traffic dangers and their personal freedom is seriously curtailed for safety reasons. This unit develops children's understanding by showing how traffic is a major environmental problem with which everybody has to grapple.

Vocabulary

bollard, bypass, chicane, environment, flyover, fumes, habitat, smog, traffic, underpass, vehicle

Geographical skills

* Ability to make a flowline diagram
* Ability to make judgements
* Use of diamond rankings
* Ability to devise enquiry questions
* Conduct a traffic survey

National Curriculum links

* Environmental issues that give localities their character
* Collect and record evidence to answer questions
* Issues arising from the way land is used e.g. conflicting views about the construction of a bypass across farmland

Assessment indicators

Children should be able to:
* describe how vehicles cause environmental damage
* suggest some solutions to transport problems
* describe how traffic effects their local area

Personal application

These statements highlight the relevance of the children's learning:
* I know how I contribute to traffic problems through my own activities
* I understand that there are no easy ways of solving traffic problems
* I know how to collect information for myself

Teaching the lessons

Lesson 1 ① ②

Key question

What causes traffic problems?

Introduction [5 min]

▦ Talk to the children about how we depend on road transport. Make a quick class travel survey. Ask who has used a car in the last day, week or month. Can the children think of anything in the classroom which did not involve a road journey at some stage?

Using the information sheet `25min`

The information on **Copymaster 33 Transport problems** explains how cars cause environmental damage and suggests that other forms of transport and especially bicycles are valuable alternatives.

Differentiate by encouraging less-able children to concentrate on the first three questions. Ask more-able children to turn the 'keeping traffic moving' diagram into a timeline using these dates: traffic lights 1920s, roundabouts 1930s, one-way streets 1950s, underpasses and flyovers 1960s, bypasses 1970s, and motorways 1980s.

Summary `10min`

Get the children to describe how they think they will travel when they are grown up. Do they think things will be the same as today, or will they be prepared to change at least some of the ways they make journeys?

Homework

Ask the children to design a poster or campaign leaflet to persuade people to cycle to school or work instead of travelling by car.

Lesson 2 ②

Key question

How might traffic problems be eased?

Introduction `5min`

Talk about traffic congestion in your area, where traffic jams occur and which are the busiest times of day.

Using the activity sheet `30min`

Divide the children into mixed-ability groups. To use **Copymaster 34 Controlling traffic**, each group of children will need scissors, glue and a sheet of paper for mounting their work. Explain that they are going colour and cut out the pictures and arrange them in order of priority. As some solutions are of more or less equal value, a diamond ranking will be particularly effective. In this system, the best solution goes at the top of the diagram, followed by the two second best on the next row. Put three solutions on the row underneath this and complete the diamond with rows of two and one at the bottom.

Differentiate by encouraging less-able children to select and write about two solutions which they think best. More-able children should write a sentence about the reasons for each device to include with their work.

Summary `10min`

Discuss with the class how each device helps to control traffic. Do different groups agree about the most effective and least effective solutions?

Lesson 3 ①

Key question

How can we collect information about road traffic?

Introduction `10min`

Get the children to find out more about traffic near the school. Look at a map with the children to identify a suitable place for a survey. See if they can suggest some questions they would like to investigate. Examples include the following.

Which are the busiest/quietest roads in our area?

Which are the busiest/quietest times of day?

What types of vehicles use local roads?

How are people trying to control traffic in our area?

Investigation `45min`

Organise a survey to answer the question that the children have decided to investigate. If they are making a vehicle count, one child in each group could keep time, another count vehicles, while another records the results. If the children are looking for evidence of traffic control, you may need to devise a trail and a simple recording sheet to help them.

Differentiate by dividing the children into mixed-ability groups with more-able children designated as scribes.

Summary `10min`

Discuss the findings of the survey with the whole class. What were the main findings? What conclusions can be drawn from them?

Extra activities ① ②

Traffic schemes

Ask the children to contact the local council and look in local papers to find out any new traffic proposals for your area.

Cars around the world

There are 400 million cars in the world today. Ask the children to draw a bar chart or percentage line to show the proportion of cars in different parts of the world using this data: USA 35 per cent, Western Europe 32 per cent, Japan 7 per cent, Latin America 7 per cent, the rest of the world 19 per cent.

Cars are very convenient. People use them to travel where and when they want. Cars also move quickly from one place to another and can carry lots of luggage. This encourages people to make journeys.

Today there are so many vehicles on the roads that it is causing problems. Cars and lorries bring noise to the towns and countryside and damage animal habitats. Fumes from car exhausts pollute the air and cause breathing problems for some people. Traffic jams are common.

Bigger, straighter roads were built to try to solve the problem of traffic jams but they too became jammed as more and more traffic used them. One answer to these problems is to get people to travel in different ways. Buses and trains can carry lots of people at once and cause much less pollution. Bicycles are even better for short journeys. They give you lots of exercise and cause no pollution at all.

Things to do

1 Why are cars convenient?

2 Make a list of the problems cars cause.

3 Say how people are trying to solve traffic problems.

4 Draw a diagram to show how people have tried to keep traffic moving.

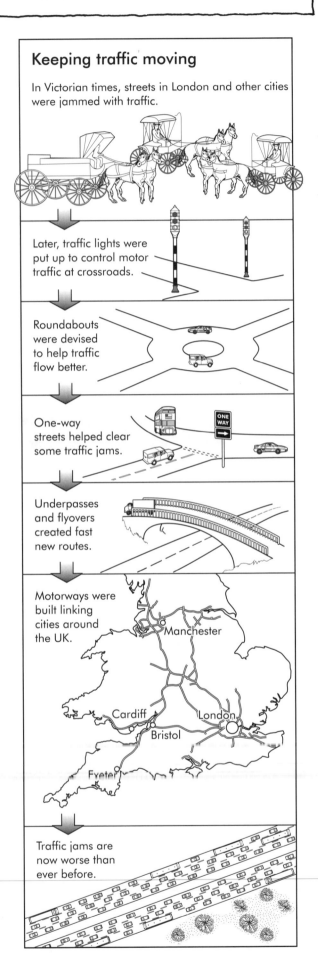

Keeping traffic moving

In Victorian times, streets in London and other cities were jammed with traffic.

Later, traffic lights were put up to control motor traffic at crossroads.

Roundabouts were devised to help traffic flow better.

One-way streets helped clear some traffic jams.

Underpasses and flyovers created fast new routes.

Motorways were built linking cities around the UK.

Manchester
Cardiff
London
Bristol
Exeter

Traffic jams are now worse than ever before.

34

Controlling traffic

1. Colour and cut out the pictures.

2. Working in your group, decide which are the best ways to control the traffic.

3. Fix the pictures on your sheet of paper with the best way at the top and the worst way at the bottom.

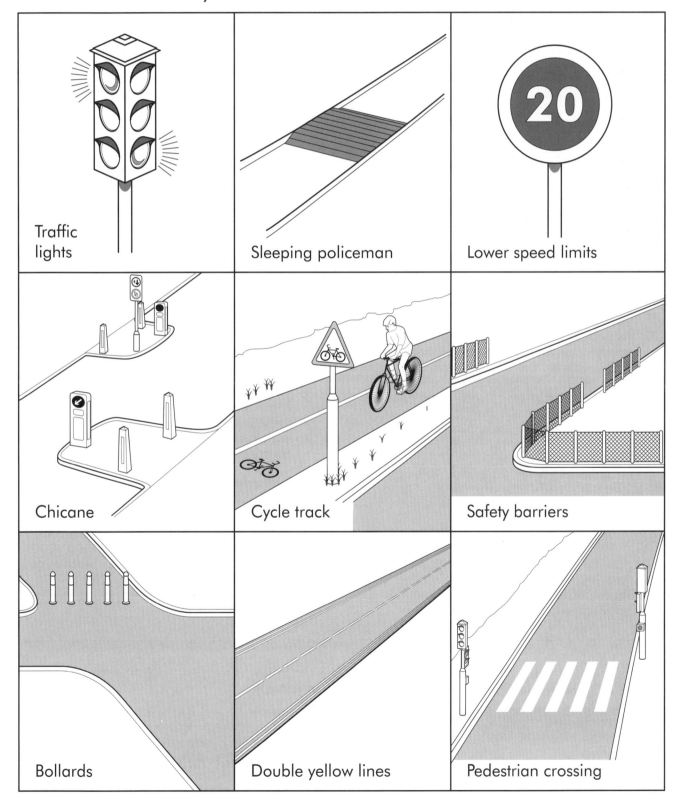

Traffic lights	Sleeping policeman	Lower speed limits
Chicane	Cycle track	Safety barriers
Bollards	Double yellow lines	Pedestrian crossing

Links around the world

Learning targets

On completion of this unit children should understand that:

1 ➤➤ modern life depends on good communications
2 ➤➤ air routes provide quick links between places
3 ➤➤ we receive news and information from all over the world

Before you start

Focus

The unit explores world communication systems and the effect they have on our lives.

Background information

The modern world is linked by a global economic system where each nation depends on others for goods and materials. However, differences in natural wealth, imperialism and other historical forces have led to increasing inequalities between nations. This is particularly apparent in Africa where many countries depend on one or two cash crops for a large proportion of their income. It also means that sudden changes in the world monetary system may have dire consequences for millions of people. Multinational businesses based in North America, Europe and Japan now control budgets which are bigger than the entire income of some of the world's poorer nations. Fast air travel and electronic communications underpin these developments.

Teaching points

Young people today will grow up to be the global citizens of tomorrow. We need to see that they understand the wider world and are equipped to play their part in it.

Progression

This unit is chiefly concerned with describing how different places are linked together. It lays the foundation for a much more adult understanding of global interdependence.

Vocabulary

communications, diet, goods, motorways, route, satellite, trade

Geographical skills

- Ability to draw annotated diagrams
- Identification of places on a world map
- Extraction of information from secondary sources

National Curriculum links

- Identify the points of reference specified on Map C (world map)
- Become aware of how places fit into a wider geographical context
- Use ICT to gain access to additional information sources

Assessment indicators

Children should be able to:
- talk about changes in transport and communications
- identify some major world air routes
- explain some of the ways they are linked to distant places

Personal application

These statements highlight the relevance of the children's learning:
- I can describe ways in which I am linked to people and places around the world
- I realise that busy air routes link prosperous parts of the world
- I do not believe all the information I receive without finding out more

Teaching the lessons

Lesson 1 ❶

Key question

How do modern communications link us with the rest of the world?

Introduction 15min

▓ Invite the children to write down three things they know about the world beyond the UK. Now ask some of them what they wrote down and how they learnt about it. Their sources of information will probably include the television, photographs and international travel. Explain that most of what we know about the world is due to improvements in transport and communication.

Using the information sheet ⌐25min⌐

There are two main ideas on **Copymaster 35 Links around the world**: (a) communications have improved dramatically in the last century, (b) modern industry depends on worldwide trade.

Differentiate by discussing the answers to the questions as a class exercise with less-able children. Find out more about satellite communications and the Internet with more-able pupils.

Summary ⌐15min⌐

Make a class list of some of the ways the place where the children live is linked to places in other parts of the world either through trade or communications.

Homework

Ask the children to bring some stamps to school for a display about world postal services.

Lesson 2 ②

Key question

How are places linked by air routes?

Introduction ⌐5min⌐

Talk to the children about any air journeys they have made. Ask where they went, how long the flight took and what it was like.

Using the activity sheet ⌐30min⌐

Look at the map on **Copymaster 36 Air routes** with the children. See that they understand that London is at a place where routes join while Moscow is on a through route and Cairo is at the end of a route. Talk about how it is possible to go directly from Tokyo to Los Angeles 'around the back' of the map.

Differentiate by encouraging more-able children to devise routes from one place to another, listing the places they would pass through. Possible journeys might include London to Sydney, Buenos Aires to Tokyo and Bangkok to Chicago.

Summary ⌐5min⌐

Select some of the cities shown on the map and ask the children to name the places they could fly to directly from that starting point.

Lesson 3 ③

Key question

How do we know what is happening around the world?

Introduction ⌐15min⌐

Discuss how news bulletins tell us what is happening around the UK and in other parts of the world. See if

the children can remember any news events. Remind them how messages are beamed around the world by satellite.

Investigation ⌐30min⌐

Divide the children into groups and give each group a recent broadsheet newspaper. They should then make a list of the different places and countries mentioned in the news reports. Ask them to locate the places in an atlas and mark them on their own blank map of the world.

Differentiate by making a wall display with less-able children by arranging the headlines (or brief summaries of the reports) on a world map.

Summary ⌐15min⌐

Compare the results from different groups. Make a master list on the board of all the countries mentioned. Do some continents seem to feature more than others? Do some parts of the world never seem to be mentioned? You might also discuss the sort of information which is reported and what you would want people in other parts of the world to know about what is currently happening in the UK.

Extra activities

Schools link

Get the children to use the Internet to attempt to establish a link with a school in another country and to exchange information about the local areas.

Made around the world

Ask the children to make a survey of ten objects in and around the classroom. They should note down from the label where each one was made, then find these different places and countries in an atlas and show their results on their own world map.

Always available

Ask the children to devise a diagram to show how the grapes we buy in a supermarket come from different parts of the world according to the season. Use the information in the table below.

Season	Countries grapes come from
Spring	Brazil, South Africa
Summer	India, South Africa, Chile
Autumn	Greece, Italy, Spain
Winter	Spain, Brazil

Links around the world

A hundred years ago, most food was grown locally and people went on holiday to seaside resorts around the UK. Countries had their own factories making things for the people who lived there.

Now, much has changed. Trains go at high speed because of better tracks and signals. Motorways have been built across Europe allowing cars and lorries to travel quickly over great distances. Enormous oil tankers and container ships carry goods across the oceans. Air travel has seen even bigger changes. Simple aircraft made from fabric and wood have been replaced by massive jets.

There have also been big improvements in sending messages and information. Television, telephones and computers now allow people to communicate across the world as easily as they once did in a village. News travels fast.

These links help people exchange goods and services. Companies can now make goods in one part of the world and sell them in distant countries. Trade has increased and many people have grown richer.

At the same time, people no longer have to rely on food they can grow for themselves. The fruit and vegetables in supermarkets can come from Africa, Asia and other faraway places. We now have a better diet than we used to have.

Things to do

1 What was life like a hundred years ago?

2 How has air travel changed?

3 What improvements have there been in sending messages?

4 What can companies now do?

5 Make a drawing to show how satellites can beam messages around the world.

6 List three of the advantages of better communications.

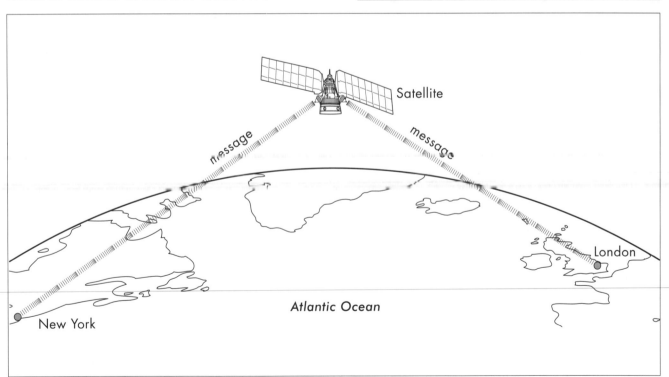

Satellite

message

message

London

Atlantic Ocean

New York

1. Colour the key.
2. Colour the cities on the map using the colours from the key.
3. Fill in the table at the bottom of the sheet.

Key	
Places where routes meet	green
Places on through routes	yellow
Places at the end of a route	red

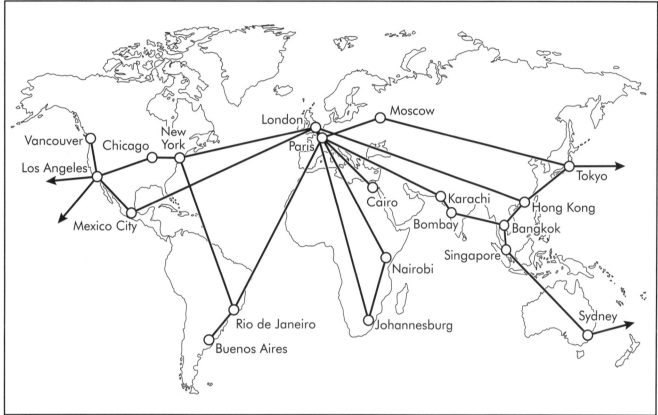

Places where routes meet	Places on through routes	Places at the end of a route

ENVIRONMENT

Focus

Environmental problems are one of the key issues facing the world at the present time. The growth of industry and economic activity since the Second World War has caused serious pollution on a global scale and is putting an increasing strain on natural resources. At the same time, there has been a massive increase in population. Human numbers have more than trebled since the start of the twentieth century and are likely to go on rising. Ultimately, there is a limit to the demands that can be put on the Earth which is a finite system.

A number of other factors have compounded the problem. One of them is inequality. About one-fifth of the world's population currently consume about four-fifths of the world's wealth. This leaves the vast majority impoverished. The contrast between the developed countries of the 'North' and developing countries of the 'South' was highlighted by the Brandt Report in 1980. Ultimately, the environmental crisis, which is the product of human activity, will only be solved when there is a much greater measure of social justice.

In recent years, there have been some serious efforts to address the problem. The Earth Summit that was held in Rio de Janeiro in 1992 was a major landmark in international cooperation and was attended by representatives from many of the world's nations. One of the outcomes was a blueprint for the planet which has come to be known as Agenda 21. Another was the notion of sustainable development.

Schools throughout Britain have enthusiastically adopted these ideas. Schemes to recycle waste and reduce consumption are widespread. Specific projects such as Eco-schools (run by the Tidy Britain Group) have also proved popular. Activities of this kind are central components in a curriculum focused on citizenship and environmental awareness.

Brainstorm

Use this brainstorm to help you develop a medium-term plan.

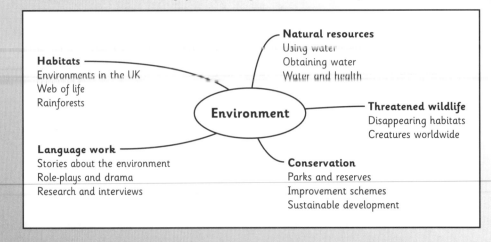

Habitats
Environments in the UK
Web of life
Rainforests

Natural resources
Using water
Obtaining water
Water and health

Environment

Threatened wildlife
Disappearing habitats
Creatures worldwide

Language work
Stories about the environment
Role-plays and drama
Research and interviews

Conservation
Parks and reserves
Improvement schemes
Sustainable development

Research findings

Even before they come to school, children acquire ideas about the environment. However, many of these notions are incomplete or confused. For example, when nursery children were asked about creatures which live in polar lands, Palmer (1998) found about a third gave completely inappropriate answers. Similarly, junior school children appear to have very muddled ideas about the greenhouse effect. In a survey of 563 children, Qualter (1995) found that 85 per cent thought that protecting rare species would help to alleviate the problem. A similar number believed that reducing nuclear bombs would be the solution. These findings are a timely reminder that, although children today have access to a lot of information about the world around them, they need help in making sense of it.

Content

This section considers different aspects of the environment in the UK and wider world.

Units 19, 20	Look at the countryside and towns respectively.
Unit 21	Considers water which is a key natural resource.
Unit 22	Focuses on the rainforest, arguably the most valuable habitat on earth. This could be used in conjunction with Unit 40 *South America*.

National Curriculum expectations

At the end of Key stage 2, it is expected that most children will be able to:

- recognise how selected physical and human processes cause changes in the character of places and environments
- describe how people can affect the environment and explain the different views held by people about an environmental change

Literacy links

Year 3	Word games: Unit 21 *Water*, Homework. Collect new words from other subjects: Unit 22 *Rainforests*, Lesson 1. Collect information from a variety of sources: Unit 19 *Caring for the countryside*, Extra activities, Green team.
Year 4	Make short notes: Unit 20 *Caring for towns*, Lesson 2.
Year 5	Write accounts based on personal experience: Unit 19 *Caring for the countryside*, Extra activities, Study visit. Compose non-chronological reports: Unit 20 *Caring for towns*, Lesson 3. Write own play script: Unit 21 *Water*, Lesson 3.
Year 6	Construct effective arguments: Unit 22 *Rainforests*, Extra activities, Rainforest drama.

Story

There is a wide range of stories on environmental issues including *The People who Hugged Trees* by Deborah Lee Rose (Rinehart 1990), a traditional folk tale from India, *Brother Eagle, Sister Sky* by Chief Seattle (Hamilton 1992) and *One World* by Michael Foreman (Andersen 1990) which stresses the idea that planet Earth is the only home we have.

ICT links

| CD-ROM | Use *Odyssey Scrapbook* (YITM 1996) to find out more about environmental issues. |
| Internet | Up-to-date information about environmental issues all over the world is available on the Internet. |

Caring for the countryside

Learning targets

On completion of this unit children should understand that:

1 ➤➤ the UK has a rich flora and fauna
2 ➤➤ many forms of wildlife are threatened
3 ➤➤ parks and nature reserves help to conserve plants and creatures

Before you start

Focus

The countryside needs to be protected to save it from development.

Background information

Originally, most of lowland Britain was covered by forest. Over the centuries, people have slowly cleared away the trees and claimed the land for farming. In modern times, the growth of urban areas and the introduction of intensive farming techniques have put the countryside under increasing pressure. Since the Second World War, the pace of change has accelerated. Marshes, downlands, woodlands and hedgerows have all been destroyed at an alarming rate. Creatures which were once common, such as the dormouse and song thrush, are now under threat. The government has responded by designating areas of high landscape value, creating Sites of Special Scientific Interest (SSSIs). Organisations such as the RSPB (Royal Society for the Protection of Birds), WWF (World Wildlife Fund for Nature), CPRE (Council for the Protection of Rural England) and The Woodland Trust are also doing what they can to protect the countryside for the enjoyment of future generations.

Teaching points

Try to stress the positive things that people can do rather than dwelling exclusively on the negative aspects of the current situation.

Progression

Young children have a natural empathy for plants and creatures. This unit builds on and extends their interest.

Vocabulary

bay, cliff, coastline, countryside, habitat, hedge, marsh, meadow, nature reserve, pond, wildlife, wood

Geographical skills

- Recognition of links and connections
- Ability to argue a case
- Ability to draw conclusions

National Curriculum links

- How people affect the environment
- How and why people seek to manage and conserve their environment e.g. by conserving areas of beautiful landscape or scientific value

Assessment indicators

Children should be able to:
- name three threatened creatures
- say what people are doing to save the countryside
- describe different habitats

Personal application

These statements highlight the relevance of the children's learning:
- I realise that some plants and creatures are only found in specific environments
- I understand that the loss of even a small habitat may affect many species
- I understand why some places need to be protected

Teaching the lessons

Lesson 1 ❶❸

Key question

What different habitats do you know?

Introduction   10 min

▦ Begin by talking to the children about their experiences of the countryside and discussing what places they like going to and why. Explain how a habitat provides an environment for a range of plants and creatures. Ask what different habitats the children can think of and what wildlife they support.

Consider contrasting places such as woods, mountains and seashores.

Using the information sheet $\boxed{30\text{min}}$

 The information on **Copymaster 37 The countryside** introduces the idea of habitats through practical examples.

Differentiate by encouraging slow-learning children to make drawings of different habitats (e.g. marshes, woods, downlands, cliffs) and to write a sentence describing them. More-able children could develop the study of the Minsmere Nature Reserve by making their own annotated map of the reserve.

Minsmere Nature Reserve

Minsmere Nature Reserve is in Suffolk in East Anglia. It is an area of marshes close to the sea. The mixture of reeds and grasses creates a very special habitat. Over 100 different types of bird live on the reserve. Many others stop there as they migrate from one place to another.

Many people visit Minsmere every year. They can follow a trail and watch the birds from sheds or hides without disturbing them.

Looking after the reserve takes a lot of work. As well as looking after visitors, the warden sees that some of the reeds are cut and cleared each year. The best time to do this is in the winter before the birds start nesting.

Summary $\boxed{5\text{min}}$

 Discuss whether one habitat is more important than another or whether they are all equally valuable.

Homework

Ask the children to create their own mini-environment in a bowl or small dish. They could cover the soil with moss, use little twigs for trees and small stones as rocky outcrops.

Lesson 2 ②

Key question

How can wildlife become threatened?

Introduction $\boxed{10\text{min}}$

 Remind the children that wildlife is threatened for a number of different reasons. For example, towns and cities are getting larger, farmers are using the land more intensively, and pollution is poisoning the environment.

Using the activity sheet $\boxed{40\text{min}}$

 The plants and creatures shown on **Copymaster 38 Threatened wildlife** come from a range of different habitats. Specific projects have helped to restore the number of barn owls in recent years. This points the way to the future and indicates that what people do can make a difference.

Differentiate by encouraging slow-learning children to

discuss the threats facing the different plants and creatures as a whole-class exercise. Divide more-able children into groups and ask them to research one of the plants or creatures shown on the copymaster.

Summary $\boxed{10\text{min}}$

 Compare the threats the children think each creature faces.

Lesson 3 ① ③

Key question

Where are the national parks?

Introduction $\boxed{5\text{min}}$

 Look at a map of the UK with the children and identify the locations of the different national parks. Ask the children which parks include the coastal areas. Ask why they think so many parks are in hills or mountains.

Investigation $\boxed{45\text{min}}$

 Ask the children to draw their own maps of the UK, showing the locations of the national parks.

Differentiate by providing slow-learning children with a photocopied map which they can colour in. Ask more-able children to compile a table with their maps, listing each park, its main physical features and the nearest towns.

Summary $\boxed{5\text{min}}$

 Talk to the children about the national park that is nearest to your area. What is it like?

Extra activities ① ② ③

Green team

Divide the children into groups. Tell them that they have been asked to devise a campaign to protect wildlife in their area. What are their plans? Discuss some of the options before letting the children work on their own. Leaflets, press releases, fund-raising events, letters to the newspapers and posters are all suitable strategies.

Study visit

Arrange a visit to a nature reserve or field studies centre in the area near your school. As well as using this as opportunity to find out about how people are caring for the natural environment, you could also develop links to other areas of the curriculum, especially science.

Wildlife spreadsheet

Set up a computer spreadsheet of endangered wildlife around the world using the following headings: 'Plant/creature', 'Habitat', 'Numbers (if known)' and 'Conservation'. The children can add to the spreadsheet over a period of time as they find out more information.

The countryside

Britain has a very varied and beautiful countryside. A mixture of fields, hedges, woods and marshes has developed over thousands of years. This provides homes or habitats for great numbers of different plants and creatures.

Each area of the UK has its own character. In southern England, there are grassy hills with colourful flowers and butterflies. Eastern England is well known for its marshes. In Wales and Scotland, clumps of heather spread across the mountains. There are cliffs and bays all around the coast of the UK. These make one of the most attractive coastlines in the world.

Today, the countryside is changing. Roads, houses and factories are taking up more and more space. Plants, birds and animals are threatened as they lose their habitats. Some have even become extinct.

There are many ways of protecting wildlife. In some places, parks and nature reserves have been set up. In other areas, people have made wildlife gardens. This is helping to keep the countryside safe for the future.

Things to do

1 How would you describe the British countryside?

2 Write one thing which is special to each part of the UK.

3 How are people protecting the countryside?

4 Make up three questions to ask the warden of Minsmere Nature Reserve.

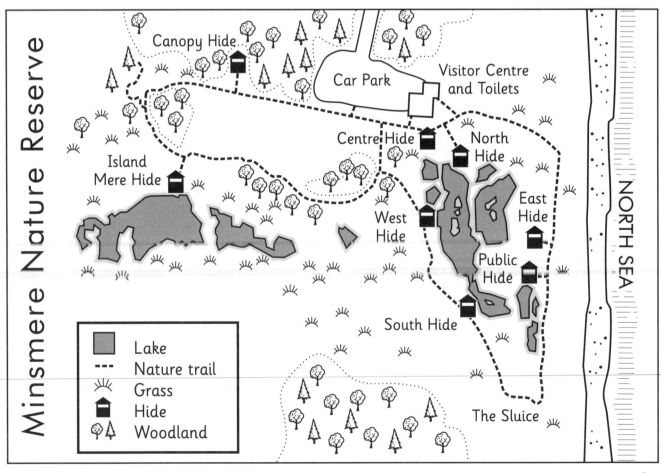

Minsmere Nature Reserve

Canopy Hide
Car Park
Visitor Centre and Toilets
Centre Hide
North Hide
Island Mere Hide
West Hide
East Hide
Public Hide
South Hide
The Sluice
NORTH SEA

Lake
Nature trail
Grass
Hide
Woodland

Threatened wildlife

1. Colour the drawings.
2. Say how each creature is threatened.

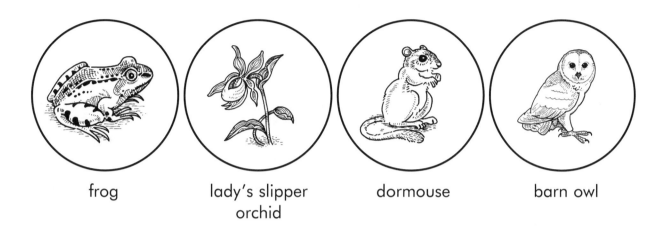

| frog | lady's slipper orchid | dormouse | barn owl |

Plant or creature	Habitat	Threat
frog	pond	
lady's slipper orchid	meadow	
dormouse	hedge	
barn owl	old building	
large blue butterfly	field	
badger	woodland	
dragonfly	marsh	
puffin	seashore	

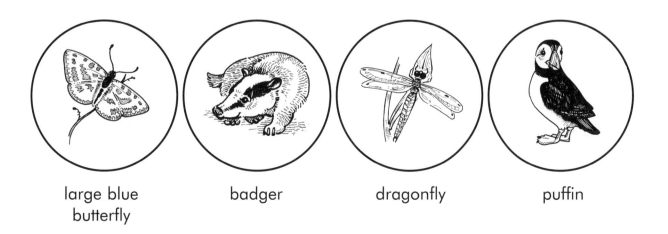

| large blue butterfly | badger | dragonfly | puffin |

Caring for towns

Learning targets

On completion of this unit children should understand that:

1 ➤➤ towns need to be cared for and maintained
2 ➤➤ most streets and buildings can be improved

Before you start

Focus

This unit considers the importance of caring for the urban environment.

Background information

In Britain, town planning dates back to Roman times. Cities such as London, York and Exeter were laid out on a grid pattern and each defended by a wall punctuated with gates. Through the centuries, people have continued to plan cities, often following formal plans with avenues and vistas as at Bath or Edinburgh. In modern times, green belts and garden cities have been established in an attempt to control the spread of buildings into the countryside. At the same time, buildings of architectural or historic merit have been given legal protection and the centres of some cities designated as conservation areas.

Teaching points

You will find it helpful to explore the local area yourself and identify ways in which it could be improved before beginning this unit.

Progression

Young children tend to think that their surroundings are immutable. This unit helps them to realise that it can be changed and improved.

Vocabulary

bollards, chicanes, council, environment, facilities, pedestrianisation

Geographical skills

* Ability to sort into lists
* Ability to make comparisons
* Ability to reach conclusions

National Curriculum links

* How and why people seek to manage and sustain their environment
* Undertake studies which focus on geographical questions
* Analyse evidence, draw conclusions and communicate findings

Assessment indicators

Children should be able to:
* describe the work of the local council
* say how their own area could be improved
* appreciate that all schemes have advantages and disadvantages

Personal application

These statements highlight the relevance of the children's learning:
* I know about some of the jobs which the council does
* I can describe an improvement scheme and the reasons behind it
* I have my own ideas for improving the local area

Teaching the lessons

Lesson 1 ❶

Key question

Who cares for towns?

Introduction `10min`

▨ Talk to the class about famous buildings around the world. Examples include the Tower of London, Edinburgh Castle, the Eiffel Tower, the Kremlin, the

Taj Mahal and the Pyramids. Make a list on the board. Explain that all buildings are created by people and that they are among the finest human achievements.

Using the information sheet `30min`

▨ **Copymaster 39 Caring for towns** describes the way the council helps to look after towns. It does many other jobs which are not described here.

Differentiate by encouraging slow-learning children to make a list on the board of special buildings in their neighbourhood and talk about the changes shown in the high street drawings on the copymaster. Discuss the advantages and disadvantages of pedestrianisation with more-able children.

Summary ⬚ 5min

Working around the class, ask the children to list the different ways the council cares for towns.

Homework

Ask the children to suggest one way in which their own street or immediate environment could be improved. They might include maps or drawings in their work as well as a short written passage.

Lesson 2 ②

Key question

How can improvement schemes help the environment?

Introduction ⬚ 10min

Discuss the ways that the council tries to improve the environment. For instance, it creates new paths and cycle routes, plants trees and sets up playgrounds. Ask the children to explain the reason for these different schemes. Explain also that before they build anything, the council asks local people for their opinions and ideas.

Using the activity sheet ⬚ 40min

Discuss the schemes shown in the pictures on **Copymaster 40 Improvement schemes** so that the children are clear about what each one involves.

Differentiate by encouraging slow-learning children to colour the drawings and write a sentence underneath. Extend the work with more-able children by asking them to describe each scheme, explain why it is needed, say who benefits, consider any disadvantages from it and so on.

Summary ⬚ 10min

Compare the children's answers. Which of the four schemes do they think is most important?

Lesson 3 ②

Key question

How could your street be improved?

Introduction ⬚ 10min

Discuss the factors which affect the quality of the environment. The following questions and answers are appropriate.

What are the things which contribute to the quality of the environment? (Traffic calming, pedestrianisation, cycle routes, trees, fountains, statues, gardens and flowers.)

What are the things which detract from the quality of the environment? (Noise, traffic fumes, vehicles travelling too fast, litter, vandalism, pollution.)

Investigation ⬚ 45min

 Divide the children into groups and explain that they are going to visit a local street. It is their job to identify good and bad features and write a short report on the quality of the environment.

Differentiate by providing slow-learning children with Copymaster 40 to complete on which they list the positive and negative features of the street. More-able children can suggest an improvement scheme of their own, providing drawings and details of what they have in mind.

Summary ⬚ 5min

Children report back to rest of the class on their findings.

Extra activities ① ②

Improvements drama

Tell the children that the council has decided to pedestrianise the road outside your school. Debate the advantages and disadvantages of the scheme, with the children taking on different roles such as parent, younger brother or sister, motorist, van driver, headteacher, grandparent.

Listed buildings

Find out from the council which buildings in your area are listed buildings. Arrange to visit them so the children can make their own sketches and write descriptions for a class display. Which places would the children put on the list and why?

Town planning

Arrange for a town planner to visit the class to talk about their work. If the children have studied a local street (*see* Lesson 3 above) they will be able to frame their own questions. Otherwise, you could find out more generally about how planners help to improve the local surroundings.

BEFORE

AFTER

Many of the world's finest buildings are in towns and cities. Over the centuries, people have built beautiful churches, museums, palaces, hospitals and theatres. Some of these, like St Paul's Cathedral in London, attract thousands of visitors each year.

However, buildings wear out as they grow older and have to be repaired. The sun,

wind, rain and snow cause a lot of damage. Other things just wear out as people keep on using them. Roads and pavements also need to be looked after.

In a town, everyone is involved in caring for their own house. Many other jobs are done by the local council. Here are some of the things that the council does to make a pleasant environment.

Things to do

1 What special buildings can you find in a town in your area?

2 Why do roads and buildings wear out?

3 Write a list of the jobs which the council does:
a) regularly
b) once in a while

4 Working from the pictures, say how the high street has been improved.

Jobs done by the town council

Caring for trees

Looking after parks and gardens

Seeing that there are playgrounds for children

Helping to keep traffic running smoothly

Repairing roads and pavements

Keeping street lamps working

Helping people repair old buildings

Clearing away litter and rubbish

Clearing snow from streets in winter

Providing sports facilities

Running museums and libraries

Planning changes and improvements

40

Improvement schemes

Say how each scheme has improved the town.

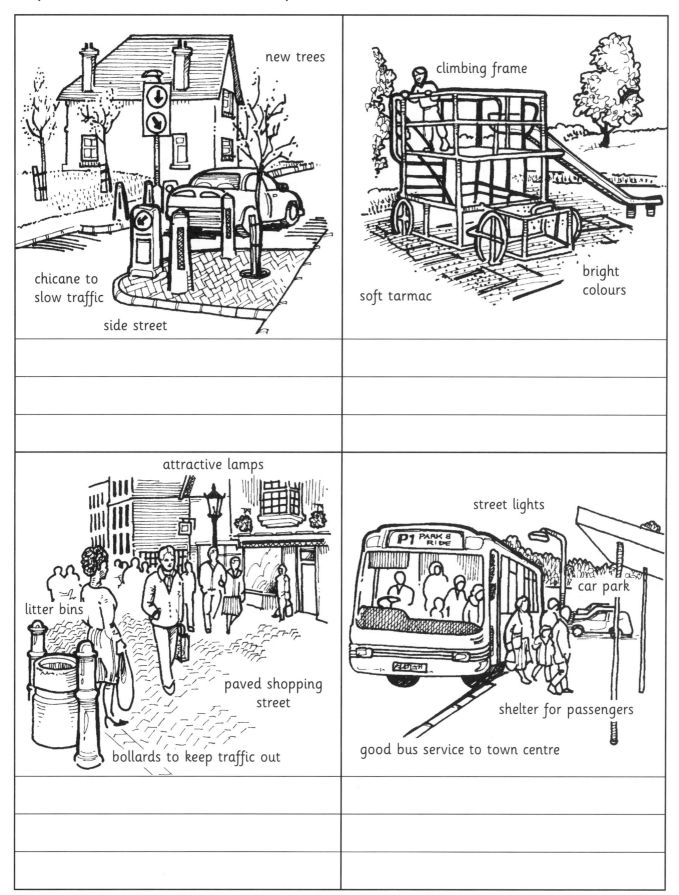

new trees

chicane to slow traffic

side street

climbing frame

soft tarmac

bright colours

attractive lamps

litter bins

paved shopping street

bollards to keep traffic out

street lights

car park

shelter for passengers

good bus service to town centre

Water

Learning targets

On completion of this unit children should understand that:

1 ➡➤ water is an important natural resource
2 ➡➤ we need to conserve water
3 ➡➤ in the developing world many people suffer from poor water supplies

Before you start

Focus

This unit considers how we use water, a key natural resource, in lots of different ways.

Background information

Most of the water in the world is found in seas and oceans which are contaminated with salt. Fresh water is much harder to find. Rivers, lakes and water-bearing rocks are the main sources of supply. In the UK, increases in demand are stretching available resources, especially in the south and east of England. One solution, which has been used since Victorian times, is to augment supplies from reservoirs in wetter areas such as Wales. In the developing world, water supply is an even more important issue. There, many people often spend a great deal of energy carrying water from rivers and pumps. Over three-quarters of all disease is caused by pollution problems which could be easily prevented.

Teaching points

You might want to use this unit in conjunction with the lessons on rivers. There is no direct mention of the water cycle as this is dealt with more fully in science.

Progression

Young children enjoy experiencing and playing with water but are unlikely to have considered how we depend on it throughout our lives.

Older children can learn about different types of water supply.

Vocabulary

canal, goods, litre, ocean, Pacific, reservoir, river, sprinkler, stream, well

Geographical skills

- Ability to make labelled drawings
- Ability to list activities in order
- Identification of problems and solutions

National Curriculum links

- Environmental issues, e.g. water pollution, that give localities their character
- How people affect the environment e.g. by building reservoirs

Assessment indicators

Children should be able to:
- describe different ways people use water
- say how we can reduce our demand for water
- explain how poor water supply affects people in other parts of the world

Personal application

These statements highlight the relevance of the children's learning:
- I can explain how I depend on water
- I understand that water is precious and needs to be saved
- I realise that access to clean water is a basic human right

Teaching the lessons

Lesson 1 ❶

Key question

Why is water important?

Introduction ⏱ 10 min

▨ Ask the children how they have used water through the day. Extend the discussion to consider how other people use water. The following questions and answers are appropriate.

How do farmers use water? (To water crops and as drinking water for animals.)

How do factories use water? (To wash and clean material and to cool machines.)

How do we use water on holiday? (For sailing, boating, swimming and surfing.)

Using the information sheet ⏱ 30 min

▨ From **Copymaster 41 Water**, children may be surprised to learn that we depend on water for nearly all the things we do.

Differentiate by encouraging slow-learning children to answer only the first two questions. Discuss where water comes from with more-able children and ask them to draw a diagram to show how it gets to the taps in our homes.

Summary `5min`

Discuss how the children would be affected if the water supply was cut off to their homes.

Homework

Get the children to create an acrostic poem using the letters from the word WATER.

Lesson 2

Key question

How can we save water?

Introduction `10min`

Explain that we can all help to save water. The following questions and answers are appropriate.

Do any of the children have water meters in their homes? (Answers will vary according to the location of the school.)

Why do we have water meters? (So that people know how much water they are using and to encourage them to use less.)

Are there any devices in school which are designed to save water? (Examples may include automatic taps, lavatories with small cisterns and rainwater butts.)

Using the activity sheet `40min`

 Copymaster 42 Saving water highlights some of the ways we can save water. The dripping tap needs to be mended, the garden sprinkler uses far more water than a watering can, the water flowing down the drain could be stored in a water butt and a bath uses much more water than a shower.

Differentiate by discussing the problems and solutions with slow-learning children, putting model answers on the board for them to copy. Blank out some of the pictures or words before giving the copymaster to more-able children so they can add their own ideas in the empty spaces.

Summary `10min`

Discuss with the children what target they would set themselves and how they would achieve it if they had to reduce their own water consumption.

Lesson 3 ③

Key question

Why is clean water important in our lives?

Introduction `10min`

Explain to the children how many people in the developing world have to collect their water from a river or well. This means they spend a lot of time carrying heavy loads and have to make do with very meagre supplies. There is also a serious danger of disease from pollution. On the board, make a list of the problems this causes.

Investigation `45min`

 Ask the children to devise a short play or drama in which a group of villagers try to convince a government officer they need piped water instead of relying on the river. Each member of the group will need a different role such as housewife, child, farmer, official, doctor. Restrict each play to a maximum of three minutes.

Differentiate by ensuring that each group contains children of different abilities to promote interaction and peer group learning.

Summary `20min`

Each group should perform their play to the rest of the class.

Extra activities ① ③

Water survey

Ask the children to record the different ways they use water over a period of a day. Examples include washing hands, cleaning things, watering plants. Record the results as a bar graph or pie chart using a computer program.

Water research

Contact suitable aid agencies (such as Oxfam and Water Aid) or use photopacks or reference books to find out how people are working to improve water supplies in different parts of the world.

41

Water

There is a lot of water in the world. Water falls from the clouds as rain and snow. It runs down slopes in streams and rivers. Eventually, it ends up in the sea.

Seas and oceans cover almost three-quarters of the Earth's surface. One ocean, the Pacific, is larger than all the continents put together. It is 14,000 kilometres across.

Sea water is full of salt which has washed out of rocks. Fresh water is much more useful because people can drink it. It comes from rivers and from wells that go deep underground. Rainwater is also stored in reservoirs.

Water is used in lots of different ways. We need it for drinking and cooking. People use it for washing clothes and when they take showers and baths. A lot of water also goes into flushing the lavatory.

Factories use water when they make goods. In the country, farmers often water the land to help plants grow. In some places, goods are carried from place to place along rivers and canals. Towns and cities have grown up along these routes.

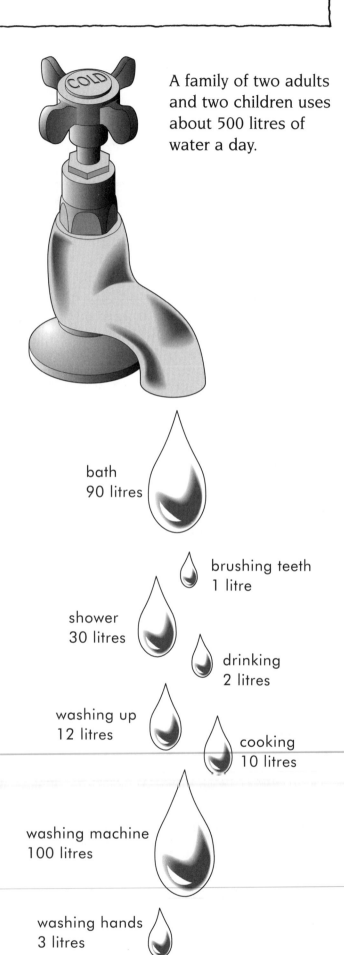

A family of two adults and two children uses about 500 litres of water a day.

bath
90 litres

brushing teeth
1 litre

shower
30 litres

drinking
2 litres

washing up
12 litres

cooking
10 litres

washing machine
100 litres

washing hands
3 litres

Things to do

1 Write down three ways we get fresh water.

2 Make labelled drawings showing some of the ways we use water.

3 Working from the diagram, write down the different ways we use water putting the smallest first and the largest last.

Saving water

1. Colour the drawings.
2. Write a sentence about each problem and the solution.

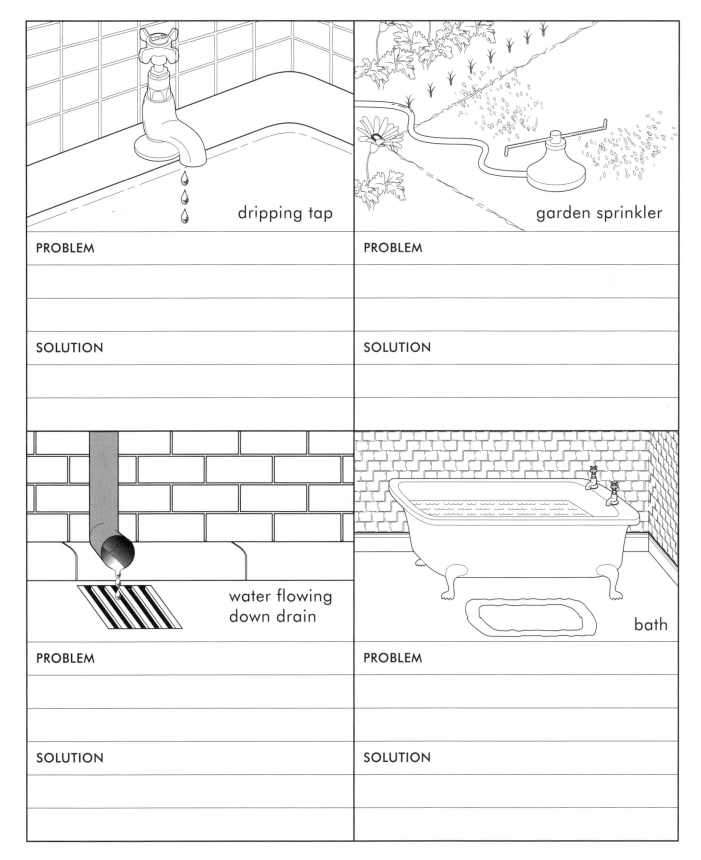

dripping tap

PROBLEM

SOLUTION

garden sprinkler

PROBLEM

SOLUTION

water flowing
down drain

PROBLEM

SOLUTION

bath

PROBLEM

SOLUTION

ENVIRONMENT
UNIT 22 | Rainforests

Learning targets

On completion of this unit children should understand that:

1 ➡➡ rainforests are a unique and valuable habitat
2 ➡➡ rainforests need protection
3 ➡➡ rainforests are important to people all over the world

Before you start

Focus

The problems facing the rainforests are considered in this unit. It is important to make it clear that while there are no simple solutions we can all help to influence what is happening ✳ and preserve the rainforests for future generations.

Background knowledge

Rainforests are the richest habitat on Earth containing over half of all known plant and animal species. The heavy rain and high temperatures near the Equator allow thick vegetation to develop. The highest trees reach to a height of 50 metres in their search for light. The forest floor, by contrast, is shrouded in perpetual gloom by the dense canopy of leaves above. Rainforests have taken millions of years to develop but are now being cleared at an alarming rate. Logging, ranching, industry and encroachment by landless peasants are all taking their toll. It is estimated that an area the size of the UK is destroyed each year. In addition, uncontrolled forest fires in Indonesia and Brazil in 1997 and 1998 have wreaked massive devastation. If these are allowed to continue, very few areas of forest will be left within a decade, leaving the world immeasurably poorer.

Teaching points

The children need to know where the rainforests are on the Earth's surface. This is a good opportunity to look at an atlas or globe and to point out the position of the Equator.

Progression

This unit illustrates environmental problems through a case study of the rainforests. It could be used to support a study on an overseas' locality or as part of a cross-curricular project on the Amazon.

Vocabulary

creatures, Equator, habitat, plants, products, rainforest, ranch, rubber, wildlife

Geographical skills

* Identification of a sequence
* Ability to make comparisons
* Recognition of habitats

National Curriculum links

* How environments change
* How people affect the environment
* How and why people seek to manage and sustain their environment

Assessment indicators

Children should be able to:
* name some rainforest plants and creatures
* know how rainforests are threatened
* understand how rainforests can be protected

Personal application

These statements highlight the relevance of the children's learning:
* I can imagine the rainforest habitat
* I know what is happening to the rainforests
* I know some of the ways my life is linked to the rainforest

Teaching the lessons

Lesson 1 ①

Key question

What is the rainforest like?

Introduction [15 min]

▨ Find out what the children already know about the rainforest and write down their ideas on the board. Use the questions and answers below to help structure the discussion.

Where are the rainforests? (Rainforests are found near the Equator especially in Brazil, Zaire and Indonesia.)

What is the weather like in the rainforest? (It is hot and wet all the year round.)

What creatures live in the rainforest? (Answers could include parrots, butterflies, monkeys, snakes, jaguars and crocodiles.)

98

What does a rainforest look like? (There are thousands and thousands of trees. Sometimes there are big rivers. From the air, the forest looks like a green carpet.)

Using the information sheet   `40min`

 Read the information on **Copymaster 43 Rainforests** with the whole class, then get the children to answer the questions. Reference books on rainforest creatures could help with Question 2. You might like to discuss Question 3 considering the advantages and disadvantages of rainforest life before the children write down their answers.

Differentiate by encouraging children with learning difficulties to complete the first two questions and colour the picture. More-able children could produce a crossword in which each clue is about the rainforest environment.

Summary `10min`

 Discuss and note on the board how the rainforest is different from your local area using these headings: 'Weather', 'Plants', 'Creatures' and 'Landscape'.

Homework

Ask the children to fix or copy a picture of the rainforest into their geography exercise books. Weekend magazines, encyclopedias, reference books and the Internet are all useful sources.

Lesson 2 ②

Key question

How do people affect the rainforests?

Introduction `5min`

 Talk to the children about how the rainforests are being cleared. Loggers are damaging large areas, fires are burning out of control and huge amounts of land are being made into ranches. It takes 22.25 ha of forest land to produce the meat for a hamburger.

Using the activity sheet `30min`

Provide the children with **Copymaster 44 Rainforest threats** and glue and scissors. They will need to make coloured drawings to go with each heading, cut around the edges of the box and fold and glue the box together.

Differentiate by making your own drawings in the empty spaces for slow-learning children to colour. Ask more-able children to design their own model, illustrating another rainforest threat such as new dams or metal factories.

Summary `10min`

 Discuss different ways of preserving the rainforest. Use this opportunity to introduce children to the concept of sustainable development.

Lesson 3 ③

Key question

Why are rainforests important?

Introduction `10min`

Although the rainforests are a long way away, they are important to us all because of the wildlife they contain and their effect on world climate. You can begin to explore this link with children by thinking about different tropical products. Make a list on the board using the table below to help you.

Rainforest products	
bananas	mahogany
pineapples	rubber
cacao	orchids
mangoes	medicines
coconuts	zoo animals
peanuts	house plants

Investigation `30min`

 Give each group of six children blank cards 10 cm wide and 5 cm deep. Get them to draw and label a different rainforest product on each one. Now ask them to fix the cards on to a large sheet of paper, putting the most important product at the top, the next most important product second and so on, with the least important product at the bottom.

Differentiate by encouraging less-able children to make labelled drawings on the cards for a wall display. More-able children should write a few sentences explaining how they have put the products in order of importance.

Summary `20min`

Compare the results from different groups. Have they all organised the cards in the same sequence? What are their reasons?

Extra activities ① ② ③

Rainforest drama

Divide the children into groups and ask them to make up a five-minute drama about the rainforest. Set the scene by telling them half the group is working for a logging company which is clearing trees with heavy machines. The other half of the group represents native people who have lived in the forest for thousands of years.

Rainforest music

Using the lessons on the rainforest as a context, get the children to make up a piece of music about the rainforest. As well as the sounds of animals, they should try to represent the noise of the rain in the trees, the peace of the early morning as the sun rises through the mist and the gurgling of the water as it flows downstream.

Rainforests are found near the Equator. Trees and other plants thrive in the hot sun and heavy rain. Many different animals make their homes in the forest. Parrots live high in the trees. Jaguars keep close to the ground.

The forest floor is dark and gloomy. The leaves on the trees keep out the sun and provide shelter from the rain. Some trees grow very tall as they reach up to get more light.

People have lived in the rainforests for thousands of years in groups of tribes. There are also rubber tappers who collect the juice from rubber trees. They all make a living without harming the forest.

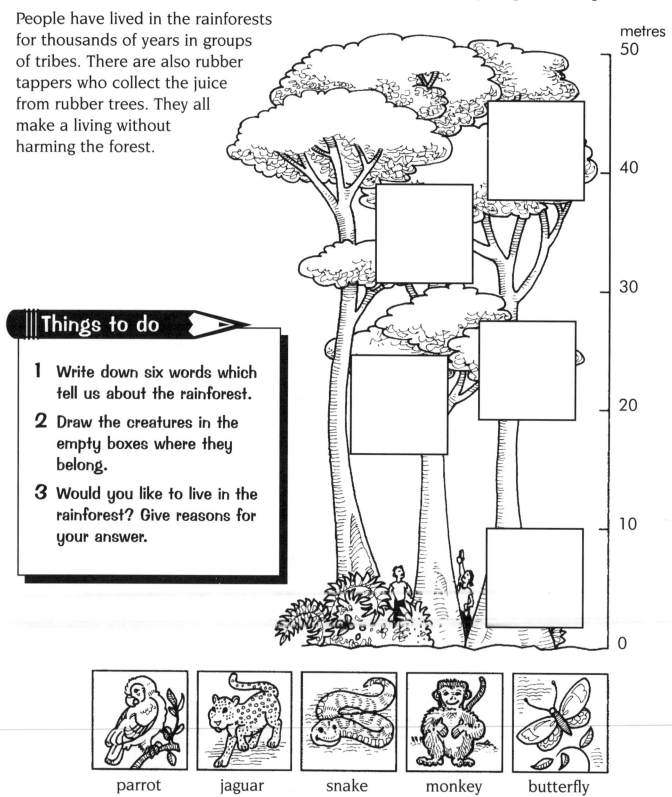

Things to do

1 Write down six words which tell us about the rainforest.

2 Draw the creatures in the empty boxes where they belong.

3 Would you like to live in the rainforest? Give reasons for your answer.

parrot   jaguar   snake   monkey   butterfly

Rainforest threats

Heavy rain washes away soil	Cattle graze on fields	Trees cut down and burnt	Thick forest with many plants and creatures

SCHOOL BUILDINGS

Focus

Many geographical ideas can be studied at a range of scales. For example, the idea of 'movement' can be illustrated in the classroom and school building. However, it can also be studied in the local environment and immediate region or, indeed, at a national or international level. The geography curriculum recognises the value of allowing children to develop key ideas of this kind. In particular, it emphasises the notions of 'process', 'pattern' and 'change'. All these concepts can be explored in small-scale environments such as the school building.

There are also strong pragmatic reasons for using the immediate area as a teaching resource. Not only is it accessible, it also places children within a scale which relates to their experience and understanding. Furthermore, there will be

ample opportunity for posing questions which the children can investigate for themselves – another aspect of good practice.

There will be a wealth of topics for children to consider. To begin, they need to explore the building and discover how the different areas are used. Once they are familiar with their surroundings, they can then begin to discuss improvements and alterations. Issues to do with safety, changes to the design, and conservation of resources are each likely to provide a strong focus.

Children spend about a third of their time in school playing in the school grounds. They often welcome projects which utilise their own observations and experience. They also interpret this kind of work favourably. If the buildings and grounds are well cared-for, the children tend to feel valued.

Brainstorm

Use this brainstorm to help you develop a medium-term plan.

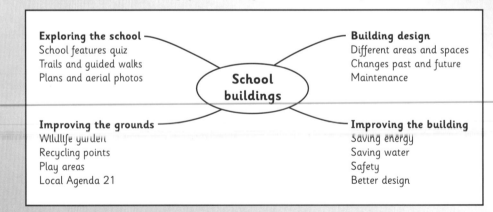

Exploring the school
School features quiz
Trails and guided walks
Plans and aerial photos

Building design
Different areas and spaces
Changes past and future
Maintenance

School buildings

Improving the grounds
Wildlife garden
Recycling points
Play areas
Local Agenda 21

Improving the building
Saving energy
Saving water
Safety
Better design

Research findings

There is considerable interest in using the school buildings and grounds as a teaching resource. The opportunity for using familiar environments such as the classroom for mapping exercises has long been exploited by educationalists. Similarly, projects such as *World Studies 8–13* (Fisher and Hicks 1985) have pointed out how children can begin to learn about the distant places through practical activities and first-hand experiences.

A lot of attention has been focused on the school grounds. Bartlett (1998) stresses how children and other members of the community should be involved in their design and management. School grounds have a number of different roles – aesthetic, recreational, educational and ecological. All these can be enhanced and developed with care. One of the spin-offs is that this involves decision-making. Scoffham (1980) argues how environmental work can help prepare children for a participatory role in civic and community affairs. This is something which is of considerable interest at the present time when there is a growing interest in citizenship.

Content

Unit 23 Introduces children to study techniques and draws their attention to things they can see and record for themselves.

Unit 24 Considers the pattern of land use in the school environment.

Unit 25 Focuses on change and improvement.

For related material *see* Unit 5 *Shaping the land* and Unit 15 *Routes and journeys*. There are links with the Local area and Settlement sections.

National Curriculum expectations

By the end of Key Stage 2, it is expected that most children will be able to:

*   explain patterns of physical and human features
*   describe how people can affect the environment and explain the different views held by people about an environmental change
*   undertake geographical investigations by asking and responding to questions and using a range of geographical enquiry skills, resources and their own observations

Literacy links

Year 3   Read information passages and identify main points: Unit 24 *Areas in school*, Lesson 1.
Write simple non-chronological reports: Unit 25 *School improvements*, Homework.

Year 4   A range of text types: Unit 23 *Exploring your school*, Lesson 1.

Year 5   Write accounts based on personal experience: Unit 25 *School improvements*, Lesson 1.

Year 6   Write non-chronological reports linked to other subjects: Unit 24 *Areas in school*, Lesson 3.

ICT links

Tape recorder	Use a tape recorder to record sounds and noise levels in different areas of the school.
Aerial photographs	Study oblique and overhead aerial photographs of the school to obtain extra information.
Photographs	Take photographs of selected features around the school for a quiz.

UNIT 23 Exploring your school

Learning targets

On completion of this unit children should understand that:

1 ➤➤ schools have different architectural features
2 ➤➤ trails provide structured routes linking points of interest

Before you start

Focus

This unit focuses on the features and characteristics of the school building and grounds.

Background information

Geography is not only about recording what the world is like. It also involves the study of how people view and respond to their surroundings. This aspect of geography relates directly to the arts and humanities which also focus on human behaviour. The school building is one of the best places to start developing children's environmental awareness. Begin by getting the children to identify the features which contribute to its character. You can then explore their views and opinions.

Teaching points

This unit involves making careful observations of the immediate surroundings. There are plenty of opportunities for reinforcement and once children have begun to see things in detail they will probably take delight in finding new examples.

Progression

From the earliest age, children learn to interact with and respond to their environment. By exploring their school and its surroundings, they will develop an increasing sense of empathy.

Vocabulary

decorations, pattern, sign, symbol, trail, Victorian

Geographical skills

- Compilation of a fact file
- Devise questions to gather information
- Make fieldwork sketches
- Respond to the characteristics of a place
- Make a trail

National Curriculum links

- Observe and ask questions about geographical features and issues
- Collect and record evidence to answer the questions
- Undertake fieldwork

Assessment indicators

Pupils should be able to:
- identify some of the features that give the school building its character
- describe how they feel about different places
- make a simple trail in a familiar environment

Personal application

These statements highlight the relevance of the children's learning:
- I have visited all the different places in my school
- I am aware of the colours, patterns and shapes around me
- I know how to make a trail for others to follow

Teaching the lessons

Lesson 1 ❶

Key question

What are the special features of our school?

Introduction [10min]

▨ Working with the whole class, make a list of clues and features which would help a stranger identify your school. Ask the children to describe the wall and roof materials, colour of the paintwork, shape of the windows, height and form of the building and so on. One of the things which is likely to emerge is that most children are able to recall very little about their environment.

Using the information sheet [25min]

 Give the children **Copymaster 45 Exploring your school**. Discuss whether your school resembles either of the schools in the drawings. Also check that the children know how to complete the fact file. Among other things, they could list the number of children and teachers, the date when the school was built, any special features about the building, and details of teams and clubs which children can join.

Differentiate by encouraging more-able children to copy the pictures of the two schools and annotate their drawings to highlight the main architectural differences.

Summary [15min]

 Ask the children to work in groups to make up puzzle descriptions of places in the school building or grounds. They should then see if the rest of the class can recognise the place.

Homework

Ask the children to write puzzle descriptions (and answers) of one or two features of the locality that they pass through every day. Assemble them in a small class book.

Lesson 2 ①

Key question

How can you conduct a school survey?

Introduction [10min]

 Remind the children that it is often small details which give a place or building its character. Ask them what they think of their own school. What features make it distinctive? What are the things they like or dislike about the building?

Using the activity sheet [30min]

 Divide the children into groups. Give out **Copymaster 46 School survey** to each group and see that they know which activity they are going to undertake. If they are looking for patterns, tell them to look up at the ceiling and down at the floor as well as straight ahead. You could help children with Activity 4 (Different places) by giving them a word bank to use in their descriptions.

Differentiation is provided. The activities are graded so that the first two (Patterns and Windows) are simpler than the third and fourth (Signs and symbols and Different places).

Summary [10min]

 Ask the groups to report back on the work they did and the places they visited.

Lesson 3 ②

Key question

How can you plan a trail around the school?

Introduction [10min]

 Explain to the children that they are going to make a trail linking places around the school which they would show to a stranger. The route has to contain six stops and follow logically around the school building and grounds.

Investigation [45min]

 Divide the children into groups and provide them with a photocopied map of the school site. Tell them to identify the stops first. Then ask them to devise the route and write a few sentences about each place.

Differentiate by providing slow-learning children with a list of the places you want them to include on their trail. Invite more-able children to select a theme for their trail, such as decorations, history or wildlife. They might also make up a quiz using photographs.

Summary [15min]

 Arrange for the groups to swap trails so that they can test out each other's work.

Extra activities ① ②

Wear and tear

Make a survey of wear and tear in your classroom and other parts of the school building. Tell the children to write down twenty different examples. See if they can distinguish between damage due to natural causes (e.g. sun and rain) and human activity (e.g. chipped paintwork and scruffed doors).

Different views

Find a viewpoint such as the top floor of the school or highest point in the school grounds. Tell the children to record what they can see to the north, south, east and west using words or pictures. Identify any unknown buildings or features from a large-scale map back in the classroom.

Exploring your school

Most of the time, we do not bother to look at the buildings where we live and work. We follow the same routine each day and get on with the things we have to do. Every so often, it is good to stop and do something different.

Finding out about your school is great fun. You have to go to places you do not normally visit. It might be that you are looking for patterns and decorations to make a quiz. You could also search for clues which show how the school has changed. Another idea is to look for noisy or peaceful places.

Different schools

Some schools are very old. They were built a hundred years or more ago in Victorian times. There were separate entrances for boys and girls. The classrooms had high ceilings to keep the air clean and the rooms were heated by coal or gas fires.

Other schools are more modern. These schools have big windows and doors which open on to the playground or garden. Sometimes there is no wall between the classroom and the corridor. The flat roof and chimney from the heater makes these schools look very different.

Things to do

1 List three features of Victorian schools.

2 List three features of more modern schools.

3 Make up a fact file of things you know about your school.

4 Write down some questions you would like to ask about your school.

School survey

1. Patterns

Sketch and label some of the patterns you can find in your classroom and other parts of the school.
Name the shapes you can see such as circles, triangles and rectangles.

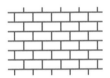

2. Windows

Make careful drawings of four different windows in your school. Say where you saw each one.

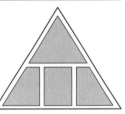
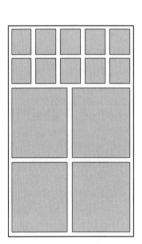

3. Signs and symbols

Make drawings of some of the signs and symbols in your classroom and other parts of the school.

QUIET PLEASE

THIS WAY

Boys   **Girls**

4. Different places

Write a sentence about how you feel in each of these places:
a) your classroom
b) the corridor
c) the library
d) the hall
e) the playground
f) the cloakroom

Areas in school

Learning targets

On completion of this unit children should understand that:

1 ➤➤ spaces in buildings are used in different ways
2 ➤➤ the way that space is used can be shown on maps and plans
3 ➤➤ over a period of time the way space is used may change

Before you start

Focus

This unit considers patterns of land use by illustrating the way spaces are used in school.

Background knowledge

On a global level, geographers consider the different spaces and areas on the Earth's surface. About two-thirds of the planet is covered by water. The remaining third consists of dry land which is divided between deserts, mountains, sheets of ice, forests, farmland and other areas. Describing and accounting for these variations is a key part of geography.

Patterns of land use can also be studied on a much smaller scale. There are different areas within a country or region. Planners and environmentalists are particularly interested in the way these patterns are changing and the affect this has on people. A similar analysis in urban areas can be equally valuable and reveal the form and structure of settlements.

Teaching points

In this unit, children learn to classify the way that spaces are used to reveal the underlying pattern and structure.

Progression

Young children will know there are different areas in their homes and schools. What they consider here is some of the ways these areas can be classified. In turn, this serves to illustrate the wider patterns of land use which children will study at Key Stage 3.

Vocabulary

area, code, key, land use, pattern, services, space

Geographical skills

- Use of a key
- Code a map
- Classification and grouping of activities
- Recognition of patterns

National Curriculum links

- Develop the ability to recognise patterns
- Analyse the evidence, draw conclusions and communicate findings

Assessment indicators

Children should be able to:
- say how spaces are used in their classrooms and schools
- describe how some activities are given more space than others
- talk about changes in land use in their school or locality

Personal application

These statements highlight the relevance of the children's learning:
- I know that different activities need their own spaces
- I realise that there is a pattern to the way spaces are used
- I understand why buildings sometimes have to be altered

Teaching the lessons

Lesson 1 ➊

Key question

How are spaces in buildings used in different ways?

Introduction [10min]

▨ Make a list on the board of the different areas and places in your classroom. Discuss how some areas, such as cupboards, are physically defined while others, such as learning areas, are more flexible and depend on the arrangement of furniture. Why is each space needed?

Using the information sheet [20min]

▨ **Copymaster 47 Different areas** explores in general terms how buildings are used for different purposes as well as considering the areas in a school and classroom.

Differentiate by discussing the answers before asking

less-able children to complete the work. Ask more-able children to devise a symbol for each of the different areas shown on the plan.

Summary

Discuss the advantages and disadvantages of having designated areas for reading, art and computer work. Discuss whether these activities could happen in the same place as more general learning and studying.

Homework

Ask the children to make a study of their own homes, listing all the different spaces and areas they can think of.

Lesson 2 ②

Key question

How do plans show the different ways space is used?

Introduction ⌈10min⌉

Discuss with the children how spaces can be classified. In school, for example, learning areas will occupy a considerable proportion of the building. However, some space will also need to be allocated for movement (corridors), life needs (lavatories) and administration (the office). Could these same categories be applied to a home?

Using the activity sheet ⌈20min⌉

Give the children **Copymaster 48 Areas in school**. Check that the children understand that they colour the code boxes next to the headings in the key.

Differentiate with more-able children by blanking out the rooms listed in the key and asking them to decide which category each one belongs to.

Summary ⌈5min⌉

Discuss the answers to Question 3. Talk about which other areas might have been shown on the plan (such as a playground, field, car park). Ask how the findings compare with your own school.

Lesson 3 ①

Key question

What are the essential areas in a school building?

Introduction ⌈5min⌉

Talk about the way we all make more use of some parts of the school than others. Ask whether there are any places the children visit very rarely and places they never visit.

Investigation ⌈30min⌉

Give each child a simple map of your school on which you have marked the different areas and spaces. Ask them to colour the plan using green for spaces which are 'essential to me', yellow for spaces which are 'useful to me' and red for spaces which are

'not needed by me'. Now invite them to redesign the school simply showing the places that they need themselves.

Differentiate by simplifying the activity for less-able children by only asking them to decide if each place is 'essential' or 'not needed'. Encourage more-able children to make up an entirely new plan rather than copying the existing buildings when they make up their own designs. They might also consider what new facilities could be added, such as a computer room or pottery room.

Summary ⌈10min⌉

Discuss the different plans that the children have produced. Which ones are most effective and why? Talk also about the advantages of grouping several hundred children together in one building. This maximises the space devoted to learning as opposed to lavatories, heating and other life needs. The same principle applies to towns which make better use of the infrastructure of essential services than do scattered settlements.

Extra activities ② ③

Local land-use map

Let the children look at a map or aerial photograph of your local area or town. Ask them if they can identify different areas such as houses, streets, shops, factories, schools, car parks and so on. Ask them to make a simple land-use map with a key and a different colour for each area.

Changes in land use

Ask the children to compare old and new maps of your school or neighbourhood. They can make a list of the main changes and suggest why each one happened. Ask them to say what other changes they think might happen in the next ten years.

Different areas

47

Buildings are designed for different purposes. For example, homes provide warmth and shelter and comfortable living and sleeping areas. Factories are places where people work together to make things. Shops have spaces where goods can be displayed in front of customers. Schools need spaces where children can be taught their lessons.

A lot of the space in a school is used for learning. The classrooms, hall, library and resources room are busy most of the day. Other spaces are used for offices and storing things. The kitchen, lavatories and boiler room provide for our everyday needs. Some areas, such as corridors, provide routes from one place to another. These can suddenly become very crowded at the end of a lesson.

The way that school buildings are used is always changing. Sometimes, the number of children in the classes goes up and another room is needed. At other times, the numbers go down, creating spare space. Space also has to be found for new machines and equipment. Ten years ago, very few schools had computers. Now, there is a computer in every classroom.

Things to do

1 What do homes provide?

2 List the different areas and spaces in your school.

3 Why are schools changing?

4 Colour the different areas on the classroom plan.

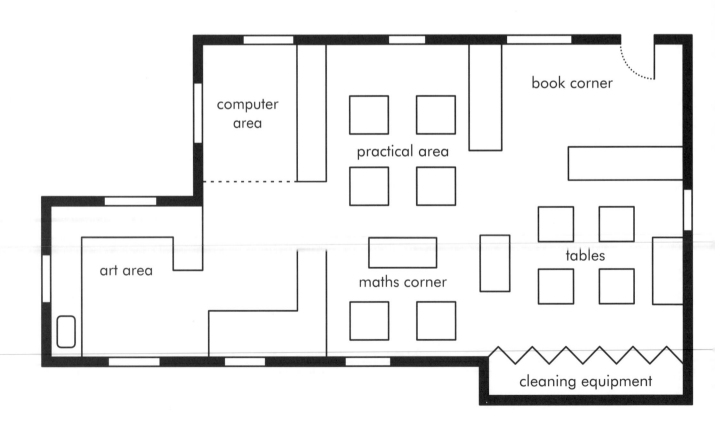

Areas in school

1. Colour the code boxes in the key.
2. Colour the school plan using the same colours.
3. Answer these questions.

Which area takes up most space?

_____

Which area takes up least space?

_____

Which part of the school seems least important?

_____

KEY

Learning areas	yellow
classrooms hall library	

Moving areas	blue
corridor	

Life needs	red
kitchen boiler room lavatories cloakroom	

Keeping things running	green
office stockroom staffroom caretaker's room	

School plan:
- stockroom
- classroom 3
- office
- staffroom
- lavatories
- kitchen
- corridor
- cloakroom
- hall
- classroom 4
- classroom 1
- classroom 2
- library
- caretaker's room
- boiler room

School improvements

Learning targets

On completion of this unit children should understand that:

1 ➤➤ schools and other buildings need regular maintenance
2 ➤➤ people can reduce the demands they make on the environment
3 ➤➤ the school environment can be altered and changed

Before you start

Focus

This unit considers different ways of improving schools and making them more sustainable.

Background information

One of the outcomes of the Earth Summit held in Rio de Janeiro in 1992 was a blueprint for action to help save the planet. Known colloquially as Agenda 21, this has been adopted in countries around the world. The way in which local action can contribute to solving global problems is one of the central ideas in Agenda 21. So, too, are the concepts of citizenship and sustainability.

One of the best places to begin Agenda 21 projects is in the school and its immediate environment. There are many different approaches. Ideally, children should work in partnership with other adults and local groups so that the local community is fully involved. Individual lessons are suggested here. These could serve as an introduction to a more substantial project.

Teaching points

A large-scale plan of the school and its grounds will be a useful resource. It is also worth finding if the local council has an Agenda 21 officer and is involved in projects or consultation exercises.

Progression

Most children are aware of how we need to care for creatures and save resources by turning off lights and taps before they come to school. This unit develops these ideas in a more substantial way by thinking in terms of practical projects.

Vocabulary

conservation, energy, environment, habitat, mosaic, mural, resources, sculpture, wildlife

Geographical skills

* Undertake a survey
* Ability to make judgements
* Draw maps and plans

National Curriculum links

* Undertake studies that involve fieldwork and classroom activities
* How and why people seek to manage and sustain their environment

Assessment indicators

Children should be able to:
* identify some simple ways of improving the school environment
* describe one improvement scheme in detail
* recognise how their personal actions relate to wider environmental issues

Personal application

These statements highlight the relevance of the children's learning:
* I know how and why buildings need looking after
* I realise that the things I do affect the environment
* I understand how to present my ideas so that others can understand them

Teaching the lessons

Lesson 1 ❶ ❸

Key question

How can we improve our school?

Introduction ⏱ 10min

▓ Discuss with the children the ways in which the things they use have to be cared for but will eventually wear out. The following questions and answers are appropriate.

How do we look after clothes? (They need washing, ironing and mending.)

How do we look after cars? (They need servicing and parts have to be replaced.)

How do we look after buildings? (They need regular cleaning, the woodwork has to be repainted, the roof has to be repaired.)

Using the information sheet `20min`

 Copymaster 49 Improving your school describes wear and tear resulting from natural forces and human activity. It also provides ideas for possible projects. You could develop these ideas as separate pieces of work in subsequent lessons.

Differentiate by asking the children to make simple drawings to illustrate each of the improvement ideas.

Summary `10min`

With the children, make a list of some of the ways your school could be improved. Consider who else would need to be involved in making any changes and how much these would cost.

Homework

Ask the children to make drawings and write a short description of three ways they or their families have improved their homes. Examples might include redecorating the walls, rearranging the furniture or putting plants and seeds in the garden. Encourage them to include environmental changes, such as energy-efficient light bulbs, better wall insulation and measures to save water.

Lesson 2 ② ③

Key question

How can we save energy in school?

Introduction `15min`

Remind the children how we depend on different resources in our daily lives. For example, we all need food to eat, water for drinking and washing, clothes for keeping warm, paper to write on and books to read. With more and more people living on the planet, we need to reduce our demand on the environment in whatever ways we can.

Using the activity sheet `30min`

 Give out **Copymaster 50 Energy survey**. Check that the children understand the questions before they begin the survey. Terms which may require explanation include 'thermostat', 'insulation', 'automatic controls', 'fluorescent' and 'rubber seals'.

Differentiate by dividing the children into mixed-ability groups so that more-able children can help slow learners complete the survey.

Summary `10min`

Discuss which single energy conservation measure is most needed in your school. See if the children can agree on the priorities.

Lesson 3 ③

Key question

How can we improve wildlife in our school?

Introduction `15min`

Make a list of the plants and creatures that the children would like to encourage in the school grounds. Examples might include butterflies, spiders, small birds, amphibians and the flowers and plants to give them food and shelter. Is there an area on the school site that could be made into a wildlife area or could habitats be created in special pots and tubs?

Investigation `45min`

 Get the children to draw up a plan to improve wildlife in your school. As well as using their own ideas, the children could consult reference books or contact a local natural history society. They could find out if any special equipment would be needed and what it would cost. Maintenance is another issue. Who would look after the plants and creatures and protect them from pests?

Differentiate by giving less-able children a clear framework – an outline plan to complete. Leave the study open-ended for more-able children so they can develop it according to their abilities.

Summary `10min`

Compare the schemes that the children have produced. Also discuss the advantages and disadvantages of creating specific habitats. Would it be better simply to let plants and creatures find their own habitats?

Extra activities ② ③

Improvement schemes

Select one of the improvement ideas suggested on the information sheet for the children to study in detail. For example, they could design their own mosaic path, make a drawing of a sculpture or decide where new signs are needed around the school.

Recycling

Ask the children to think about how your school could save natural resources by recycling waste products. Are materials such as paper, glass and metal currently being recycled? Are there other materials such as cloth which could also be saved?

Local Agenda 21

Find out how the council is implementing Agenda 21 in your area. What are the priorities and are there any specific projects involving schools? Set up a link with local organisations to explore some of the issues and problems that the children have identified.

Improving your school

Schools need be cared for and looked after. The weather causes a lot of damage. The heat of the sun makes the paintwork peel and crack. Strong winds loosen tiles on the roof, letting in the rain. In winter, snow and ice freeze in pipes causing them to burst.

People also damage the building without knowing it. For example, carpets and floors wear out as people walk across them. Switches and taps have to be repaired. Dust and rubbish have to be cleaned up.

The caretaker and cleaners spend their time making the school run smoothly. Builders, painters and decorators also visit from time to time to do different jobs.

Improvement projects
Wherever you are, there will also be ways of improving your school. Some of these will cost money. Others, such as cleaning up litter, can be done for nothing. Here are some ideas.

Signs
Make up some new signs to help people find their way around your school.

Mosaic path
Design a mosaic path to provide a new route and make your school more attractive.

Litter bins
Create models of litter bins using animal shapes which other children would like to use.

Mural
Paint a mural to brighten up a dull brick wall.

Sculpture
Design a sculpture for a space in your school grounds.

Nature garden
Plan a nature garden for plants and creatures.

 Things to do

1 How does the weather damage a school?

2 How do people damage a school?

3 Who works to look after the school?

4 Write out a list of six ways of improving your school. Put the most important thing first and the least important thing last.

50

Energy survey

1. Make a survey of how energy is used in your school. Answer each question by putting a cross in the 'No' box or circling the score in the 'Yes' box.

2. Add up the total score.

Questions	Answers No	Yes
Are the windows double-glazed?		15
Are there conservation reminder signs?		5
Do the lights have an automatic control?		5
Is the ceiling insulated?		15
Is there a thermostat in the room?		10
Are there curtains at the windows?		5
Are there carpets on the floors?		5
Do the windows have rubber seals?		5
Do the radiators/heaters have reflecting panels?		5
Does the room have thick walls?		10
Are the lights fluorescent?		5
Are you wearing suitable clothes for the season?		10
Do the windows give reasonable light?		5
Total		

3. Show your findings by colouring the correct number of sections on the conservation line.

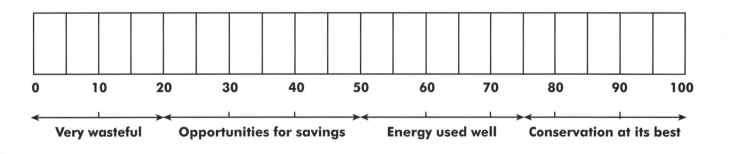

LOCAL AREA

Focus

The study of place is central to geography. This has been recognised from the outset by the National Curriculum which specifies place studies at both Key Stage 1 and Key Stage 2. Work on the local area is a key feature of both programmes of study. It is important to recognise that the local area is essentially small-scale. It consists of the school building, school grounds and immediate streets and buildings. Within this environment there will be rich opportunities for fieldwork and for developing topics such as houses, shops, transport and the environment. One aspect which is likely to prove particularly fruitful is the investigation of local issues. Inspection reports reveal that good standards are often achieved 'when work is based on practical experiences in the classroom, school grounds, local area or further afield'. In addition, 'enthusiasm for relevant local issues, in conjunction with high expectations by teachers can achieve some outstanding results' (Smith 1997).

Landscapes	Hills, valleys, woods, slopes, rocks
Rivers	Ponds, streams, lakes, rivers, marshes, estuaries
Weather	Sheltered and exposed sites
Houses	Cottages, terraces, flats, housing estates
Shops	Corner shops, shopping precincts, supermarkets
Services	Fire and Rescue, police, ambulance, hospitals, dentists
Work places	Farms, factories, offices, warehouses, workshops
Leisure	Parks, museums, sports centres, swimming pools
Transport	Roads, railways, paths, stations, garages
Environment	Nature reserves, recycling points, park and ride, pedestrianisation
Local issues	Road widening, new buildings, improvement schemes

Geographical features of the local area

Brainstorm

Use this brainstorm to help you develop a medium-term plan.

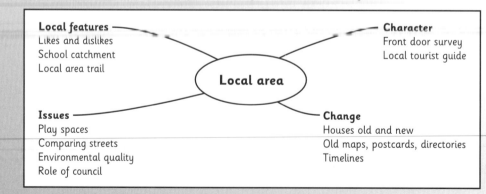

116

Research findings

Children's perceptions of their local area have been thoroughly investigated in the last few decades. Working largely in the London area, Bowles (1995) has explored how children's ideas of the local area expand as they grow older. Another major factor is car travel which gives children in suburban and rural districts a much wider range. Chambers (1998) reports how children in inner-city Liverpool want to see a reduction in violence and street crime to make their environment a better place. Finally, Hart (1979) made a far-reaching study of how environmental experience contributes to children's emotional and psychological development. He concludes that interaction with their surroundings allows children to grow and mature. It follows that there are strong reasons for allowing children to explore the place where they live. Schools have a key part to play in nurturing these experiences, especially given fears over safety in the present climate.

Content

Unit 26	Allows children to establish the extent of their local area.
Unit 27	Explores the things which give the local area its character.
Units 28, 29	Focus on changes and issues.

There are strong links with the School buildings section and supporting material can be found in the Settlement section.

National Curriculum expectations

At the end of Key Stage 2, it is expected that most children will be able to:

- undertake geographical investigations by asking and responding to questions and using a range of geographical enquiry skills, resources and their own observations
- recognise how selected physical and human processes cause changes in the character of places and environments
- describe how people can affect the environment and explain the different views held by people about an environmental change

Literacy links

Year 4	Use writing frames: Unit 27 *Special character*, Lesson 3. Summarise key ideas in writing: Unit 28 *Change*, Lesson 2.
Year 5	Convey feelings or moods in a poem: Unit 27 *Special character*, Lesson 1. Collect information from a variety of sources: Unit 29 *Local issues*, Extra activities, Public enquiry.
Year 6	Write a balanced report of a controversial issue: Unit 29 *Local issues*, Lesson 1. Develop a journalistic style: Unit 29 *Local issues*, Extra activities, Newspaper reports.

Story

Shaker Lane by Alice and Martin Provensen (Penguin 1987) describes what happens when a reservoir threatens a close-knit rural community.

ICT links

Photographs	Record features of the local area using photographs. These can then be put on CD-ROM and viewed, captioned and enhanced on computer.
Aerial photographs	Use aerial photographs of the school and its surroundings as a source of information and to look for changes in the environment.
CD-ROM	*Local Studies* (Soft Teach 1995) is a versatile program which allows children to construct their own map and add information about selected 'hot spots'.

Your local area

Learning targets

On completion of this unit children should understand that:

1 ➤➤ the places we visit regularly form the local area
2 ➤➤ each of us has a slightly different local area

Before you start

Focus

This unit introduces children to the notion of the local area.

Background information

The study of place is one of the major concerns of geography. The local area is a rich location for primary-school study because it is familiar and accessible, yet for most children is undefined, a taken-for-granted context for their daily lives.

Children should experience the key elements of a place and a settlement to enrich their local experience and provide the basis for comparisons with more distant places. They should explore and analyse landscape, water features, weather, buildings, transport, shops and services, leisure facilities, other places of work, and issues of use and conservation of environment and human issues in the community.

Children should ask the key questions of place: 'How did this place come to be?', 'What is the special character of this place?', 'What are the resources of this place?', 'How is this place linked to other places?' and 'What is it like to live here, what are the issues?'.

Teaching points

Children should be introduced to the key elements which structure life in the locality and, by using a range of questions for their investigations, be able to give a balanced view of the local area.

Progression

Many infants are taken on environmental walks. Here, in this section, children begin to consider the shape and structure of their local area.

Vocabulary

area, boundary, community, distance, newsagents, route

Geographical skills

- Ability to sort places using distance rings
- Ability to draw maps
- Recognition of patterns

National Curriculum links

- Become aware of how places fit into a wider geographical context
- Develop the ability to recognise patterns
- Follow routes

Assessment indicators

Children should be able to:
- describe their local area
- identify their local area on a map
- explain why the local area varies from one person to another

Personal application

These statements highlight the relevance of the children's learning:
- I can tell a visitor about the place where I live
- I know some parts of the district better than others
- I know what activities I can do in my local area

Teaching the lessons

Lesson 1 ①

Key question

What is your local area?

Introduction ⏱10min

▦ Discuss how we need a range of things in our daily lives. We go to school (work), buy things (shops), need to stay healthy (sports facilities) and like to relax (visiting friends). We find these facilities in our local area. Check also that the children can distinguish between the terms 'community' (a group of people), 'local area' (a place) and 'neighbourhood' (a place and the people in it).

Using the information sheet `20 min`

The first three questions on **Copymaster 51 The local area** are based on the text. Questions 4 and 5 depend on the children's local knowledge. Children who are new to the class should discuss their answers with other children. The drawing at the bottom of the page shows houses from different periods from the nineteenth century onwards.

Differentiate by asking slow-learning children to make drawings of the local area and write a sentence under each one. Extend the work by providing more-able children with materials to help them find out about the history of their area.

Summary `10 min`

Ask the children to talk about the places they would show a visitor. Ask them for one word that sums up the character of their local area.

Homework

Ask the children to write a poem celebrating the things they like about their local area.

Lesson 2

Key question

How large is your local area?

Introduction `5 min`

Remind the class that the local area is the area around their home which they visit regularly. Theoretically, the local area will be circular in shape but in practice it is often distorted by physical factors (e.g. rivers and hills) and the concentration of facilities in the town centre.

Using the activity sheet `30 min`

Discuss **Copymaster 52 My local area** with the class and how they are going to decide if a place is 'near', 'quite near' or 'far away'. The simplest criterion is physical distance but pupils who travel by car may have different ideas.

Differentiate by providing more-able children with a photocopied map of the area so that they can find the different places they have listed. Now ask them to draw a boundary round the edge to show the extent of their local area. What is the approximate radius in terms of distance and journey time?

Summary `10 min`

Discuss what the children have discovered.

Lesson 3

Key question

Which areas can you use for play?

Introduction `10 min`

Talk to the children about the different places where they play and the games that they like most. Think about a range of environments such as places to explore, places where you can be quiet and places for team games. Remind the children about games they play at different times of year, such as tobogganing in winter and swimming in summer.

Investigation `30 min`

Ask the children to draw a map of local play places. Ask them to say which games they play at each place and to write down the names of any local features.

Differentiate by allowing the children to complete the maps in different ways according to their abilities. Remind them that the map needs to be clear enough for a stranger to understand it. More-able children should use symbols and add a key.

Summary `10 min`

Discuss whether the children agree about the best playing areas in the local area. Make a list of playing areas on the board and ask them to vote for their number one choice.

Extra activities

Route cards

Tell the children to devise a set of cards that will help them to explore their school grounds or local area. Each card should contain a different instruction, such as 'turn left', 'turn right', 'turn around' 'jump', 'skip'. Add other activity cards to the set, for example 'draw a pattern', 'collect a leaf' and 'listen to different sounds'. The children can then follow the route and play the game in pairs or small groups.

Trail

Devise a trail which will link together some of the key places and features of the local area. Ask the children to make drawings, collect information and perhaps take photographs at each stop.

Aerial photographs

Look at an aerial photograph of your local area. Ask the children to identify the places they visit regularly. What are the things beyond the edge of their local area?

51

The local area

Most of us spend our time at home or going about our daily business. This involves travelling to school or work, shopping, attending church, visiting friends or playing games. We have to move around to get to different places.

Your home and the area around it which you visit regularly is known as the local area. The size of the local area varies from one person to another. Babies have a very small local area because they are unable to move about very much. School children travel about more freely so their local area is larger. People who go long distances for their work have the biggest local area of all.

Exploring your local area can be fun. As well as familiar buildings and places, you are likely to discover new things. These might include secret paths and routes, different places to play and exciting things to see.

You may also be able to find out how your local area is changing. Old newspapers, maps and photographs tell us what places were like in the past. If you talk to people who have lived in the area for a

long time, they will be able to tell you more.

So many changes are happening today that many places alter even in a few years. It is interesting to think about how they may develop in the future.

Things to do

1 What is the local area?

2 Why do babies have a small local area?

3 List four ways you can find out what your area used to be like.

4 Imagine you have been asked to show a friend or visitor round your local area. What would you show them?

5 Make a list of changes which you remember happening in your area.

52 | My local area

1. Tick the boxes in the table to show how far you go to different places.

2. Draw a picture of your house in the middle of the diagram below.

3. Draw and name at least three places you visit in the other circles.

Place	Very near	Not so near	Far away
School			
Church/place of worship			
Club			
Playing field			
Swimming pool			
Sports centre			
Friend's house			
Newsagent			
Post office			
Supermarket			

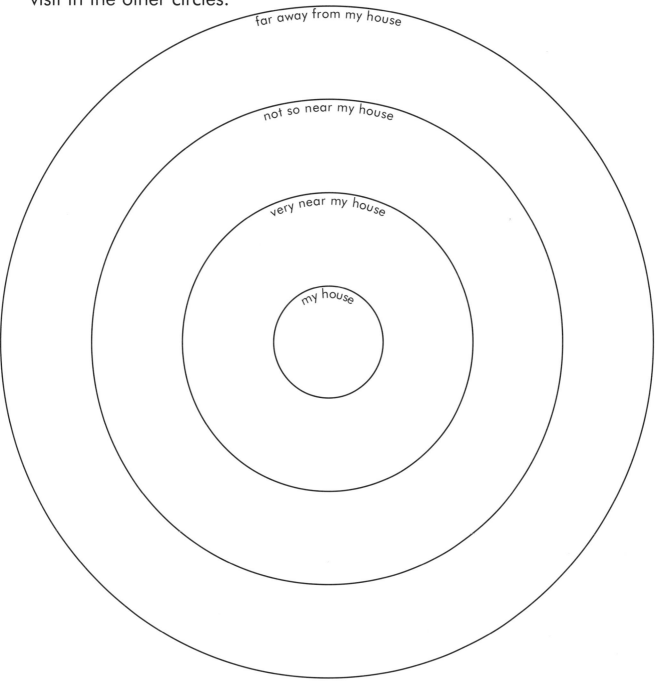

far away from my house

not so near my house

very near my house

my house

Special character

Learning targets

On completion of this unit children should understand that:
1 ➤➤ the mixture of features gives a place its character
2 ➤➤ each place has a unique character

Before you start

Focus

This unit considers the way in which the physical, human and environmental features combine to give a place its character.

Background information

Places are not merely buildings and open spaces but whole environments created by people. The local area supports or even frustrates our lives, sometimes pleasing and sometimes disturbing us. It evokes feelings and emotions. To understand a place, we have to be actively involved with it.

The special character of a place is evident in a variety of ways. A careful look will reveal small features unnoticed from day to day, some old, some bizarre, all of them interesting. Children are good at finding these things when inspired to do so. At the same time, they should be made aware of opportunities for engaging in change and improving the quality of their environment.

Teaching points

There will be a wealth of different visual and architectural features even in an apparently bland environment. Children can also record street names and landmarks as well as finding out about local groups and organisations that are active in the community. Fieldwork is a key component.

Progression

Rather than simply expressing subjective judgements about their local environment, this unit gives children reasons for substantiating or changing their opinions.

Vocabulary

character, community, environment, features, landscape, recreation ground, tower block, valley

Geographical skills

- Identification of local features
- Expression of opinions
- Draw a map
- Communication of ideas to others

National Curriculum links

- The main physical and human features and environmental issues that give a locality its character
- How localities may be similar and how they may differ

Assessment indicators

Children should be able to:
- list special features in their local area
- talk about what it is like to live in their locality
- communicate their findings to others in an interesting way

Personal application

These statements highlight the relevance of the children's learning:
- I know what gives my area its character
- I understand how people have used and responded to the local landscape
- I realise there are places which I like and others I dislike

Teaching the lessons

Lesson 1 ❶

Key question

What gives a place its character?

Introduction 〔10min〕

▦ Discuss the things that make your locality distinctive. Make a list on the board using the following headings: 'Physical features' (weather and landscape), 'Human features' (settlement, work and transport) and 'Environmental issues' (pollution and conservation).

Is there anything unusual about your area, such as historic buildings or links with famous people or events?

Using the information sheet `15 min`

Ensure that the children understand what 'character' means. **Copymaster 53 Places have character** explains the sort of thing that give a place its character.

Differentiate by asking the children to use the words they have selected in Question 3 in a poem or word picture of their area. The children will tackle this task at various levels depending on their ability.

Summary `10 min`

Make a list on the board of all the things which the children have identified as giving the locality its character. Which ones seem the most important?

Homework

Ask the children to write down ten street names or other local features, working from a map, asking adults or making personal observations.

Lesson 2

Key question

What local features matter to you?

Introduction `10 min`

Discuss how each part of the UK has its character. East Anglia has a flat landscape with half-timbered houses. Pennine villages are built of local stone and nestle in sheltered valleys. Around the coast, there are seaside resorts with grand promenades. Compare postcards of different places and explain to the children that they are going to analyse the character of their own area.

Using the activity sheet `30 min`

You can change the list of words on **Copymaster 54 Local features** by blanking out any that are inappropriate and adding suitable alternatives. You could also use the copymaster to analyse the features of contrasting places either in the UK or overseas.

Differentiate by completing Question 1 as a class exercise with slow-learning children. Give more-able children maps of the area so they can research any local names which they do not know.

Summary `10 min`

Get the children to use Copymaster 54 and ask them to describe the character of their own area. Ask them what else they would want to include that is not covered by the table. Weather conditions, building materials and local issues are some of the things they might mention.

Lesson 3

Key question

What is it like to live in your area?

Introduction `5 min`

Discuss with the children what it is like to live in the local area. Ask them what things they like and dislike about it. Ask them which features of the local environment they would miss if they were exiled to a desert island.

Investigation `30 min`

Ask the children to describe their local area using a writing frame. Prompts could include 'places I like', 'things I can do there', 'places that frighten me', 'local plants and creatures', 'common smells and sounds' and so on.

Differentiate by providing less-able children with a few simple prompts. Extend the work as an exercise in expressing opinions with more-able children.

Summary `10 min`

Read some of the best pieces of work out loud to the rest of the class.

Extra activities

Front door survey

Ask the children to make a study of just one aspect of the local area such as house front doors. Which colours are they painted? Do they have any glass or decorations? What is the design of the door knocker? Is the entrance in good repair? Is it welcoming? Encourage the children to devise their own survey questions.

Local guidebook

Collect information for a guidebook on your local area. Each child could contribute something different, such as a drawing, a survey, a poem. Some might focus on the odd or unusual features of your area. Others could describe their favourite places or find out about an aspect of local history.

Places have character

Every place is special in some way. Think about the shape of the land. Think about the buildings which people have put up. Think about the natural environment and places for wildlife. These are the things which give a place its character.

Some places have grown up in valleys. Others are on rivers or the coast. The landscape makes a big difference to the way we feel about a place.

History adds to the character. Most places have some ancient buildings. These may provide clues to old ways of living or forgotten industries. Sometimes there are links with famous people from the past.

The things you can do also make a place special. For example, there may be opportunities for sport or play or the chance to join different groups and clubs. In towns, there are cinemas and sports centres. Villages have farms, woods and countryside to explore.

The more you find out about a place, the more you will understand about its character. Wherever you live there are things to be proud of. Finding out about them can be good fun.

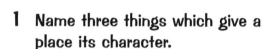

Things to do

1 Name three things which give a place its character.

2 How does history add to the character of a place?

3 Make a list of words which describe your area.

4 Write down three things you enjoy doing. Say where you can do each one in your local area.

colourful

beautiful

interesting

ugly

dull

NEW!

1. Tick the circles next to the words which describe the landscape, buildings and environment in your area.

2. Write down the local names and say a few words about the things you have ticked.

LANDSCAPE		
cliff	○	
coast	○	
flat	○	
hill	○	
lake	○	
marsh	○	
mountain	○	
river	○	
slopes	○	
valley	○	
BUILDINGS		
church	○	
factory	○	
hospital	○	
hotel	○	
inn	○	
museum	○	
petrol station	○	
offices	○	
old houses	○	
tower blocks	○	
ENVIRONMENT		
canal	○	
field	○	
main road	○	
nature reserve	○	
old ruins	○	
park	○	
railway line	○	
recreation ground	○	
wasteland	○	
wood	○	

UNIT 28 | Change

Learning targets

On completion of this unit children should understand that:

1 ➤➤ we live in a different way now from how we did in the past
2 ➤➤ many places change gradually but steadily
3 ➤➤ change will continue to affect places in the future

Before you start

Focus

This unit concentrates on the way places are changing.

Background information

Britain has changed enormously since the beginning of the nineteenth century. The Industrial Revolution brought a huge increase in population and led to the growth of towns. Today, modern electronics and fast communications and travel have heralded a new wave of development. Geographers are particularly interested in change as planning and development decisions require accurate predictions. This is a complex process which involves balancing the needs of many different groups of people.

Teaching points

An appreciation of change is required by most school subjects, especially history, but even older children find the concept difficult to appreciate, usually because of the timescales involved.

Progression

Young children can appreciate changes in their own bodies and immediate families. This unit encourages them to think about changes in their local area.

Vocabulary

allotments, countryside, motorway, nature reserve, supermarket, travel

Geographical skills

- Making of annotated drawings
- Reading and interpretation of maps
- Ability to make comparisons
- Ability to argue a case

National Curriculum links

- Recent or proposed changes in a locality
- Undertake studies that focus on geographical questions
- Interpret maps at a variety of scales

Assessment indicators

Children should be able to:
- describe changes in their local area
- describe changes in social behaviour
- talk about how their locality might alter in the future

Personal application

These statements highlight the relevance of the children's learning:
- I know that modern life has advantages and drawbacks
- I can find out how my area has changed by looking at maps and using my eyes
- I do not expect my area to stay the same as I grow older

Teaching the lessons

Lesson 1 ①

Key question

How do places change?

Introduction ⌛10 min

▦ In the last two centuries, lifestyles have altered considerably. Discuss some of the main changes. The following questions and answers are appropriate.

How has work changed? (People work shorter hours and do more paperwork.)

How has diet changed? (We tend to eat less bread and more processed food.)

How has leisure changed? (We watch television instead of playing games.)

How have holidays changed? (Many more people go abroad instead of staying in the UK.)

Using the information sheet   15 min

Copymaster 55 Places change focuses on how towns have grown progressively bigger and the impact this is having on the countryside.

Differentiate by encouraging less-able children to colour the drawings on the page rather than making their own versions for Question 3.

Summary   10 min

Divide the class into two groups. Ask one group to argue that changes have improved people's lives while the other group argues that it has made them worse.

Homework

Ask the children to design a house for 100 years into the future.

Lesson 2   ②

Key question

What clues tell you changes have happened?

Introduction   10 min

Discuss how in many places change is a gradual but steady process and how maps and visual clues tell us about the past. The following questions and answers are appropriate.

How do we tell if a building is old? (The size of the windows, the building materials and decorations are good clues.)

What evidence of past lifestyles could you find in the street? (Bootscrapers, coal holes, cobbles, stables, old advertisements, water pumps and so on.)

Using the activity sheet   30 min

The maps on **Copymaster 56 More and more buildings** show the stages by which a hamlet can be transformed into an urban area over a period of years. Detailed comparisons are needed for this exercise and it helps if the children colour the maps beforehand using red for roads, green for the orchard and orange for the motorway.

Differentiate by talking to less-able children about the information shown on each map. Ask more-able children to make a timeline illustrating the changes.

Summary   5 min

Make a list on the board of the key features marked on the 1850 map and discuss the main changes since then.

Lesson 3

Key question

What will the future be like?

Introduction   5 min

Talk to the children about the changes they have witnessed in their own lives. Some of them may have moved home, others will have seen roads being built or open spaces developed. Make a list on the board.

Investigation   40 min

Divide the children into groups and provide each group with a sheet of A2 paper. Ask them to divide the paper into four and to indicate the changes they think might happen at five-year intervals using drawings, words and plans in each quadrant. If possible, provide large-scale maps so the children can make their ideas as realistic as possible.

Differentiate by encouraging slow-learning children to just consider the changes that might happen ten years ahead. More-able children could say why each change is needed, give a rough idea of the cost and the benefits and drawbacks of the changes.

Summary   20 min

Ask each group to report back to the rest of the class. Ask why the children think the places they have selected are particularly likely to change.

Extra activities

Changing shops

Visit a local shopping street and record the numbers and names of the different premises and the trades conducted there. Give the children the relevant street directories (or extracts from them) when they return to school so they can find out how many of the shops have changed their use. They could find out how many shops are still selling the same type of goods, whether any buildings have been knocked down and whether any trades have completely disappeared.

Local changes

Get the children to look in the local newspaper to find out about how your area is changing. Ask the children to cut out articles for a wall display. Tell them to prepare a brief chart listing the reasons for and against each scheme.

Places change

Two hundred years ago, most people lived in the countryside in scattered farms and villages. They grew their own food, walked from place to place and played games in the fields and woods.

Today things are very different. Towns and cities have been built across the UK. As a result, more and more people now live in built-up areas. They have warm, dry homes, buy their food from supermarkets and travel about by car.

You can find out about these changes by looking for clues of the past. For example, old houses are often found in the middle of towns and villages close to a church. Narrow, twisty roads follow the route of old cart tracks. Patches of countryside have been made into nature reserves.

Some people are worried by what is happening. They think that towns are spreading too far into the countryside. This is threatening plants and creatures. Also people have less and less space where they can enjoy themselves.

Elizabethan 1590

Georgian 1750

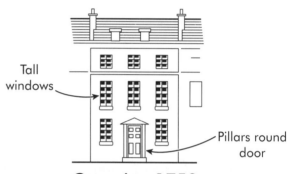

Victorian 1870

Inter-war 1930

Post-war 1970

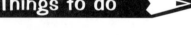

Things to do

1 Write a sentence about how most people lived 200 years ago.

2 Write a sentence about how most people live today.

3 Make drawings of:
   a) a twentieth-century house
   b) a house from a previous century

4 Describe how people's lives and environment might change in another hundred years.

More and more buildings

In 1850, St Mary's School was in the country but it is now surrounded by buildings.

1. List six features shown on the 1850 map.

2. Write a sentence describing the changes shown on the other maps.

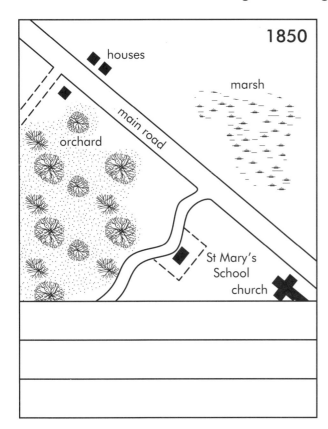

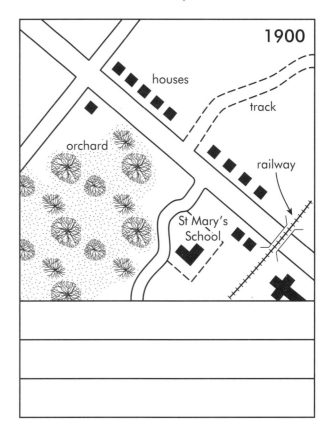

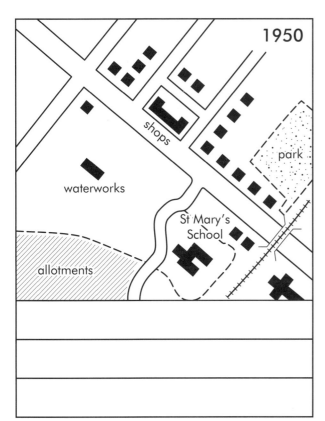

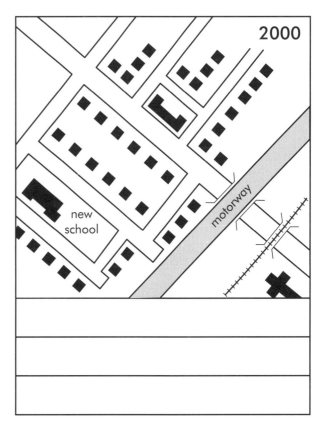

UNIT 29 | Local issues

Learning targets

On completion of this unit children should understand that:

1 ➤➤ the council works to improve the local environment
2 ➤➤ we can assess the quality of the environment using surveys
3 ➤➤ a range of issues affects the local area

Before you start

Focus

This unit focuses on the issues which affect a locality and the ways they can be addressed.

Background information

Work on issues and local planning problems has stimulated some of the best geography teaching in recent years. Not only does it engage the children in a meaningful way, it also allows them to formulate and investigate their own enquiry questions. The interplay of the physical landscape and human activity is often particularly well illustrated in these studies. There is also ample opportunity for role-play and imaginative thinking. In any area, there will be a wealth of different problems to study. The need for an environmentally sensitive perspective adds another dimension.

Teaching points

Children often see issues in a simplistic way and fail to realise the solutions are often based on compromise. They need to appreciate that there are often many different points of view.

Progression

Young children will have discussed what they like and dislike about their local area. This unit shows our personal views have to be balanced against other people's needs and interests.

Vocabulary

community, council, development, environment, issue, opinion, vandalism

Geographical skills

• Recognition of issues
• Use of a number scale
• Devising of a street profile

National Curriculum links

• Recent or proposed changes in a locality
• Issues arising from the way land is used
• How and why people seek to manage and sustain their environment

Assessment indicators

Children should be able to:
• talk about the issues affecting their local area
• appreciate that people have different angles and viewpoints
• know how to compare different environments

Personal application

These statements highlight the relevance of the children's learning:
• I know that I am part of a community
• I can compare different places and areas
• I realise that what I want has to balanced against the needs of others

Teaching the lessons

Lesson 1 ①

Key question

What issues affect our area?

Introduction [10 min]

▨ Ask the children to make a list of some of the issues that affect their lives at home. For example, they will probably have to abide by certain rules, such as tidying the mess that make, agreeing with the rest of the family which television programmes to watch and going to bed before a certain time. Discuss why these rules are needed and what happens when there is a disagreement.

Using the information sheet [20 min]

▨ The information on **Copymaster 57 Local issues** explains how the council works to look after the local area and reconcile different interests. You may

130

want to explain that the council consists of elected members who determine policies and instructs paid officers to put them into practice.

Differentiate by encouraging less-able children to concentrate on drawing speech bubbles listing local problems and ignore the other questions. More-able children could develop the last question by writing a short report illustrated with maps and diagrams.

Summary `10min`

Discuss the different issues that the children have identified. Which ones seem most pressing to the children personally and to the community at large?

Homework

Ask the children to write a letter asking the local council to take action about one of the issues they have identified.

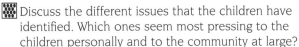

Lesson 2 ②

Key question

How can we compare local streets?

Introduction `10min`

Discuss the different factors which contribute to the quality of a street or area. Noise, fumes and litter are some of the negative factors. Tree planting and conservation measures and proper maintenance are some ways places can be improved. Now tell the children that they are going to visit a couple of local streets to study the quality of the environment. Remember that some of the class may live in the streets you have selected. Be sensitive to their feelings and try to value the good things as well as identifying problems.

Using the activity sheet `30min`

Divide the children into groups and give each group **Copymaster 58 Street survey**. Check that the children understand how to answer the questions in the table. They can complete their profiles when they return to school. Explain that they should put a cross on each axis to show the score and create the profile by linking the points together with straight lines.

Differentiate with slow-learning children by demonstrating on the board how to complete the street profile. More-able children can use their field-work observations and the data from Copymaster 58 in an action plan for local improvements.

Summary `10min`

Discuss the street profiles the children have produced. Discuss whether the profiles are an accurate reflection of their feelings. Would they have obtained different results if the survey had been done at another time of day or in different weather conditions?

Lesson 3 ③

Key question

What can we discover about local issues?

Introduction `5min`

Talk about the issues currently affecting your area. Brainstorm some ideas and make a list on the board as a revision exercise.

Investigation `30min`

The children could use the local newspaper to find out more about what is happening locally. As well as news reports, the letters page is one of the best sources of information as it indicates how people are thinking and includes a range of opinion.

Differentiate by selecting and photocopying some reports yourself to help slow-learning children. Extend the work with more-able children by arranging a site visit. Alternatively, ask a planner or councillor to come and talk to the class.

Summary `15min`

Ask each group to report back to the rest of the class on the issues they have found out about.

Extra activities ② ③

What matters most?

Children could conduct a survey of ten children to find the most pressing issue in school at the moment, the biggest issue in the local area and what most children think is an important world issue.

Newspaper reports

Make a class newspaper about local issues, each child contributing an article on a topic which interests them. Print out the results on a computer using one of the prepared newspaper programs.

Public enquiry

Children could make a detailed study of one issue that affects your local area using information from planning documents, the local press, campaign leaflets and so on. What are the advantages and disadvantages of the scheme? Why is it needed? Who is liable to benefit and who will lose out? Give the children different roles and discuss the proposal in a debate or mock public enquiry.

57 | Local issues

Wherever you live, there are bound to be issues and problems. Many places suffer from traffic and car fumes. Litter, rubbish and vandalism are very common. Noise is another problem.

Sometimes, people can solve these problems themselves. However, the local council also tries to help. It cares for the roads, open spaces and public buildings round about you.

One of the aims of the council is to improve the local environment. This can involve creating parks and gardens or building leisure and sports centres where people can relax.

The council also makes decisions on new plans and developments. For example, it approves road schemes and decides where to build houses and factories.

Sometimes these decisions are very difficult as people have different opinions on how to use a piece of land. They also disagree on how best to spend the money the council has available.

Things to do

1 Make a list of different issues or problems.

2 Draw three speech bubbles and write inside them the problems that affect you most.

3 Write a few sentences about the work of the local council.

4 Say how you would improve your local area.

Street survey

1. Write down the name of the street or place you are studying.

2. Answer the questions in the table by filling in the box which matches your opinion.

Questions	← ————————————	1	2	3	4	5	————————————→
Litter	A lot of litter						Very clean
Noise	A lot of noise						Very quiet
Air	Air bad to breathe						Clean, fresh air
Buildings	In poor repair						In good repair
Plants	No trees or gardens						Plenty of plants
Safety	Lots of dangers						Very safe
Wires	A lot of ugly aerials						No wires
Pavements	Uneven, poor repair						Clean and smooth

3. Show your results of the street profile here.

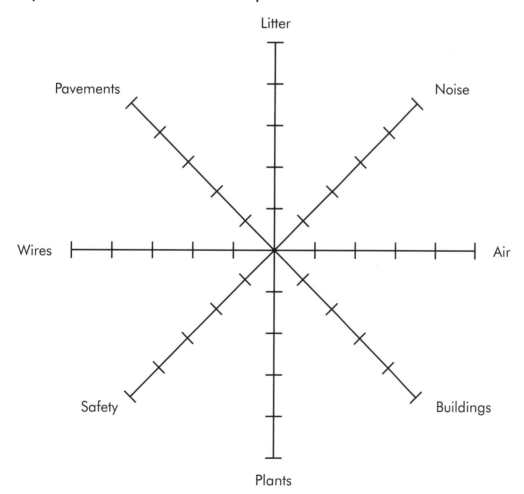

UNITED KINGDOM

Focus

The UK has a greater diversity of scenery than almost any other part of the world. Many of these variations can be accounted for by the underlying geology. The hard rocks of the north and west have resisted erosion. Here, glaciers have scooped out deep valleys such as the Scottish glens and the cwms of North Wales. Further south, softer rocks have resulted in a lowland landscape characterised by gentle slopes and low scarps.

The way in which people have interpreted this landscape makes a fascinating story. The forests which once covered large parts of the country have been cleared away. Settlements have developed where people could satisfy their basic needs for shelter, food, water and work. The hill forts of southern England, the lost villages of Lincolnshire and the old castles in Wales and Scotland are all part of a complex interaction between people and their surroundings.

Perhaps the most profound changes began in the nineteenth century when factories and cities sprang up on the coalfields of the Midlands, Wales and northern England. In the twentieth century, modern transport and electronic communications have brought yet more changes. In many areas, the countryside has been placed under intense pressure. Woodlands, hedges, marshes and old meadows have been lost in the process. It remains to be seen whether we can conserve what remains for future generations or whether this too is lost to development.

At the current rate of urbanisation, which is conservatively estimated at 11,000 ha a year, a fifth of all England will be built on by the middle of the twenty-first century.

Brainstorm

Use this brainstorm to help you develop a medium-term plan. It shows you how to make a 'web' for any chosen place.

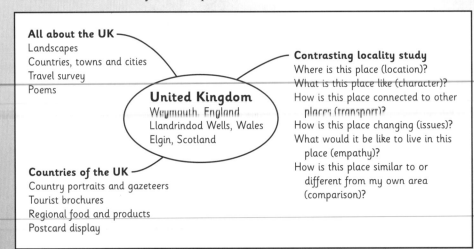

All about the UK
Landscapes
Countries, towns and cities
Travel survey
Poems

United Kingdom
Weymouth, England
Llandrindod Wells, Wales
Elgin, Scotland

Countries of the UK
Country portraits and gazeteers
Tourist brochures
Regional food and products
Postcard display

Contrasting locality study
Where is this place (location)?
What is this place like (character)?
How is this place connected to other places (transport)?
How is this place changing (issues)?
What would it be like to live in this place (empathy)?
How is this place similar to or different from my own area (comparison)?

Research findings

Apart from direct experience, photographs will be a valuable way of teaching children about other parts of the UK. Research shows that children tend to see visual images differently to adults and need help in learning to 'read' them (Mackintosh 1998). In particular, it appears that rather than seeing them as a whole, they view photographs as a series of different parts which they favour according to individual preferences. Exercises and interviews in which children talk about and draw what they see can help to reveal their understanding. It is also useful to select images which challenge stereotypes and exploit their curiosity.

Content

Unit 30	Provides an overview of the UK.
Units 31, 32, 33	Are case studies of places in England, Wales and Scotland which are designed to support work on a contrasting UK locality.

Supporting material can be found in Unit 15 *Routes and journeys*, Unit 16 *Types of transport* and Unit 19 *Caring for the countryside*.

National Curriculum expectations

By the end of Key Stage 2, it is expected that most children will be able to:

- know the location of key places in the United Kingdom, Europe and the world
- explain the physical and human characteristics of places, and their similarities and differences
- recognise how selected physical and human processes cause changes in the character of places and environments

Literacy links

Year 3	Make clear notes: Unit 32 *Llandrindod Wells*, Lesson 1. Write simple non-chronological reports: Unit 33 E*lgin*, Lesson 2.
Year 4	Summarise key ideas in a paragraph: Unit 30 A*ll about the* UK, Lesson 1. Collect information from a variety of sources: Unit 30 A*ll about the* UK, Lesson 2.
Year 5	Make notes for different purposes: Unit 33 E*lgin*, Lesson 1.
Year 6	Write a balanced report of a controversial issue: Unit 31 *Weymouth*, Lesson 3.

Story

The Katie Morag stories by Marie Hedderwick are all set in western Scotland and provide a wealth of information about island life.

ICT links

Postcards	Use postcards, travel brochures and photographs to provide information about places around the UK.
E-mail	Exchange information with another school by e-mail.

All about the UK

Learning targets

On completion of this unit children should understand:

1 ➤➤ the physical features of the UK
2 ➤➤ the different countries of the UK

Before you start

Focus

This unit introduces children to the main physical and human features of the UK. It is designed to provide an overview for more detailed work on themes, localities and mapwork.

Background knowledge

There are four countries in the United Kingdom. Wales was effectively joined to England in 1301, Scotland was included in 1603 and Ireland in 1801. The Union Jack, the national flag, reflects these different national elements containing the crosses of St George (England), St Andrew (Scotland) and St Patrick (Ireland). There are big variations in landscape and climate across the United Kingdom. The English lowlands are the most crowded areas.

Teaching points

It is useful to distinguish between the United Kingdom which is a political entity and the British Isles which is a group of islands off the north-west coast of the European mainland.

Progression

Many children will have been taught to recognise the shape of the British Isles in Key Stage 1. This unit provides an overview of the UK and background information for the study of a contrasting locality.

Vocabulary

Belfast, Cambrian Mountains, Cardiff, Edinburgh, England, English Channel, Grampian Mountains, Irish Sea, Lake District, London, North Sea, River Severn, River Thames, River Trent, Scotland, United Kingdom, Wales

Geographical skills

- Ability to read a map
- Use of secondary sources of information

National Curriculum links

- Identify the points of reference specified on Map A (UK)
- Become aware of how places fit into a wider geographical context
- Use ICT to gain access to additional information sources

Assessment indicators

Children should be able to:
- name and locate the countries of the UK
- identify where they live on a map of the British Isles
- describe different areas of the British Isles in simple terms

Personal application

These statements highlight the relevance of the children's learning:
- I can tell a visitor from another country about the features of the UK
- I know how to find out information from books, CD-ROMs, atlases and other sources
- I can describe what makes the UK distinctive as a European country

Teaching the lessons

Lesson 1 ❶

Key question

What are the physical features of the UK?

Introduction `15min`

 Show the class a wall or atlas map of the British Isles. Point out the different countries, their distinctive shapes and the way they are arranged with Scotland in the north, Wales in the west and Northern Ireland across the Irish Sea. Find out if any of the children have visited the different countries either for a holiday or to see friends and relations. Ask what they did and saw and what impressions they formed.

Using the information sheet [40min]

Talk about the places and features shown on the map on **Copymaster 59 The British Isles** and ask the children to identify where they live.

Differentiate by encouraging slow-learning children to colour the countries on the map and complete Question 1. Challenge more-able children to include a variety of information in their fact files. For example, can they find a way of using the compass and scale bar as well as find the names of towns, seas, mountains and other landscape features?

Summary [10min]

Working around the class, compare the sentences the children have written and the information they have put in their fact files.

Homework

Ask the children to find and copy out a poem about the British Isles or make up one themselves.

Lesson 2 ②

Key question

What are the countries of the UK?

Introduction [5min]

Remind the children about the different countries which make up the United Kingdom, their different sizes, shapes and physical relationship to one another.

Using the activity sheet [40min]

Divide the children into four groups and give each one a different UK country to investigate. The children should begin by brainstorming everything they know about the country they are studying. They should then use atlases and reference books to add to their knowledge. It will enhance the work if you are able to supply postcards, holiday brochures and other material. For example, the Katie Morag stories by Marie Hedderwick are all set in western Scotland and contain some valuable details about the Western Isles. Use **Copymaster 60 Portrait of a country** to record the results and get the children to colour their country on the UK map.

Differentiate either by organising the children into ability groups with learning assistants helping children who need support or put them in mixed groups for team work.

Summary [15min]

Ask each group to report back on their study to the rest of the class.

Lesson 3

Key question

Can you design a tourist brochure?

Introduction [15min]

Discuss what the children would tell someone who lives abroad about the UK. Ask what they think they would want to know. Put up a list on the board using these headings: 'Landscape', 'Weather', 'Cities', 'Food', 'Daily life', 'Sports', 'Festivals' and 'Environmental issues'.

United Kingdom portrait [60min]

Tell the children they have been asked to compile a portrait of the United Kingdom for a child who has never been here. Use the questions on the board, which they have already formulated, to help structure the work. If possible, provide atlases, reference books and other materials. Depending on the time available, you may want each child to focus on just one or two questions. They could then compile their work in a group booklet.

Differentiate by encouraging the children to present their work using a variety of formats such as maps, diagrams, annotated drawings and computer printouts. The range of techniques that they use will depend on their ability.

Summary [10min]

Get each group to identify the single most important thing they would want to include in a class portrait of the United Kingdom.

Extra activities

Travel survey

Make a survey of some of the places in the UK that the children have visited. Ask each child to name one destination and write a few words about it. Display the work around a large wall map with lines of light string or wool identifying the locations.

Local food

Discuss some of the foods and dishes which come from different parts of the UK. Examples include Yorkshire pudding, Cornish pasties and Leicester cheese. Give the children photocopied maps of the UK on which they can record where each item of food comes from.

Grand tour

Ask the children to devise a route around the UK linking points of interest. Suitable places include castles, cathedrals, museums, parks, mountains and beaches. Show the route on a map together with a brief itinerary.

The British Isles

The British Isles is made up of over 900 islands. The mainland of Britain is the eighth largest island in the world. It is nearly 1,000 kilometres long and 500 kilometres wide.

The British Isles is divided into different countries. England is the largest. Northern Ireland is the smallest. Scotland and Wales both have lots of mountains. Each country has its own capital city, traditions and customs.

The Grampians are the highest mountain range in the British Isles. The Severn is the longest river. Lough Neagh is the largest lake. Eastern England is very flat where some places are below sea level and have to be protected by walls.

SCOTLAND

Grampian Mountains

Edinburgh

North Sea

NORTHERN IRELAND

Lough Neagh

Belfast

Pennines

Lake District

Irish Sea

N

River Trent

Cambrian Mountains

ENGLAND

River Severn

WALES

River Thames

London

Cardiff

English Channel

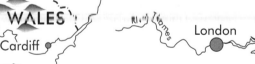

| 0 | 50 | 100 | 150 | 200 | 250 | 300 km |

Things to do

1 Write a sentence containing one fact about:
   a) England
   b) Scotland
   c) Wales
   d) Northern Ireland

2 Make a fact file about the British Isles using the map to help you.

Name of country	
	People and places
Mountains, rivers and countryside	What other things give the country its character?

UNIT 31 Weymouth

Learning targets

On completion of this unit children should understand that:

1 ➤➤ Weymouth is a port and holiday resort
2 ➤➤ Weymouth is changing and growing larger

Before you start

Focus

The development of Weymouth shows how people interact with their environment in different ways.

Background knowledge

There has been a port at the mouth of the River Wey for thousands of years. The Isle of Portland and Chesil Beach create a natural haven which is sheltered from the prevailing south-west winds. From the Iron Age onwards, Weymouth has served as a trading post with Europe and the Mediterranean. The Romans settled in the area and built roads leading inland to towns such as Dorchester. In the Middle Ages, Weymouth benefited from the wool trade. It also provided an anchorage for the navy which confronted the Spanish Armada and was the place where rats first came ashore carrying the bubonic plague.

In the eighteenth century, Weymouth grew dramatically as a sea-bathing resort. Royal patronage by George III led to the development of the Esplanade. The arrival of the railway in 1857 saw a new rush of Victorian development spreading outward from the Georgian core. Since then, Weymouth has continued to expand. Ribbons of villas and bungalows now connect it to surrounding villages and 14,000 caravans have been set up around the bay. There is a regular ferry service to the Channel Islands and there are new trading estates on the edge of the town. The old harbour has recently been redeveloped for tourists.

Progression

This unit will extend the children's understanding of towns and settlements. It also links to work on holidays and transport and could serve as the introduction to a more detailed study of a contrasting UK locality.

Vocabulary

beach, estuary, ferry, harbour, marina, pedestrianised, pier, port, resort, shelter

Geographical skills

- Use and interpretation of maps
- Use of alphanumeric coordinates
- Identification of geographical features

National Curriculum links

- Contrasting UK localities
- Different types of settlement
- How places are changing

Assessment indicators

Children should be able to:
- say why Weymouth was built in a specific location
- describe some key features of the town
- list some of the issues currently affecting Weymouth

Personal application

These statements highlight the relevance of the children's learning:
- I can imagine what a place might be like by looking at a map
- I can find out about places I would like to visit from a map
- I realise that some changes bring benefits and others bring disadvantages

Teaching the lessons

Lesson 1 ❶

Key question

What is Weymouth like?

Introduction [15min]

▓ Remind the children about different types of town – industrial centres, market towns, strongholds and ports. Talk briefly about the history of Weymouth from its early beginnings as an Iron Age trading centre, to the modern ferry links with the Channel Islands. Explain how Weymouth acquired significance as a naval base in the Middle Ages and as a holiday resort in modern times. The following questions and answers are appropriate.

When was Weymouth first set up? (In the Bronze Age to provide links with Europe.)

Why was it a good site for a port? (The estuary of the River Wey provided shelter.)

How did Weymouth develop? (It became a naval base and holiday resort.)

What is Weymouth like today? (Buildings have spread over the surrounding countryside and parts of the centre have been redeveloped for tourists.)

Using the information sheet `25min`

Talk about the map on **Copymaster 61 Weymouth** before the children begin the Things to do. Ask them to locate the harbour and beach and trace the course of the River Wey. The historic town developed near the river mouth where it was easy for boats to dock. The breakwaters to the south are part of the Portland Harbour naval base constructed in the nineteenth century, while the old castle (Sandsfoot Castle) dates back to the time of Henry VIII.

Differentiate by encouraging slow-learning children to concentrate on Question 1.

Summary `10min`

Talk to the children about other ports and holiday resorts around the British Isles. Ask in what ways they are similar to or different from Weymouth.

Homework

Get the children to use a road atlas or map to make a list of place names ending in 'mouth' such as Bournemouth, Exmouth and Sidmouth. Also look for a river with a similar name e.g. Exmouth is on the River Exe.

Lesson 2

Key question

What features give Weymouth its character?

Introduction `10min`

Introduce the lesson by making a list on the board of different geographical features. Physical features include rivers, hills, cliffs, beaches and other aspects of the natural landscape. Human features include shops, churches, houses, factories and other buildings constructed by people.

Using the activity sheet `25min`

Check that the children remember how to use grid references before using **Copymaster 62 Weymouth map**. Talk about how to deal with features such as the beach which cross more than one square.

Differentiate by checking that children with special needs use suitable colours for the key and map. Ask more-able children how each feature reflects an aspect of Weymouth's past. For example, the ferry and marina relate to the port, while the Jubilee Clock and statue of King George III date from the time when Weymouth was a fashionable resort.

Summary `10min`

Ask the children to decide which features best capture the character of Weymouth. Make a list on the board in order of importance with the most significant at the top and the least significant at the bottom.

Lesson 3

Key question

How is Weymouth changing?

Introduction `5min`

Consider the way places are always changing, even in minor ways. Get the children to recall the different repairs and alterations to the school over the last year.

A changing environment `30min`

Write each of the changes listed in the table below on separate pieces of card. Divide the children into groups and give each group a set of cards. Get them to write down why they think each change has happened and whether it has improved or damaged the environment.

Ring road built round town
Masts and aerials on nearby hills
Caravan parks extended
Main street pedestrianised
New supermarkets built on edge of town
Old brewery made into tourist shopping village
Piers and bandstand demolished
New parks and gardens along seashore
Inner harbour made into marina
Many new houses and bungalows
Bird reserve set up
Dogs banned from main beach

Summary `15min`

Ask each group to report back to rest of the class and compare their opinions and ideas.

Extra activities

Weather in Weymouth

Ask the children, by using the weather reports in one of the national broadsheet newspapers, to make a chart of weather in Weymouth over a period of two or three weeks. How does it compare with the weather in your area? Is it generally sunnier and warmer?

A holiday in Weymouth

Ask the children to design a publicity leaflet advertising Weymouth as a holiday resort. Include details of travel arrangements and suggestions for things to do over a period of a week.

Weymouth in history

Ask the children to draw pictures of the types of boats you would find in Weymouth harbour nowadays and the types you would have found in the past.

141

61 | Weymouth

Weymouth is an old town on the south coast of England. It was set up thousands of years ago in the Iron Age. Local people wanted to trade goods with the rest of Europe. They used the estuary of the River Wey as a harbour for their boats.

Today, Weymouth is popular with tourists. Visitors come to swim in the sea and enjoy the long sandy beaches. In summer, Weymouth is a busy holiday resort. People stay in hotels or in caravans near the town.

Weymouth has grown a great deal since it was founded. The old town is now surrounded by roads and houses. The high street has been pedestrianised and the harbour turned into a marina. There is also a new ferry service to the Channel Islands.

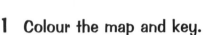

Things to do

1 Colour the map and key.

2 Give two reasons why Weymouth is a good place for a port.

3 Say what would make you want to visit Weymouth.

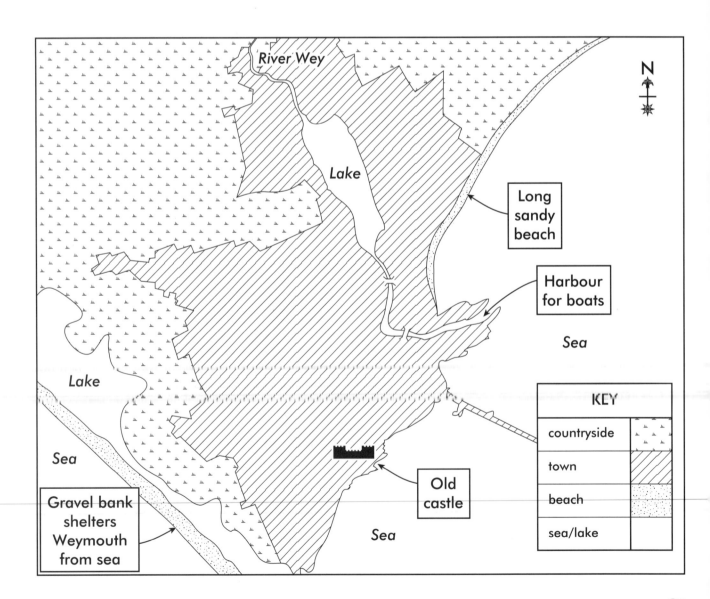

River Wey

Lake

Long sandy beach

Harbour for boats

Sea

N

Lake

Sea

Gravel bank shelters Weymouth from sea

Old castle

Sea

KEY	
countryside	
town	
beach	
sea/lake	

1. Make a list of the different features shown on the map.
2. Write down the correct grid reference next to the feature in your list.
3. Colour the map.

Feature	Grid reference	Feature	Grid reference

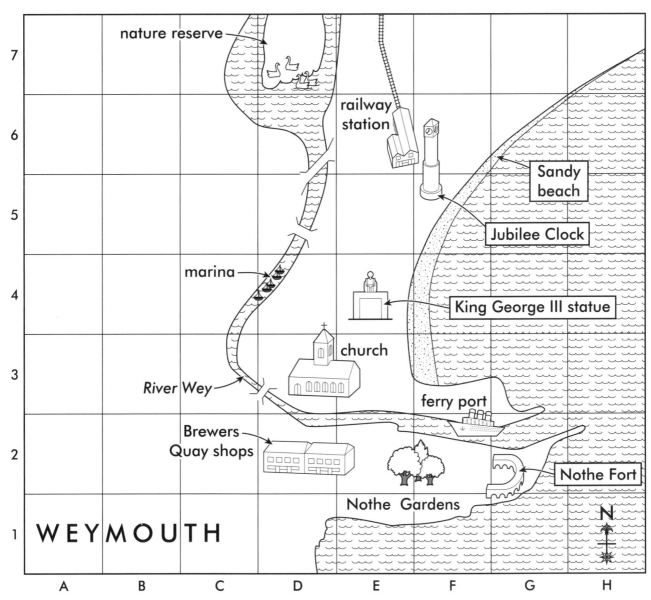

UNIT 32 | Llandrindod Wells

Learning targets

On completion of this unit children should understand that:

1 ➡➡ tourists visit Llandrindod Wells for its facilities and countryside
2 ➡➡ places in the UK have similarities and differences
3 ➡➡ Wales has distinctive physical and human features

Before you start

Focus

This unit provides a case study of a town in Wales which has developed into a tourist centre. Children can compare it with their own locality and identify similar and contrasting features.

Background knowledge

Llandrindod Wells is situated in mid-Wales and has been the administrative centre and county town of Powys since 1974. It is over 200 metres above sea level and surrounded by the Cambrian Mountains. As the name indicates, Llandrindod owes its development to the mineral water springs which are found in the area. The construction of a railway in 1865 brought large numbers of visitors who thought their health would be improved by drinking the waters. Big houses and hotels were built as well as a beautiful park and pump room where people could drink the water and enjoy a quiet, relaxing time.

Today, Llandrindod Wells is a busy tourist centre throughout the year. Visitors enjoy the attractive Victorian architecture and the pump room and make tours into the surrounding countryside. The town has many leisure facilities – a boating lake, sports centre, golf course, theatre and a bowling club which organises international competitions.

Progression

This unit will develop the children's ability to study and analyse the character of places.

Vocabulary

buzzard, countryside, features, kite, landscape, locality, mountains, pump room, routes, source, spring, villas

Geographical skills

* Knowledge of map of Wales
* Identification of factors which give places their character
* Making of comparisons between places

National Curriculum links

* Contrasting UK localities study
* Features which give localities their character
* How localities are set within a broader geographical context

Assessment indicators

Children should be able to:
* describe the features which give Llandrindod Wells its character
* explain how tourism has developed in Llandrindod Wells
* compare Llandrindod with their own locality

Personal application

These statements highlight the relevance of the children's learning:
* I know what makes a place interesting
* I know it is important to select criteria when making comparisons
* I can identify Wales on a map and some of the key features

Teaching the lessons

Lesson 1 ①

Key question

Why do tourists visit Llandrindod Wells?

Introduction [15 min]

▓ Locate Llandrindod Wells on a map of Wales. Note the main routes leading to the town and its proximity to the West Midlands. Find out the names of the surroundings mountain ranges, rivers, lakes and reservoirs. Give the children a brief summary of how the town has developed. The following questions and answers are appropriate.

How did the Victorian railway influence the development of Llandrindod Wells? (It provided better access to the town and encouraged people to visit it.)

How do people travel to Llandrindod Wells nowadays? (By car, coach, bicycle and train.)

144

What is tourism? (People who take holidays and visit places for leisure, relaxation and interest are known as tourists.)

What sort of places attract tourists? (Tourists are attracted by the sea, sunshine, sport, attractive countryside and ancient ruins.)

Using the information sheet `30min`

The text and pictures on **Copymaster 63 Llandrindod Wells** provide a portrait of Llandrindod and introduce children to some of the main features of the town.

Differentiate by encouraging less-able children to colour and label the drawings, cut them out and fix them in their books. More-able children could write about how each of the different buildings contributes to the town.

Summary `10min`

Ask the children what they would most like to do on a visit to Llandrindod Wells and why.

Homework

Ask the children to design an advertisement for a brochure to attract tourists to Llandrindod Wells. Extend the activity by asking pupils to make a similar advertisement for their own locality to display for comparison.

Lesson 2 ②

Key question

How can we compare different places in the UK?

Introduction `10min`

Discuss with the children the way that all towns have a range of facilities and features. Some of these relate to the landscape and physical setting. Others are to do with buildings and economic activities. It is the variety of features which gives a place its character. The following questions and answers are appropriate.

What type of town is Llandrindod Wells? (An old market town, administrative centre and tourist resort.)

What factors have helped Llandrindod to grow larger? The Victorian railway, proximity to the West Midlands, and the natural spring water.)

What type of place is your own locality? (Children should discuss key features.)

How can we find out about places? (Using books, tourist leaflets, photographs and guides.)

Using the activity sheet `30min`

Copymaster 64 Similar or different provides information about the landscape, history, and work and leisure facilities in Llandrindrod Wells. Using these headings, the children should list the features in their own locality to make a comparison. The 'comparison scale' gives the children an opportunity to make a balanced judgement. You may find it helpful to get them to give reasons for their choices.

Differentiation is provided. The activity is designed for all children. Those with special educational needs could work in groups with a support assistant or in pairs with a more-able child.

Summary `10min`

Prepare your own master sheet of local features so that you can compare the children's ideas with your own. Discuss the features which are found both in Llandrindod Wells and your own locality.

Lesson 3 ③

Key question

What is Wales like?

Introduction `20min`

Talk about the way that countries are described in guides and gazeteers by a list of facts and figures. These tell people about the rivers, mountains, main towns and so forth. Now get the children to look at an altas map of Wales to see what information they can find out for themselves.

Welsh fact file `40min`

 Ask the children to draw a map of Wales showing the main mountains, rivers, lakes and towns. Ask them to write down ten other facts about Wales using textbooks, reference books, photographs, pamphlets and other sources of information. If possible, mark the location of each fact on the map using the numbers 1 to 10. Finally, add a title in English and Welsh (Wales is *Cymru*).

Many children will need a photocopied map of Wales to help them with this task but more-able children can draw their own outlines.

Summary `10min`

Discuss the ways in which Llandrindod Wells is set in a typically Welsh landscape. What aspects give it this distinctive character? What other Welsh places would you like to learn about and why?

Extra activities ③

Slate mines

Ask the children to find out about slate mining in North Wales using reference books, maps and other sources of information (e.g. schools television programmes). Ask the children to make diagrams showing how roofing slates are produced. They could make a survey of slate roofs in your own area.

Reservoirs

Look at a map to find Lake Vyrnwy and other reservoirs. Who uses the water? Why is this a good place for reservoirs? Compare the rainfall figures for the Welsh mountains with your own part of the world and discuss what makes it so wet.

Llandrindod Wells

Llandrindod Wells is a town in mid-Wales. It is surrounded by countryside and high mountains. Every year, thousands of tourists come to Llandrindod by car, coach, bicycle and train. They make tours in the mountains and walk in the valleys and forests. They also come to see the wildlife. Unusual birds such as kites and buzzards are found in the area.

Visitors enjoy visiting the buildings in the town. Natural spring water is available in the pump room. There is also a theatre, leisure centre, bicycle museum, international bowling club and a beautiful boating lake.

Many local people earn money working for tourists. They work in hotels, shops and restaurants. Each year in August, there is a special festival when people

dress in Victorian clothes, arrange fairs and workshops and remember the ways of the past. This brings even more visitors to Llandrindod.

Things to do

1 Make a list of the things tourists like to do when they visit Llandrindod Wells.

2 Label the pictures of Llandrindod Wells using this list:
boating lake
bandstand
bowling green
high street
railway station
hotel

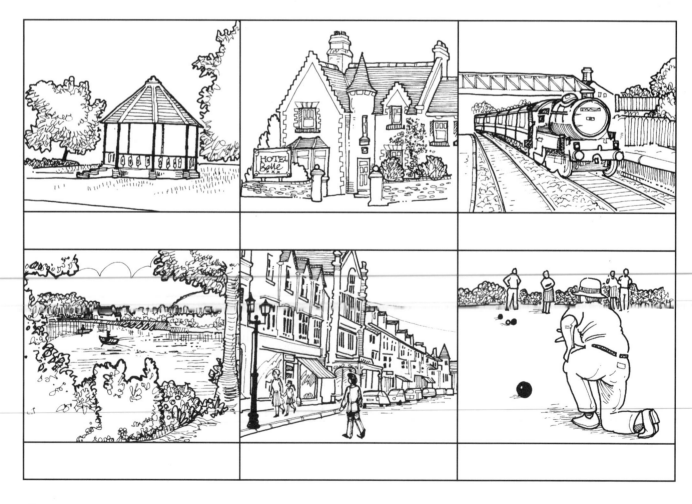

Similar or different?

1. Name your locality and fill in the empty boxes in the table below.
2. Decide whether your place is similar to or different from Llandrindod Wells by colouring one of the circles on the companion scale.

	LLANDRINDOD WELLS	
LANDSCAPE	In valley of River Ithon. Surrounded by mountains. Lakes and reservoirs nearby.	
HISTORY	First visitors came to use spring water. Railway prompted further growth. Now the centre for visitors to mid-Wales.	
WORK	Many people work in hotels, restaurants and shops. Industrial estate and nearby farms also provide jobs.	
LEISURE	Range of leisure facilities – golf course, theatre, bicycle museum, Victorian festival, parks and bandstand, bowling green.	

①	②	③	④	⑤	⑥	⑦	⑧	⑨	⑩
Very different		**Quite different**			**Quite similar**			**Very similar**	

Elgin

Learning targets

On completion of this unit children should understand that:

1 ➤➤ Elgin is an ancient town in Scotland
2 ➤➤ Elgin is both similar to and different from other towns
3 ➤➤ there are beautiful valleys and mountains around Elgin

Before you start

Focus

In this unit, children will learn about an ancient Scottish town.

Background knowledge

Elgin is in north-east Scotland on the Moray Firth. Its strategic position in the valley of the River Spey, relatively mild climate and fertile soil encouraged settlement from the earliest times. By the eleventh century, a substantial castle had been built and the area was popular with royal hunting parties. It also became the seat of the Bishop of Moray. Elgin flourished and many fine buildings were built in the seventeenth century, reflecting the prosperity of the merchants and craftsmen. In the nineteenth century, the coming of the railway fuelled business fortunes.

Today, Elgin is a busy place with a population of 20,000 people. The graceful ruins of the cathedral and the parks and leisure facilities attract tourists. Industrial estates on the outskirts supply local farmers and the North Sea oil industry. There are also specialist businesses like coppersmiths who tend the whisky distilleries that are scattered around the Spey valley. Further afield, there is the major RAF base at Lossiemouth, the Baxters food factory at Fochabers and a fishing port at Buckie.

Teaching points

It is useful if the children know the location of Elgin within Scotland, its relation to Aberdeen, Inverness, Lossiemouth and Aviemore and have some general idea of the course of the River Spey from its source in the Cairngorms.

Progression

This unit is designed to extend children's awareness of the character of the UK in general and Scotland in particular.

Vocabulary

coppersmith, forestry, merchant, oil platform, River Spey, Scotland, vat, whisky

Geographical skills

- Knowledge of UK map
- Making of a land-use map
- Use of a colour code
- Making of comparison lists

National Curriculum links

- Contrasting UK localities
- The characteristics and locations of settlements reflect their economic activity

Assessment indicators

Children should be able to:
- say what Elgin is like
- explain what makes Elgin different from other places
- compare Elgin with their own locality

Personal application

These statements highlight the relevance of the children's learning:
- I understand how Elgin and other towns develop
- I see what is special about a place from a town plan
- I can describe what is special about the Scottish countryside

Teaching the lessons

Lesson 1 ①

Key question
What is Elgin like?

Introduction [10min]

▨ Make a list on the board of what the children think northern Scotland might be like. Sort their ideas into groups using these headings: 'Landscape', 'Weather', 'Towns', 'Work', 'Environment'. Find out if any of the class have been to Elgin or the Scottish Highlands. Describe what it is like, mentioning the North Sea and the oil platforms, fishing at Buckie, RAF Lossiemouth which is a base for search and rescue, and Aviemore in the Grampian Mountains.

Using the information sheet `30min`

 As well as reading the text on **Copymaster 65 All about Elgin**, ensure that the children look at the maps. This will help them with their answers.

Differentiate by discussing the answers with the class to help slow-learning children. More-able children could concentrate on Question 4, providing maps and drawings to support their written work.

Summary `5min`

 Choosing children from around the class, ask them for facts about Elgin and make a quick list of half a dozen or so on the board. Discuss which ones seem the most significant.

Homework

Ask the children to find out with the aid of an atlas how they would get from where they live to Elgin. Tell them to provide a simple plan with distances if possible.

Lesson 2 ②

Key question

What is special about Elgin?

Introduction `5min`

 Remind the children that all towns have similar features because they cater for the needs of local residents. However, many places have a distinct regional character. Elgin is no exception.

Using the activity sheet `30min`

 On **Copymaster 66 Elgin town plan**, the children may find it useful to colour the buildings, river and roads as an orientation exercise before they complete the activities.

Differentiate by encouraging all the children to complete the first two activities but more-able children should also write the report. This is an open-ended task which could also serve as a formative assessment.

Summary `10min`

 Discuss how the different features shown on the plan reflect the history and character of the town. For example, the castle indicates Elgin's strategic importance on the route along the east coast of Scotland, while the cathedral shows that it was a centre of some significance.

Lesson 3 ③

Key question

What is the countryside like around Elgin?

Introduction `10min`

 This lesson is based on a walk along the River Spey Long Distance Path. You will need to provide the children with a copy of the description below and the simple outline map of the valley on Copymaster 65. An Ordnance Survey map of the area would also be useful.

Investigation `45min`

 Ask the children to devise an illustrated trail leaflet for a walk along the River Spey using an A4 sheet of paper folded into three vertical strips.

Differentiate by giving slow-learning children an abbreviated text and drawings to work from.

Stop 1 Spey Bay The trail starts at Spey Bay where the river meets the sea. This secluded place was once busy building ships and unloading fish. The old ice house which was once used for storing fish is now a museum.

Stop 2 Fochabers Castle At Fochabers, there is a castle and bridge where the main road crosses the river. The famous Baxters food factory is also here.

Stop 3 Craigellachie village At Craigellachie there is the last major bridge for many miles. Smaller bridges are often washed away when the river floods in winter. The village was once at a railway junction.

Stop 4 Tomintoul village The trail continues to Tomintoul. The village, which is high in the hills, is frequently cut off in winter by snow. There are magnificent views across the surrounding mountains and purple heather moorland.

Stop 5 Peat workings Tourists come to visit the peat diggings, a source of fuel and garden fertiliser. Some people think that the peat should be left in the ground as it takes thousands of years to form and provides a unique habitat for plants and creatures.

Summary `5min`

 Discuss which stops on the trail the children would find most interesting and why.

Extra activities

Made in Scotland

Make a display of labels and different goods and products that come from Scotland, some of which the children could provide. As well as Baxters food products, you might include some shortbread, Dundee marmalade, tartan cloth and the label from a whisky bottle.

The Scottish mountains

Using postcards and photographs from calendars, the children could make a study of the Scottish mountains. What are the different peaks and how high are they? How do people use the mountains in summer and in winter? What are the environmental issues which currently affect the region?

Elgin is a town in the valley of the River Spey in north-east Scotland. It has a castle and an old cathedral which is now in ruins. There are also some fine houses that were built by merchants hundreds of years ago.

In Victorian times, a railway was built linking Elgin with Aberdeen and the rest of Scotland. The town grew larger and industries such as fishing, forestry and making whisky were developed.

Today, Elgin has a population of about 20,000 people. It has all the things you would expect to find in a town, such as a museum, hospital, schools and council offices.

Elgin also has some special factories and businesses. Coppersmiths make vats for storing whisky. Engineers make the things that are needed on oil platforms. The railway line is also important. Timber from forests in the mountains is stored in the goods yard before it is taken away on trains.

These different activities make Elgin a busy place. It is also popular with tourists who visit in the summer months. Some people like to walk the River Spey Long Distance Path which goes up the valley into the mountains. Others want to see the historic town.

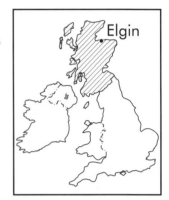

Things to do

1 Where is Elgin?

2 What happened to Elgin in Victorian times?

3 Write down three businesses which make Elgin special. Say what happens at each one.

4 What would you like to see and do if you went to Elgin?

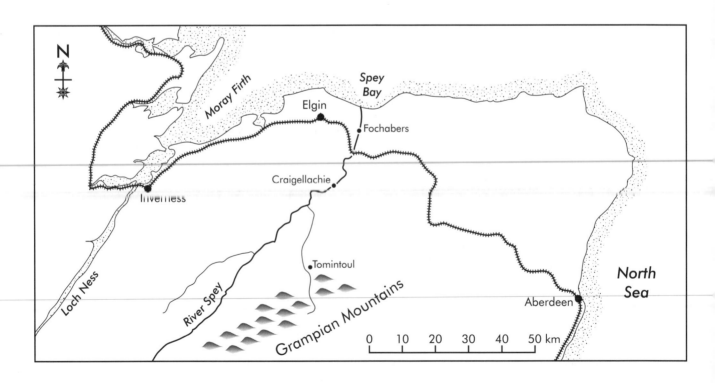

Elgin town plan

1. Make a list of the buildings and places shown on the plan of Elgin.

2. Write an A next to the buildings you might find anywhere. Write an S next to the buildings that are special features of Elgin.

3. Write a report about how Elgin is similar to and different from the place where you live.

Building or place	Code

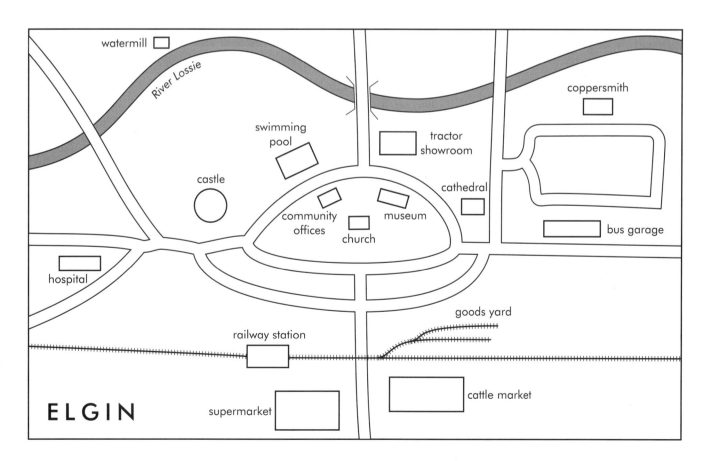

EUROPE

Focus

Europe is one of the smallest continents being about 4,000 km across in any direction. It is bounded on the west by the Atlantic Ocean and on the south by the Mediterranean Sea. The eastern border has always been less well defined. The Ural Mountains and Caspian Sea create the boundary with Asia. This division makes Moscow a major European city and the Ukraine the largest European country.

Historically, Europe traces its roots to Greco-Roman culture. For centuries, it has been the bastion of Christendom resisting waves of invaders from the east. Today, Europe still functions as a social and political entity. Seen in this way, the European Union is the latest expression of a long and deeply rooted tradition.

Although the UK has always sought a measure of independence, it is geographically part of Europe and separated from the mainland by only 30 km of water. The layers of clay, sand and chalk which make up the Weald extend across the Channel to northern France. The weather and climate of the UK also resembles that of the nearby land mass.

Today, many primary school children travel abroad for excursions or holidays. France, Spain and Greece are particularly popular destinations. On a purely practical level, it makes sense to build on their experience. However, the curriculum also requires children to learn about Europe. In geography, thematic studies should be taught at a range of scales and in different contexts including the European Union. If children are to be equipped for the twenty-first century, they need to be introduced to this perspective.

Brainstorm

Use this brainstorm to help you develop a medium-term plan.

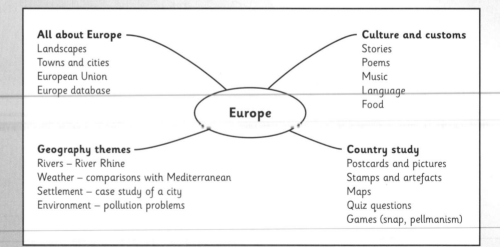

All about Europe
Landscapes
Towns and cities
European Union
Europe database

Culture and customs
Stories
Poems
Music
Language
Food

Europe

Geography themes
Rivers – River Rhine
Weather – comparisons with Mediterranean
Settlement – case study of a city
Environment – pollution problems

Country study
Postcards and pictures
Stamps and artefacts
Maps
Quiz questions
Games (snap, pellmanism)

Research findings

By the time they reach the age of eleven, most children are aware of Western Europe (Wiegand 1991 *Education 3–13*). The processes by which they acquire this information are, however, imperfectly understood. Travel and personal experience seem to be a powerful force. In a study conducted in Yorkshire schools, Wiegand (1991 *Geography*) found that children who had travelled were more willing to view stereotypes cautiously and to match them against their own observations than those who had not. Halocha (1998) compared the influence of a number of different information sources on a group of fifty-four year 5 and year 6 children. He concluded that teachers' own experiences appeared to have the greatest impact on children's learning. Penpals and materials from children in linked schools were also valuable ways of developing ideas. There is also evidence that primary school children prefer people who they perceive as being similar to themselves. For this reason, it may be best not to dwell too much on the differences and contrasts.

Content

Unit 34 Gives an overview of Europe and the European Union.

Unit 35 Is based on a tour of Western European capitals.

Unit 36 Focuses on France, Spain, Italy and Germany.

Related material can be found in Unit 6 *The River Rhine* and Unit 18 *Links around the world*.

National Curriculum expectations

By the end of Key Stage 2, it is expected that most children will be able to:
- know the location of key places in the United Kingdom, Europe and the world
- explain the physical and human characteristics of places, and their similarities and differences

Literacy links

Year 3 Word games: Unit 34 *All about Europe*, Extra activities, Word search.

Year 4 Summarise a sentence or a paragraph: Unit 34 *All about Europe*, Lesson 1. Design an advertisement: Unit 35 *European tour*, Lesson 2.

Year 5 Identify features of recounted texts: Unit 35 *European tour*, Lesson 1. Locate information confidently and efficiently: Unit 36 *Four European countries*, Lesson 1.

Year 6 Appraise a text quickly and effectively: Unit 35 *European tour*, Lesson 3.

Story

Anno's Journey by Mitsumasa Anno (Bodley Head 1977) is a story without words that portrays a journey across Europe using meticulous and very detailed drawings.

ICT links

E-mail Exchange letters and information with a twin school by e-mail.

Satellite images Use satellite images to provide information about landscape and weather in Europe.

Photographs Look at photographs, postcards, travel posters and other images of places and landscapes in Europe.

CD-ROM *Exploring Maps* (YITM 1996) uses maps of Europe, the UK and other parts of the world to develop children's skills.

All about Europe

Learning targets

On completion of this unit children should understand:

1 ➤➤ the landscape and features of Europe
2 ➤➤ the growth and aim of the European Union

Before you start

Focus

This unit introduces an overview of the physical and human geography of Europe and is designed to provide a context for studies of specific countries and localities.

Background knowledge

Europe is one of the smallest continents. It is also one of the hardest to identify as it merges with Asia on its eastern edge. The boundary follows the Ural mountains, touches the shore of the Caspian Sea and turns westwards along the crest of the Caucasus mountains.

Europe is approximately 4,000 kilometres from east to west and 3,000 kilometres from north to south. The climate varies from the cold of the Arctic to the heat of the Mediterranean. Evergreen and temperate forests are the natural vegetation for many areas, although in the east grasslands (steppes) are an important feature.

Europe has a deeply indented coastline which is rich in natural harbours. The North Sea, Baltic Sea, Black Sea and Mediterranean Sea have all served as the focus for different civilisations. The Alps, Carpathians and Scandinavian mountains are the main mountain ranges.

Teaching points

Children will need an atlas map of Europe.

Progression

Children should learn about geographical themes such as rivers and the environment in a range of contexts including Europe. As they revisit Europe in different ways, they will build up an increasingly complex view of the continent and become more aware of its general geography.

Vocabulary

Alps, Danube, Equator, Europe, European Union, France, Germany, London, Moscow, Paris, Rhine, Spain

Geographical skills

- Identification of features on a map
- Making of a map
- Recognition of continents

National Curriculum links

- Using an atlas
- Setting thematic studies in a context from the European Union
- Working at a range of scales

Assessment indicators

Children should be able to:
- name three cities and three countries in Europe
- identify the countries of the European Union on a map
- describe the physical and human features of Europe

Personal application

These statements highlight the relevance of the children's learning:
- I can describe different parts of Europe
- I know I am a citizen of both the UK and Europe
- I can compare some of the countries of Europe

Teaching the lessons

Lesson 1 ❶

Key question

What is Europe like?

Introduction 〔10min〕

▓ Show the children a world map or globe. Talk about the way the land is divided into great blocks separated by the oceans. The following questions and answers are appropriate.

What is a continent? (A large block of land.)

What are the names of the continents? (Europe,

Africa, Asia, North America, South America, Oceania and Antarctica.)

Which continent do we belong to? (Europe.)

What are the different countries of Europe? (Children should volunteer names.)

Using the information sheet `30min`

 Read **Copymaster 67 Europe** with the class and get them to answer the questions.

Differentiate by encouraging more-able children to make their own Europe quiz using the copymaster and atlas. Slow-learning children may need to discuss the answers to each question as a group.

Summary `5min`

 Reinforce what the children have learnt by making a list on the board of ten different things about Europe.

Homework

Ask the children to bring some European stamps to school for a class stamp album.

Lesson 2 ②

Key question

What is the European Union?

Introduction `15min`

 Introduce the lesson by telling the children about the European Union and how it was created.

> The European Union was created after the Second World War when much of Europe lay in ruins. People decided that they would work together to keep the peace. France, Germany, Italy and the Low Countries were the first to join in 1957. Today, there are fifteen countries in the European Union. The main areas of cooperation are trade, farming, fishing, employment, finance and environmental protection. Day-to-day administration is handled by the European Commission based in Brussels.

Using the activity sheet `30min`

 On **Copymaster 68 The European Union**, the children discover how the European Union has grown since 1957. First they choose a colour for the empty boxes in the key. Then they colour the countries on the map using the same system.

Differentiate by blanking out the names on the map before photocopying the copymaster for more-able children to identify the countries for themselves using an atlas.

Summary `5min`

 Talk about countries like Norway and Switzerland who have voted not to join the European Union while Poland and the Czech Republic are keen to become members.

Lesson 3 ①

Key question

Can you describe some of the features of Europe?

Introduction `10min`

 The children should look at a map of Europe in an atlas. Discuss some of the things that it shows, such as rivers, mountains, countries and capitals.

Europe map `45min`

Ask the children to draw their own map of Europe. This should show the United Kingdom, France, Spain, Italy and Germany, the Alps, River Rhine and Mediterranean Sea and North Sea. Remind the children to add a key and north compass point and to draw a border round the edge of the map.

Differentiate by providing less-able children with a photocopied map to complete.

Summary `10min`

 Ask the children a few simple questions about the map of Europe. The following questions and answers are appropriate.

Which is the largest country in western Europe? (France.)

What is the name of the sea which separates Europe from Africa? (Mediterranean.)

Which are the most northerly countries? (Norway and Russia.)

Extra activities ① ②

Europe Day

Celebrate Europe Day (9 May) by allowing children throughout the school to choose from a range of workshops. These could involve listening to and acting out folk tales, watching slide shows given by parents and outside talkers, making a study of the day's weather across Europe, cooking traditional food, dressing up in national costumes and learning famous songs.

Word search

Ask the children to devise a word search containing the names of twelve European countries.

Europe is one of the smallest continents. It is about 4,000 kilometres across and lies about half way between the Equator and the North Pole.

In northern Europe, the weather is often very cold. Snow and ice last many months of the year. In the southern Europe, there is plenty of hot summer sunshine.

Most of Europe was once covered with grasslands and forests. Great rivers like the Rhine and Danube flow across the land. Many rivers begin in a great range of mountains called the Alps.

Europe is divided into more than forty countries. France, Germany and Spain are some of the biggest countries. Belgium is one of the smallest. The United Kingdom is in between in size.

In Europe, large numbers of people live in cities. London, Paris and Moscow are famous places. There are many other towns where people work in factories, banks and offices.

In some places, pollution is a serious problem. Rivers and seas are dirty and the air is bad to breathe. New laws will help to make the environment better.

Things to do

1 How far is it across Europe?
2 What is the weather like in northern Europe?
3 Name two European rivers.
4 Name a high mountain range.
5 Name three European cities.
6 How many countries are there in Europe?
7 Name two pollution problems.
8 How are people trying to solve pollution problems?

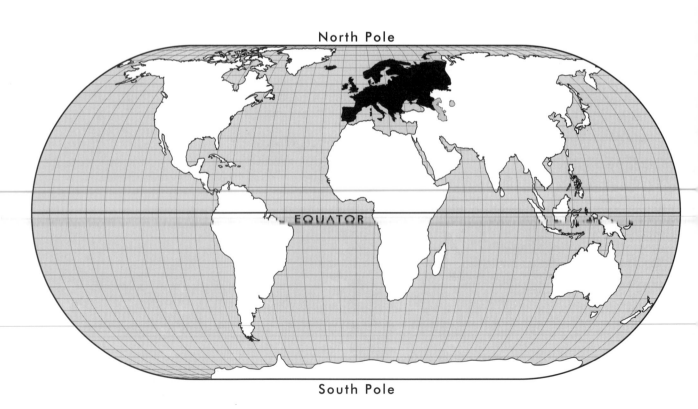

North Pole

EQUATOR

South Pole

The European Union

Date	Colour code	Country
1957		Belgium (B), France, Germany, Italy, Luxembourg (L), Netherlands (N)
1973		Denmark, Ireland, United Kingdom
1981		Greece
1986		Portugal, Spain
1995		Austria, Finland, Sweden

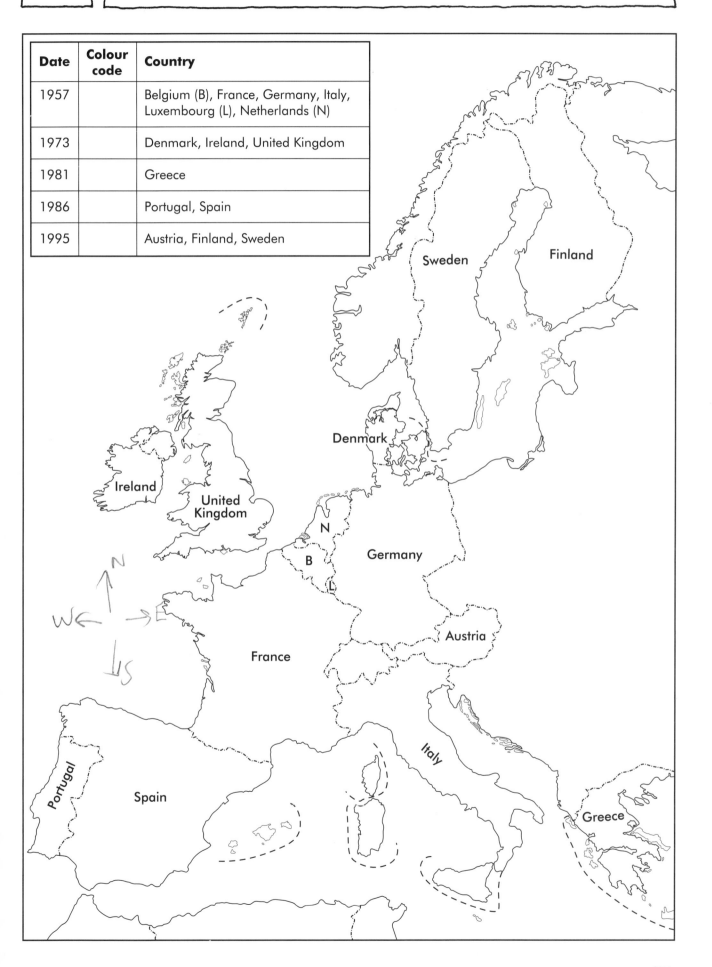

European tour

Learning targets

On completion of this unit children should understand that:

1 ➤➤ there are different countries in and features of north-west Europe
2 ➤➤ people plan a route when they go on a journey
3 ➤➤ major cities have certain features

Before you start

Focus

This unit focuses on the area of Europe which is closest to Britain. It is structured round a holiday tour which involves visiting different countries, cities and landscapes.

Background information

Much of north-west Europe is relatively flat. There are extensive lowlands in the Netherlands and Belgium which were created in recent geological times. Further south, the land rises gently reaching heights of over 500 metres in the older, harder rocks of the Ardennes, Eifel and Hunsrück. Several major rivers traverse the region including the Rhine, Meuse, Moselle and Seine. These provide important routes for communication. Europe's largest port, Rotterdam, stands on one of the branches of the Rhine.

Apart from the hills, the whole area is densely settled. There are many large cities such as Brussels, Antwerp, Cologne, Amsterdam and Berlin. As well as being centres of trade and administration, these places also have considerable architectural and historical interest. In the Ruhr and along the Franco-Belgian border, the old coalfields have led to extensive industrial activity. Much of the intervening countryside remains surprisingly rural. In northern France, the area around Rheims and Épernay is famous around the world for its champagne wine.

Teaching points

Check that there is a suitable map of Western Europe in the atlases you give to the children.

Progression

This unit is designed to extend and consolidate children's knowledge and understanding of Europe. It also relates directly to the wider theme of journeys and travel. Children who may have visited other parts of the UK now learn about Europe.

Vocabulary

capital, country, Europe, gorge, journey, leaflet, route, sights, vineyard

Geographical skills

• Development of images of different places
• Following of a route on a map
• Use of secondary sources of information

National Curriculum links

• Thematic studies especially rivers, settlement and environmental change in a European context
• Use secondary sources of evidence
• Knowledge of the map of Europe

Assessment indicators

Children should be able to:
• name the countries in mainland Europe which are closest to Britain
• talk about some of the physical and human features of north-west Europe
• describe a major European city

Personal application

These statements highlight the relevance of the children's learning:
• I can imagine a coach tour itinerary
• I can plan a realistic route for a long journey
• I am able to collect information from a variety of different sources

Teaching the lessons

Lesson 1 ❶

Key question

What is north-west Europe like?

Introduction 5min

▦ Find out what the children know about tours. Discuss how they are organised. Ask where the children would go if they wanted to go on one. Ask if any of the children have been to north-west Europe.

Using the information sheet ⌗30min⌗

▓ Copymaster 69 European tour describes the places people visit on a typical five-day tour. The route takes in scenic landscapes and historic cities and links different countries each of which has its own traditions and customs.

Differentiate by encouraging less-able children to draw a picture of a coach and list the places visited on the tour underneath instead of answering Question 2. More-able children could describe some of the other activities they would like to do on the tour such as taking photographs.

Summary ⌗5min⌗

▓ Discuss how the tour would be good value for money.

Homework

Ask the children to bring postcards, pictures, stories or artefacts from north-west Europe to school for a class display. They should write a short explanation of what they bring.

Lesson 2 ① ②

Key question

How can we show the features on a route?

Introduction ⌗5min⌗

▓ Talk about the things you need to consider when devising an advertising leaflet. For instance, it could include pictures, maps, diagrams, itineraries and prices. Show the children some examples – you can obtain these from travel agents.

Using the activity sheet ⌗60min⌗

▓ Before they begin the work on **Copymaster 70 European tour map**, ensure that the children can identify the land and sea on the map. Get them to follow the route and discuss what the pictures show.

Differentiate by providing less-able children with headings to help them structure their leaflet. More-able children could work out the distances between stops and devise slogans.

Summary ⌗5min⌗

▓ Ask the children what they think they would most like about the tour. Can they think of anything they would dislike or find unpleasant?

Lesson 3 ③

Key question

What can you discover about a European city?

Introduction ⌗10min⌗

♣ Divide the children into groups and get them to make a list of things they would like to investigate about a European city. For example, they might want

to find out about famous buildings, the people who have lived there, when the city was founded or how it is changing.

Investigation ⌗40min⌗

♣ Now select a city for each group to investigate using these questions. It will be valuable to provide reference books, leaflets, postcards and holiday brochures. Other useful sources of information include atlases, textbooks and CD-ROMs. Cities such as Athens, Rome and Venice may be particularly suitable because there are many resources available. It may also be possible to interview parents or members of staff who have travelled abroad.

Differentiate by making sure that slow-learning children have a clear task to do so that they contribute to the group. Differentiation will mostly depend on the depth and quality of the work the children produce. Select a more-able child as the group leader who will write down key questions and set the others a task.

Summary ⌗20min⌗

♣ Ask each group to present a brief report of their findings so the rest of the class can learn what they have been doing.

Extra activities

Postcard collection

Ask the children to bring postcards of European scenes to school for a class display. Give each one a title and caption and arrange them around a map of Europe with a line or string to the correct location.

Travel survey

Ask the children to conduct a survey to find out whether any of their friends have travelled abroad and the places they have visited. Depending on the circumstances, the survey might be an in-depth interview with a few children or a more general study involving the whole class. You could record the results on a spreadsheet or data handling package.

Database

Set up a spreadsheet or database about the different countries of Western Europe. You could include information about the landscape, rivers, cities, population, language, main transport routes and environmental problems.

Roberto looks after tourists on holiday.

'The coach leaves from London early in the morning. I have to see that everybody has their tickets, money and passports.

We take the ferry across the English Channel and spend the first night in Brussels. This is an old city but it is also the modern centre of the European Union. There is a huge sculpture in the shape of an atom in one of the parks. It is called the Atomium.

The next day, we go to Amsterdam which is famous for its canals and museums. Our tour also includes a visit to a diamond factory. Many people buy jewellery and presents here.

One of the most exciting parts of the trip is the boat trip on the Rhine. The river flows in a deep gorge past the Lorelei Rock. There is a story that a wicked enchantress lived here. She used to charm sailors with songs to make them crash their boats.

After that, we drive across Luxembourg and France. There are lots of vineyards in this area. We go to Épernay to visit a wine cellar.

Paris is the last stop. Notre Dame Cathedral and the Eiffel Tower are two famous sights. There are also lots of museums and cafés.

I enjoy travelling and the trips are good fun. I tell people about the history of the places which we visit.

Sometimes people lose their money or have an accident. If this happens, I help them with their problems.'

Things to do

1 Write down three jobs Roberto has to do.

2 Make a list of places on the tour. What one thing would you want to see at each place?

3 Which place would you most want to go to? Say why.

European tour map

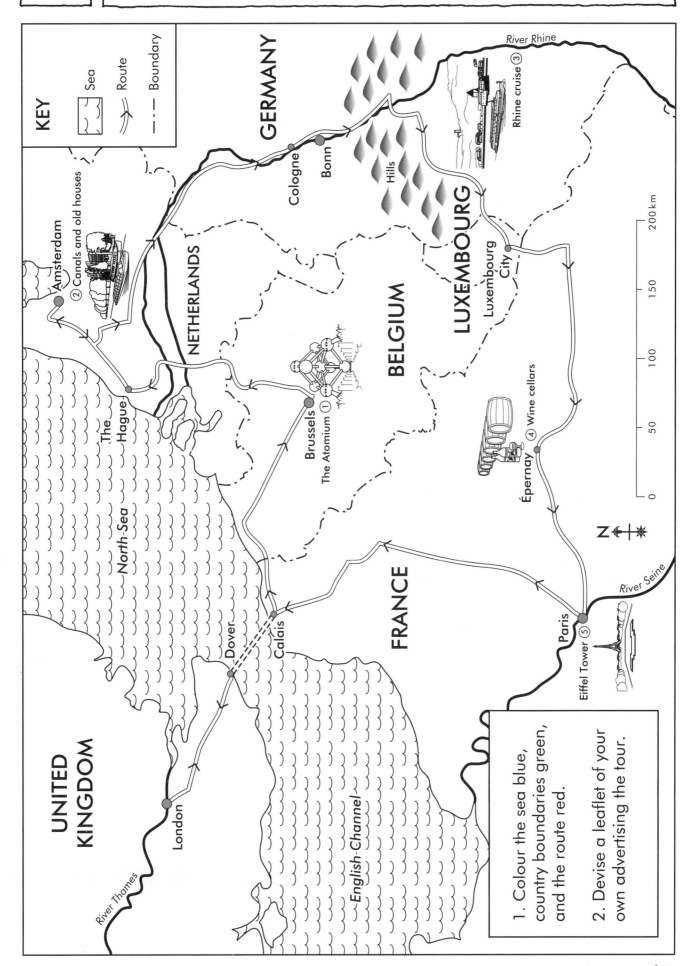

KEY

Sea	
Route	
Boundary	

GERMANY

River Rhine

Rhine cruise ③

Cologne

Bonn

Hills

Amsterdam

② Canals and old houses

NETHERLANDS

LUXEMBOURG

Luxembourg City

The Hague

BELGIUM

Brussels
The Atomium ①

④ Wine cellars

Épernay

200 km

150

100

50

0

North Sea

N

FRANCE

River Seine

Dover

Calais

Paris

Eiffel Tower ⑤

UNITED KINGDOM

London

River Thames

English Channel

1. Colour the sea blue, country boundaries green, and the route red.

2. Devise a leaflet of your own advertising the tour.

Four European countries

Learning targets

On completion of this unit children should understand that:

1 ➤➤ France, Spain, Italy and Germany each have their own distinctive character

2 ➤➤ there are key points on the map of Europe

Before you start

Focus

This unit focuses on four major countries in Western Europe – Germany, France, Spain and Italy.

Background information

France is our closest neighbour on mainland Europe. Its climate varies from temperate maritime in the north-west to Mediterranean in the south. The main mountains are the Alps, Pyrennees and Massif Central. The population is distributed fairly evenly. Its capital city is Paris.

Germany was reunited in 1989. Its climate is similar to the UK's but it has colder winters and hotter summers. It has a flat, low plain in the north and hills and mountains in the south. It is the most populous country in Europe with many large industrial cities. The capital city is Berlin.

Italy consists of a long peninsula and two large islands – Sicily and Sardinia. It has a Mediterranean climate. The Apennines form the central spine of mountains. There are two active volcanoes – Etna and Vesuvius. The population is concentrated along the coast. There is an industrial area in the north in the valley of the River Po. The capital city is Rome.

Spain has the Catalans (Barcelona) and the Basques (Bilbao) who form distinct national sub-groups. It has a Mediterranean climate in the south. There is a high mountainous plateau including the Pyrenees and Sierra Nevada. The population is concentrated near the Mediterranean and Atlantic coasts but is sparse inland.

Teaching points

This unit raises questions about images and national identity. Some children may hold negative stereotypes about the French diet or about modern Germans because of the actions of their forebears during the Nazi era. Providing unbiased information and celebrating cultural diversity can help to modify these ideas.

Progression

At Key Stage 1, children start to develop an awareness of the wider world. This unit is intended to help children develop an increasingly balanced view of neighbouring countries and peoples.

Vocabulary

area, capital, country, customs, landscape, population, region, weather

Geographical skills

- Identification of places and features on maps
- Interpretation of charts and diagrams
- Ability to make comparisons

National Curriculum links

- Recognise countries on Map B (Europe)
- Ask questions about geographical features and issues
- Analyse evidence, draw conclusions and communicate findings

Assessment indicators

Children should be able to:
- recognise the shape of Germany, France, Spain and Italy on a map
- know about some of the local traditions and customs
- talk about the differences between the countries they have studied

Personal application

These statements highlight the relevance of the children's learning:
- I can describe something which I like about France, Spain, Italy and Germany
- I can describe how my life might be different if my family went to live in another European country
- I can put events and places in a framework

Teaching the lessons

Lesson 1 ❶

Key question

How can you compare life in the UK with life in other European countries?

Introduction [15min]

Put four headings on the board: 'Germany', 'France', 'Spain' and 'Italy' and note down all the things that the children know about each country. Try to include similarities rather than differences. For example, if a child says the French eat frogs legs and snails, make the point that they also eat a lot of food which is the same as ours. This will help to avoid unfortunate stereotypes. Now see that the children can find each country in an atlas working from the index. Focus their attention by asking questions about the name of the capital city, main rivers, surrounding countries and so on.

Using the information sheet 30 min

Ensure that the children understand the different diagrams on **Copymaster 71 Country facts**. They are all drawn to scale for visual comparison.

Differentiate by encouraging less-able children to work in groups to produce a profile of just one country. More-able children can add extra information from their atlases, e.g. the latitude and longitude of the capital and the distance from one side of the country to another.

Summary 10 min

Ask some of the children to read out the sentences that they have written and to put them on the board under the appropriate country headings.

Homework

Ask the children to make up a quiz with five questions about one of the countries they have studied.

Lesson 2 ①

Key question

How are France, Spain, Italy and Germany different from each other?

Introduction 10 min

Ask the children what they think a country is. There is a wide range of possible answers but the following factors are particularly significant: own laws, own language, own traditions and customs, own currency, own head of state, own stamps, own flag, capital city and distinct area or territory. Explain that four of these factors are highlighted in the game they are about to play.

Using the activity sheet 60 min

Ask the children to colour the pictures, flags and country outlines on **Copymaster 72 Country game**. They should then cut them out carefully to make sixteen playing cards which can be used in different ways as explained below.

Country profiles: working individually, the children muddle up the cards, reassemble them in country sets and glue them down on a sheet of paper together with any other information they want to add.

Snap: working in pairs, the children shuffle their cards, make two equal sets and turn them over alternatively as in a game of snap.

Pelmanism: working in pairs, the children place their cards face down on the table and collect them in pairs as in pelmanism.

Differentiate by selecting an activity from the choices given above to match the children's abilities. More-able children could write out the rules to go with their game.

Summary 5 min

Ask which of the different clues on Copymaster 72 tells us most about a country. Discuss whether the map, flag, key building or language is most significant.

Lesson 3 ②

Key question

Have you a knowledge of country shapes?

Introduction 10 min

Summarise what the children have learnt from the previous two lessons. Discuss how we can find out about other countries.

Investigation 40 min

Ask the children to draw a map of one of the four countries (Germany, France, Spain or Italy) on a large sheet of card working either individually or in small groups. Using travel brochures, the children should then cut out photographs and arrange them as a collage filling the shape they have drawn, together with an short description.

Differentiate by drawing the country shapes on sheets for slow-learning children in advance. More-able children can work individually and add specific places to their maps.

Summary 20 min

Groups and individuals should present their findings to the rest of the class highlighting their choice of information and main findings.

Extra activities

Recipes

Ask the children to find out about traditional dishes from different parts of Europe, such as pasta from Italy, paella from Spain and cabbage and sausages from Germany. Put some of the recipes together with pictures or drawings in a zigzag book. Can any of the children explain how the dishes relate to the climate of the area?

Music

Children could listen to folk tunes and other music from the countries they have studied. They could try to learn some of the words and sing the songs. This could form the basis of a class assembly.

Language awareness

Put together a number of phrases in the languages of the four countries which can be used in school. Examples include 'Good morning children' and 'My name is … '.

Highest mountains

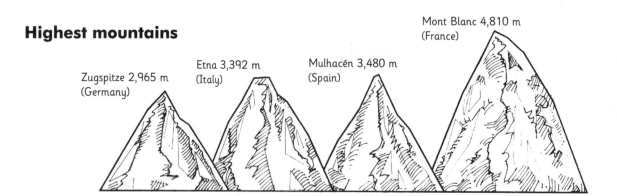

Mont Blanc 4,810 m
(France)

Mulhacén 3,480 m
(Spain)

Etna 3,392 m
(Italy)

Zugspitze 2,965 m
(Germany)

Longest rivers

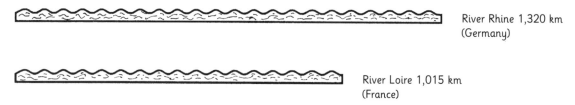

River Rhine 1,320 km
(Germany)

River Loire 1,015 km
(France)

River Ebro 925 km
(Spain)

River Po 650 km
(Italy)

Population

Germany
82 million

France
60 million

Italy
57 million

Spain
39 million

Area

Italy
300,000 square kilometres

Germany
350,000 square kilometres

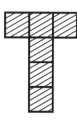

Spain
500,000 square kilometres

France
550,000 square kilometres

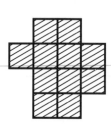
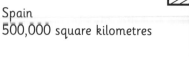

Things to do

1 Make fact files about Germany,
France, Spain and Italy.

2 Write a sentence saying
something important about each
country.

72

Country game

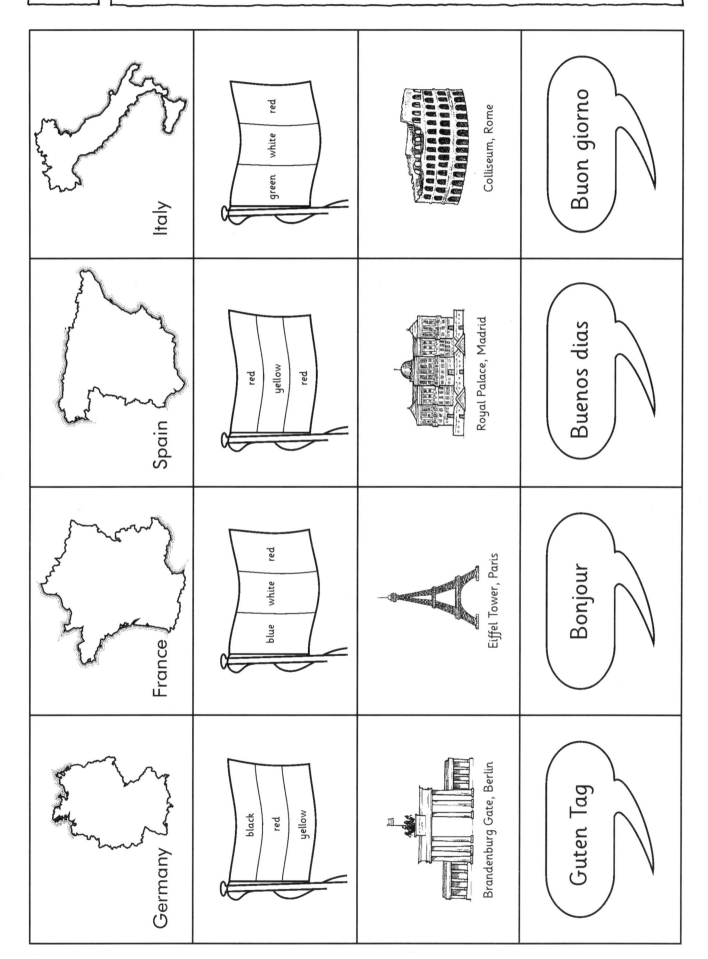

Italy	green white red	Colliseum, Rome	Buon giorno
Spain	red yellow red	Royal Palace, Madrid	Buenos dias
France	blue white red	Eiffel Tower, Paris	Bonjour
Germany	black red yellow	Brandenburg Gate, Berlin	Guten Tag

OUR WORLD

Focus

The Earth and the solar system were probably created about 4,600 million years ago from the dust of ancient stars. Originally without oceans or atmosphere, the Earth has gradually evolved into its present form over geological time. Even now, the Earth's crust is remarkably thin, varying in thickness from about 5 km to 45 km. Beneath this, there are several thousands of kilometres of molten and semi-molten rock.

Scientists now know the Earth's crust is broken into plates which fit together like the parts of a giant jigsaw. The continents are carried around on the plates by subterranean currents. Where the plates collide with each other or where they move apart, there are earthquakes and volcanic eruptions. This is particularly evident around the Pacific Ocean where a circle of volcanoes creates a 'ring of fire'.

As well as learning about the continents and oceans, children also need to know about people and living conditions in different parts of the world. The geography curriculum focuses attention on specific localities and small-scale studies. This has the advantage of teaching children about real people and their everyday lives. In any project, the underlying objectives should be to challenge stereotypes, celebrate different cultures and create positive images.

In recent years, some excellent television programmes and photopacks have been produced to support these studies. It may also be possible to obtain first-hand accounts about different places from the children's parents or other members of the local community. Twinning and direct school-to-school links are also very valuable. Stories and folk tales add another dimension.

Brainstorm

Use this brainstorm to help you develop a medium-term plan.

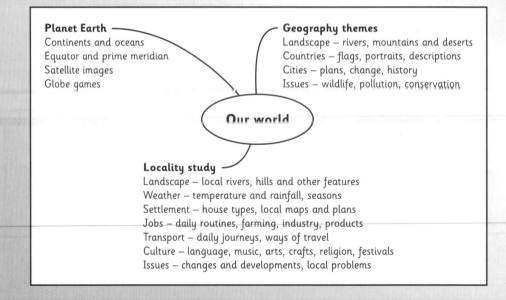

Planet Earth
Continents and oceans
Equator and prime meridian
Satellite images
Globe games

Geography themes
Landscape – rivers, mountains and deserts
Countries – flags, portraits, descriptions
Cities – plans, change, history
Issues – wildlife, pollution, conservation

Our world

Locality study
Landscape – local rivers, hills and other features
Weather – temperature and rainfall, seasons
Settlement – house types, local maps and plans
Jobs – daily routines, farming, industry, products
Transport – daily journeys, ways of travel
Culture – language, music, arts, crafts, religion, festivals
Issues – changes and developments, local problems

Research findings

Young children appear to have considerable difficulty reconciling what they are taught about the Earth with their common-sense notions. Thus, while they will state that the Earth is round like a ball, they tend argue that it is flat when questioned in greater detail according to Nussbaum (1985). Further research into children's knowledge of the world by Wiegand (1991) indicates that a seven-year-old can typically name about six countries, while an eleven-year-old can name fifteen or more. However, throughout the junior years, children seem to be largely unaware of the developing world (Africa, Asia and South America). The dangers of ignoring this gap are emphasised by Scoffham (1998) who argues that a positive teaching programme can help to change children's attitudes and perceptions. In this way, it is possible to challenge negative stereotypes and introduce the children to the notion of global citizenship at a time when they are likely to be particularly receptive.

Content

Unit 37 Considers the Earth in space and the way the surface is divided into continents and oceans.

Units 38, 39, 40 Focus on the developing world. As well as illustrating different geographical themes, these units are intended to provide a general introduction to more detailed studies of specific localities.

National Curriculum expectations

At the end of Key Stage 2, it is expected that most children will be able to:
* explain the physical and human characteristics of places, and their similarities and differences
* know the location of key places in the United Kingdom, Europe and the world

Literacy links

Year 3 Use the term adjective appropriately: Unit 39 *Asia*, Lesson 1.
Make clear notes: Unit 38 *Africa*, Lesson 1.

Year 4 Design an advertisement: Unit 39 *Asia*, Extra activities, Travel poster.
Identify features of instructional texts: Unit 40 *South America*, Lesson 2.

Year 5 Compose short explanatory texts: Unit 38 *Africa*, Extra activities, African wildlife.
Traditional stories, myths and legends: Unit 38 *Africa*, Extra activities, Myths and legends.

Story

There are many stories which support work on overseas localities including B*ringing the Rain to Kaput Plain* by Verna Aardema (Macmillan 1981), T*he Day of Ahmed's Secret* by Florence Pary Heide (Gollancz 1994) and T*he Village in the Forest by the Sea* by Beverley Birch (Bodley Head 1995).

ICT links

CD-ROM *My Amazing World Explorer* (Dorling Kindersley 1996) takes children on a light-hearted journey around the world and is an excellent way of developing their locational knowledge. D*iscover India* (Action Aid 1995) is particularly useful as a way of supporting the study of an Indian locality.

Internet Use the Internet to obtain information about different countries and news events around the world.

E-mail Arrange to swap information with a school in a developing country using e-mail.

Planet Earth

Learning targets

On completion of this unit children should understand:

1 ➤➤ key features of the globe
2 ➤➤ names and shapes of the continents
3 ➤➤ that weather varies around the world

Before you start

Focus

The shape of the Earth and the distribution of the continents and oceans forms the basis of this unit.

Background information

At the Equator, the Earth has a diameter of 12,757 km and a circumference of 40,077 km. This makes it a medium-sized planet, much smaller than Jupiter and Saturn but larger than Mercury and Mars. Scientists believe the Earth is about 4,600 million years old. Originally, the Earth consisted of a great ball of incandescent rock and gas. Very gradually, this has become cooler. The crust has solidified and the steam and gas from countless volcanoes has accumulated to create the atmosphere and oceans. The land, which was once joined together in a supercontinent, has drifted apart in great blocks. However, it is still possible to see from a world map how Africa and South America were once joined together.

Teaching points

This unit relates closely to work on 'the Earth and beyond' in science as well projects on the weather and seasons.

Progression

Children should have been introduced to the globe, continents and oceans in Key Stage 1. This unit builds on that experience.

Vocabulary

axis, continent, Equator, globe, North Pole, ocean, pattern, prime meridian, South Pole, sphere

Geographical skills

* Use of a globe
* Use of a world map
* Making of a chart

National Curriculum links

* Use and interpret globes
* Use contents pages and index of an atlas
* Recognise points of reference on Map C (world map)

Assessment indicators

Children should be able to:
* recognise the Equator, poles and other features including the British Isles on a globe
* name and locate the seven continents and four oceans on a world map
* draw and label a recognisable freehand map of the world

Personal application

These statements highlight the relevance of the children's learning:
* I know that the Earth spins and is part of the solar system
* I can locate world news items on a globe
* I know how to find out about weather around the world

Teaching the lessons

Lesson 1 ❶

Key question

What do you know about the Earth in space?

Introduction [15min]

▦ Bring a globe into the classroom and look at it with the children. Begin by demonstrating how the Earth spins on its axis. Ask them to find the Equator, prime meridian and British Isles. Remind the children of the four compass points.

Using the information sheet [30min]

▦ Read **Copymaster 73 Planet Earth** with the class. There is a lot of information on this page and it is important to ensure that the children understand the vocabulary.

Differentiate by encouraging more-able children to use the information on the copymaster to make an

Earth facts quiz. The key thing for less-able children to understand is that the Earth spins on an axis which is marked by the North and South Poles. This accounts for the pattern of day and night.

Summary `10min`

▓ With the children, compile a list of facts about the Earth on the board.

Homework

Ask the children to work from an atlas to make a list of ten different countries, places or features which are either on or very close to the Equator.

Lesson 2 ②

Key question

What are the different continents and oceans?

Introduction `10min`

▓ Ask the children to look at a world map in an atlas, or, better still, project a blank outline map of the continents on to the wall using an overhead projector transparency. Ask them to locate the British Isles, then help them to identify the continents and oceans. Point out how Europe is joined to Asia and that Oceania is actually a collection of South Pacific islands. You might also discuss the differences between a flat map and a globe, the key point being that you can 'go off the edge and round the back' of the map.

Using the activity sheet `40min`

 As well as completing the activities specified on **Copymaster 74 Continents and oceans**, the children could colour the continents to clarify the shapes of the land.

Differentiate by writing the first letter of each continent and ocean on the map and blank out Question 3 before giving the copymaster to less-able children. With more-able children, blank out the dots on the edges of the map so that they have to decide where to draw the Equator and prime meridian.

Summary `10min`

▓ Consolidate the children's knowledge by asking them questions about the world map. Which is the largest continent? Which two continents are entirely north of the Equator? Which ocean lies between Africa and South America?

Lesson 3 ③

Key question

How does weather vary around the world?

Introduction `10min`

▓ Talk to the children about differences in weather around the world. Which places would they expect to be hot? Which places would they expect to be cold? Are there any places which might be very wet or dry?

Investigation `75min`

 Let each child select a different city from the places listed around the world in the broadsheet weather reports. Ask them to make a day-by-day chart of the temperature in that place over a period of week, together with a short written report about the weather conditions. Put the work up as a wall display around a large world map with lines of wool or string linking the report to the correct place on the map.

Differentiate by encouraging less-able children to work in pairs and simply record the temperature. More-able children can present their charts and reports using a computer.

Summary `10min`

♣ Select children to report on their findings bearing in mind the following questions. Which places are hotter/colder than the UK? Are places near the Equator always the hottest? Is there any obvious pattern to the weather in each place?

Extra activities

Globe game

You need an inflatable globe and a 'feely bag' containing common letters from the alphabet for this game. Give the globe to one of the children in the class. Get a second child to choose a letter from the bag. The child with the globe now has to find and point to a country beginning with that letter. When successful, they then pass the globe to someone else for the next round. After a few rounds you can ring the changes by asking the children to search for cities instead. Seas, oceans, continents and mountain ranges provide an extra dimension.

Latitude and longitude

Explain to the children how lines of latitude and longitude create a grid which covers the Earth's surface. Now make up a quiz involving the latitude and longitude of specific places.

Satellite images

Look at a poster or photograph of the Earth taken from space. Talk about the different features which the children can see. Get them to explore the picture by writing down three or more things under each of the headings 'What I know for certain', 'What I can guess', and 'What I would like to know more about'.

73

Planet Earth

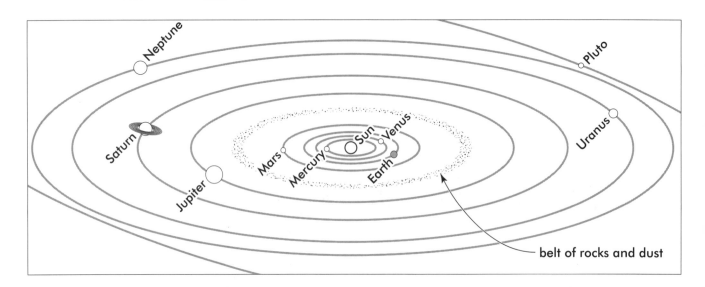

belt of rocks and dust

The Earth is one of nine planets that go round the sun. Mercury and Venus are closer to the sun than the Earth and much hotter. Planets such as Jupiter and Saturn are further away and much colder. They are made up of great masses of frozen gas.

The Earth spins as it travels through space. It takes 24 hours for the Earth to spin right around. This movement creates night and day.

As the Earth spins, two points stay still. These are the North Pole and South Pole.

Halfway between the North and South Poles there is an imaginary line round the middle of the Earth. This is called the Equator. All places are either north or south of this line.

Another imaginary line, called the prime meridian, goes from the North Pole to South Pole through London. All places are either east or west of this line.

Places near the Equator are very hot because the sun is often directly overhead. The Poles are cold because the sun stays low in the sky.

Most of the Earth's surface is covered by great sheets of water. These are called oceans and they are very deep.

Between the oceans there are great blocks of land called continents. There are seven continents in all. The one we live on is called Europe. The others are Africa, Asia, Antarctica, Oceania, North America and South America.

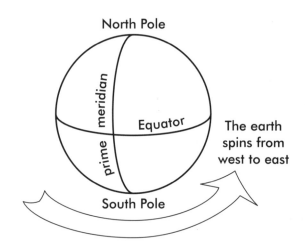

The earth spins from west to east

Things to do

1 Write sentences to describe these things: the Equator, prime meridian, North Pole, South Pole, continent, ocean.

2 Copy the drawing of the Earth in space into your book.

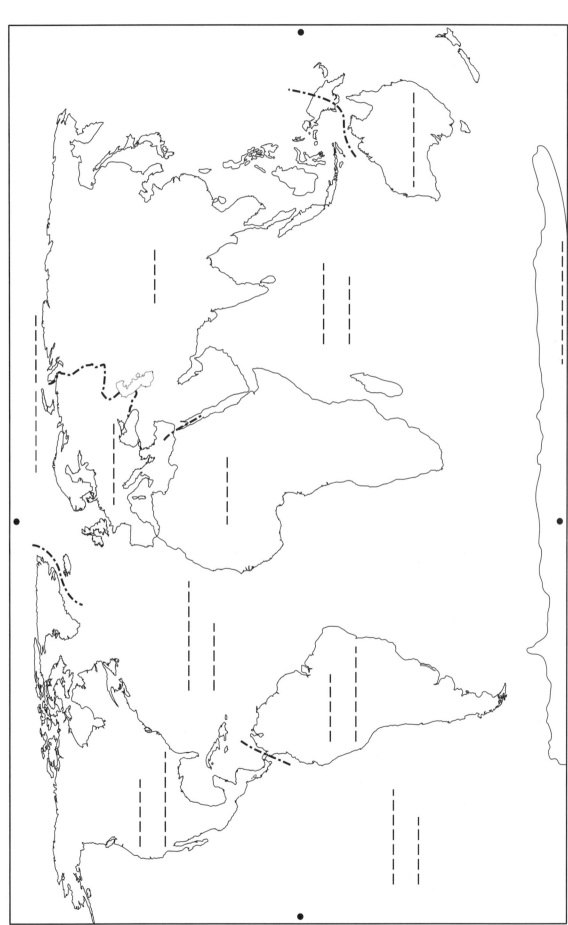

1. Label these continents.
North America, South America,
Europe, Asia, Africa, Oceania,
Antarctica.

2. Label these oceans.
Pacific Ocean, Atlantic Ocean,
Arctic Ocean, Indian Ocean.

3. Draw and label lines to
show the Equator and the
prime meridian by joining the
dots on the edges of the map.

Africa

Learning targets

On completion of this unit children should understand that:

1 ➤➤ everyday life in Africa is both similar to and different from that in the UK
2 ➤➤ Africa is divided into many different countries

Before you start

Focus

As well as giving an overview of Africa, this unit aims to show how people live their lives and to promote positive images.

Background information

Africa is the second largest continent. Most of Africa lies within the tropics and has either a hot desert climate (Sahara and Kalahari) or a pattern of wet and dry seasons (the savannahs). There are extensive areas of rainforests along the coast of West Africa and around the River Zaire. Despite being near the Equator, the highest peaks, such as Mount Kenya, are covered in snow throughout the year.

Africa is divided into over fifty countries, many of which became independent in the 1960s and 1970s. The extensive farmlands and abundant natural resources should be more than adequate for the relatively small population. In fact, many people live in poverty without adequate food, safe water or sanitation. This is partly due to the legacy of centuries of colonialism which thrived on plantation crops, slavery and other forms of 'asset stripping'. Since then, civil wars and military dictatorships have caused much hardship. Short-term economic solutions have failed and the debt of African nations has reached crisis level. Aid agencies do what they can to help address the problems of poverty and starvation but it is a complex problem in which politics plays a major role.

Teaching points

Many children think that Africa is a single country and have no conception that it is a huge land mass. They are also amazed to learn that there are modern cities in Africa. Use a locality photopack to develop the work – there

is an excellent range of material on Kenya. You could also make links to the study of Egypt in history.

Progression

As children progress through the junior school they will be increasingly able to make comparisons between places in Africa and the UK.

Vocabulary

Africa, cacao, continent, country, game reserve, Kenya, shamba, Swahili, ugali

Geographical skills

- Reading and use of a map
- Making of comparisons
- Recognition of country shapes

National Curriculum links

- Contrasting localities in Africa, Asia or South America
- Use secondary sources of evidence

Assessment indicators

Children should be able to:
- name and identify three countries on a map of Africa
- describe how people's lives are different in Africa and the UK
- describe how people's lives are similar in Africa and the UK

Personal application

These statements highlight the relevance of the children's learning:
- I know that children in Africa do many of the same things we do in the UK
- I understand that people have to work all over the world
- I can use atlases, books and ICT to find out more about distant places

Teaching the lessons

Lesson 1   ❶

Key question

What is Africa like?

Introduction   ⌊10 min⌋

▦ Begin by finding Africa on a globe or atlas map. Look for the Equator, the River Nile and Lake Victoria. Ask the children to name some of the larger countries. Point out the location of Kenya in the heart of East Africa. The following questions and answers are appropriate.

What are the main rivers in Africa? (Niger, Nile, Orange, Zaire, Zambezi.)

What are the largest countries in Africa? (Algeria, Sudan, Zaire.)

Which places does the Equator pass through? (Lake Victoria and Mount Kenya, Zaire.)

Using the information sheet 50min

 Read **Copymaster 75 What is Africa like?** with the class, taking care to make sure that they understand the vocabulary.

Differentiate by making up some questions for slow-learning children to answer to replace Questions 1 and 2. Ask more-able children to copy the map of Kamasong and make a map of their own area as part of their answer to Question 3.

Summary 5min

 Ask the children what they would most like about living in Kamasong.

Homework

Ask the children to find six things about Africa from books, atlases, travel brochures, a CD-ROM or other sources.

Lesson 2 ①

Key question

What sort of jobs do peope do in Africa?

Introduction 5min

 Remind the children that Africa covers a vast area, that it is divided into lots of different countries and that people live modern as well as traditional lives.

Using the activity sheet 30min

Copymaster 76 People in Africa focuses on people and the work that they do. It is designed to help children empathise and relate to Africa in a positive way. The drawings show both men and women to reflect what happens in reality – women actually undertake most of the agricultural work in Africa.

Differentiate by blanking out one or two of the pictures and country outlines and ask more-able children to make their own drawings in the empty spaces. Support less-able children by writing the first letter of each country name in the correct part of the map.

Summary 5min

Discuss how many of the jobs shown on the copymaster are not done in England and the reasons why.

Lesson 3 ②

Key question

Which countries is Africa divided into?

Introduction 10min

 Remind the children that Africa is a vast block of land about thirty times the size of the UK. Look at an atlas map to see how it is divided into lots of different countries. Talk about some of the main features; for example, how many countries lie on the Equator, which countries are landlocked?

Investigation 45min

 Give the children a photocopied map of Africa or provide them with an atlas. Ask them to list six different African countries and show their outlines.

Differentiate by selecting countries for slow-learning children to study. Ask more-able children to make their own tracings or even freehand drawings of the countries.

Summary 5min

 Ask the children which countries they selected and why. They might have been attracted by the name, the history of Egypt and Benin or the location of Gambia completely surrounded by Senegal.

Extra activities ① ②

African wildlife

Ask the children to work individually or in pairs to find out about an African creature and to write a report for a wildlife gazetteer.

African diary

Ask the children to imagine that they are on holiday in Africa and to devise a postcard with a picture on the front and a description of what they have been doing on the back.

Myths and legends

Give the children some traditional African myths and legends to read. Ask them to make notes and write a short précis of the story.

What is Africa like?

Daniel lives in Kamasong, a village in Kenya in East Africa. He has four brothers and three sisters. There are altogether eight children in the family.

Daniel and his family live in a round house. The walls are made of painted earth which dries hard in the sun. The roof is thatched with grass. Inside the house it is cool and dark as the windows are very small. Most people in Kamasong live in round houses like this. A few richer families live in rectangular houses with tin roofs.

Daniel gets up at 6.00 a.m. every morning. School begins at 8.15 a.m. and ends at 5.00 p.m. The last hour of the day is used for games. Daniel's favourite lessons are art, science and Swahili. In his spare time he likes going to his scout group and reading stories.

Many people in Kamasong keep animals such as cows, sheep, chickens and goats. Maize is the main crop. This is ground into flour to make a thick porridge called ugali. Other crops include potatoes, carrots, peas and onions.

Daniel's family has its own vegetable plot. This is called a shamba. Daniel helps to look after the plants and to dig out the weeds. He also grows flowers which are sold in the market to make a special powder which kills insects. He spends the money he earns on books and clothes.

Kamasong has a church, health centre, shops and a bar as well as a school. The houses are scattered over the hillside. It takes Daniel about an hour to walk to the centre of the village. When he is older, he wants to visit Nairobi. This is the capital city of Kenya about 300 km away.

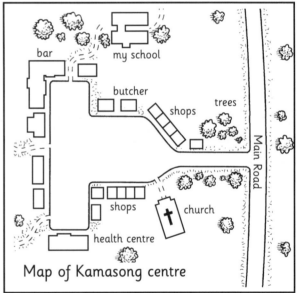

Map of Kamasong centre

Things to do

1 Make up three questions about Kamasong and write down the answers.

2 Make notes on these themes: Daniel's house, Daniel's day, Kamasong.

3 List the main differences between Kamasong and your area.

People in Africa

1. Make a list of the jobs shown in the drawings.
2. Using an atlas, draw lines from the drawings to the correct places on the map.
3. Make your own drawing of someone at work in Egypt.

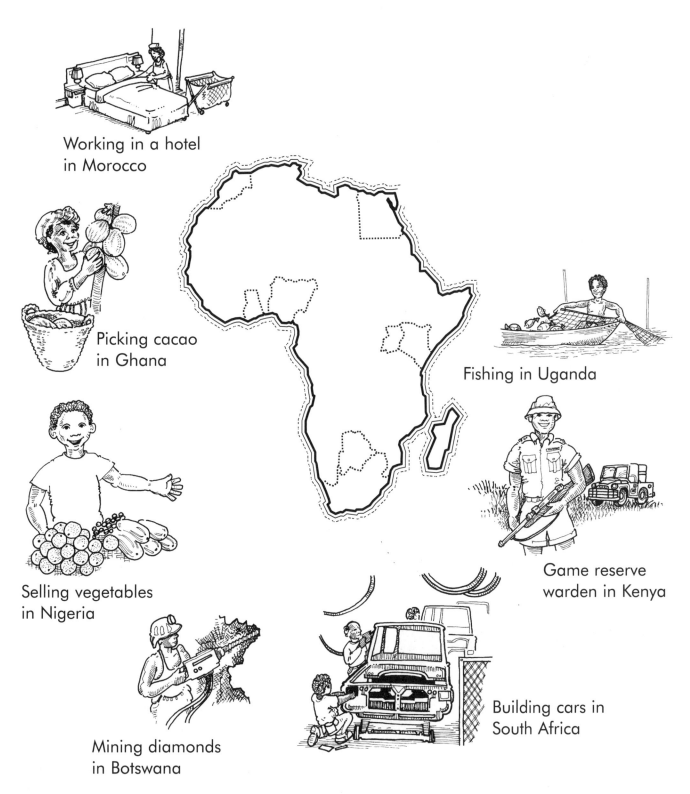

Working in a hotel in Morocco

Picking cacao in Ghana

Fishing in Uganda

Selling vegetables in Nigeria

Game reserve warden in Kenya

Mining diamonds in Botswana

Building cars in South Africa

Asia

Learning targets

On completion of this unit children should understand:

1 ➡➡ about the landscape, places and environment of Asia

2 ➡➡ the countries and key features of Asia

3 ➡➡ that many of the things we use come from places overseas

Before you start

Focus

This unit provides an overview of the physical, human and environmental features of Asia.

Background information

Asia stretches 9,000 kilometres from the Arctic in the north, to tropical islands south of the Equator. It is the largest of all the continents with over half the world's population and many great cities. However, it is so vast that many areas are almost completely empty. These include the mountains of Tibet, the plains of Siberia and the deserts of Arabia.

Asia has many environmental problems. In Russia, rapid industrialisation under Communism has led to massive pollution. Examples include the shrinking of the Aral Sea, the disaster at Chernobyl and scuppered nuclear submarines in the Arctic. Meanwhile, in South-East Asia, many valuable habitats have been lost through forest clearance. Tackling these problems is a major challenge, particularly for countries which are relatively poor.

Teaching points

Use this unit alongside photopacks and locality studies of specific places.

Progression

During the junior school years, children should develop an increasing knowledge of the continents and the wider world.

Vocabulary

civilisation, continent, desert, monsoon, plain, product, rainforest, religion, resources

Geographical skills

- Ability to read for information
- Making of a picture map
- Recognition of countries and continents

National Curriculum links

- Contrasting localities in Africa, Asia or South America
- Become aware of how places fit into a wider geographical context
- Use and interpret globes and maps and plans at a variety of scales

Assessment indicators

Children should be able to:

- name three countries in Asia
- describe the landscape and climate of Asia
- explain one of the issues affecting the environment

Personal application

These statements highlight the relevance of the children's learning:

- I know that children in Asia do many of the same things we do in the UK
- I understand that people have to work all over the world
- I can use atlases, books and ICT to find out more about distant places

Teaching the lessons

Lesson 1 ❶

Key question

What is Asia like?

Introduction ⟨10 min⟩

▓ Use a globe or atlas to find Asia and discuss some of its key features. The following questions and answers are appropriate.

Which are the largest countries in Asia? (Russia, China and India.)

Which countries in south and east Asia are made up of islands? (Indonesia, Philippines, Japan, Sri Lanka.)

How long are the Himalayas? (About 2,000 kilometres.)

Which are the main rivers? (Ganges, Indus, Chang Jiang, Huang He, Lena.)

Using the information sheet ⟨40 min⟩

▓ **Copymaster 77 What is Asia like?** is divided into sections with thematic headings to make it easier to follow. You might ask the children to find the places and features mentioned on a map.

Differentiate by making a class list of key facts for less-able children to copy into their books. Add the headings 'Weather', 'History' and 'Countries' to the fact file for more-able children.

Summary 5 min

Compare the answers that children have given to Question 1.

Homework

Ask the children to make up an acrostic with the names of twelve Asian countries or cities concealed within it.

Lesson 2 ②

Key question

How can you make a picture map of Asia?

Introduction 10 min

Remind the children about the key features of Asia from the previous lesson. The following questions and answers are appropriate.

What different landscapes are there in Asia? (Desert in Arabia and Gobi, mountains in Tibet, rainforest in South-East Asia, coniferous forest in Russia and tundra in northern Siberia.)

Where did the world's first civilisations begin? (In India, China and the Middle East.)

Using the activity sheet 40 min

On **Copymaster 78 Asia map**, check that the children can distinguish between land and sea on the map. The drawings show a mixture of landscape and built features reflecting the character of the continent.

Differentiate by enlarging Copymaster 78 to A3 size to make it easier for children to handle. Ask more-able pupils to add four drawings of their own.

Summary 5 min

Discuss which country or place the children would most like to visit and why.

Lesson 3 ③

Key question

What products come from Asia?

Introduction 10 min

Make up a word search containing the names of these six countries – China, Japan, India, Russia, Turkey, Saudi Arabia. Divide the children into groups and ask them to find the names.

Investigation 30 min

Ask the children to name and draw all the things they can think of which come from these different

countries. It is helpful if you can provide reference books and other sources of information.

China	Japan	Russia	India	Turkey	Saudi Arabia
Rice	Cars	Spaceships	Tea	Carpets	Oil
Silk clothes	Radios	Satellites	Jewels	Apricots	Dates
Shoes	Televisions	Binoculars	Cotton	Tomatoes	Spices
Toys	Computers	Timber	Films	Clothes	Camels

Differentiate by encouraging less-able children to focus on a couple of countries such as Japan and India. Fast-learning children could use their drawings to make a 'products' picture map.

Summary 5 min

Compare the results from different groups and identify some of the products in the classroom which come from the countries studied.

Extra activities ① ② ③

Travel poster

Tell the children to make a travel poster for one of the countries or areas of Asia which they would like to visit.

Visitors

Arrange for someone from Asia (parent or friend) to visit the class to talk about their country. Ask them to bring pictures, music, clothes and other details of daily life so that they will be able to answer the children's questions.

Celebrations

Find out more about the religions and customs of Asia. For example, Muslims make a pilgrimage to Mecca each year during Ramadan and the Chinese celebrate the New Year at a different time to us. There are natural opportunities here for links with art and RE.

177

What is Asia like?

Landscape

Asia is the largest continent. It has many of the world's highest mountains and longest rivers. The peaks of the Himalayas stretch for 3,000 km between India and China. From here, water flows to the sea down the Indus, Ganges, Chang Jiang and other rivers.

People

The great religions of the world began in Asia, along with the first civilisations. Over half the world's population lives on this continent. The most crowded parts are in the south and east. Here, many people depend on the monsoon rains to grow crops of rice each year.

Cities

There are many large cities in Asia. Tokyo, Bombay and Beijing are three of the most important. However, other parts of Asia are almost completely empty. These include the mountains of Tibet, the plains of Siberia and the Gobi desert. The harsh weather makes it difficult for people to live in these areas.

Resources

Asia is so vast that it has many resources. Saudi Arabia and the countries of the Middle East are famous for oil. Tin comes from South-East Asia. Iron, coal, gold and diamonds are found in Russia.

Work

In Japan, there are lots of factories, banks and offices. India and China make clothes from cotton. Tourists also come from all over the world to visit the old cities and temples.

Issues

In Indonesia and other parts of South-East Asia, the rainforests are being cut down for wood and to make farmland. In Russia, there is serious pollution from factories. All over Asia, cities are growing larger and larger.

Things to do

1 Write down three things about Asia which you would like to remember.

2 Make a 'word picture' of Asia using five adjectives and the nouns they describe. Start with 'largest continent'.

3 Make a fact file about Asia using these headings: landscape, people, cities, resources, work and issues.

Asia fact file

Mountain ranges	Himalayas (Mt Everest)
Main rivers	Indus, Ganges, Chang Jiang, Huang He
Main deserts	Gobi, Arabian
Chief countries	Russia, China, India, Japan, Iran, Indonesia
Main cities	Tokyo, Beijing, Jakarta, Bombay, Bangkok

Asia map

1. Colour and cut out the pictures.
2. Fix them in the correct places on the map.

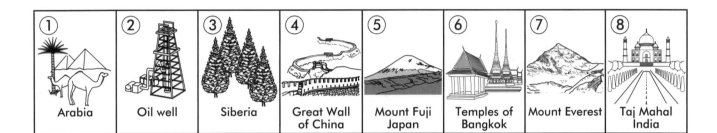

| ① Arabia | ② Oil well | ③ Siberia | ④ Great Wall of China | ⑤ Mount Fuji Japan | ⑥ Temples of Bangkok | ⑦ Mount Everest | ⑧ Taj Mahal India |

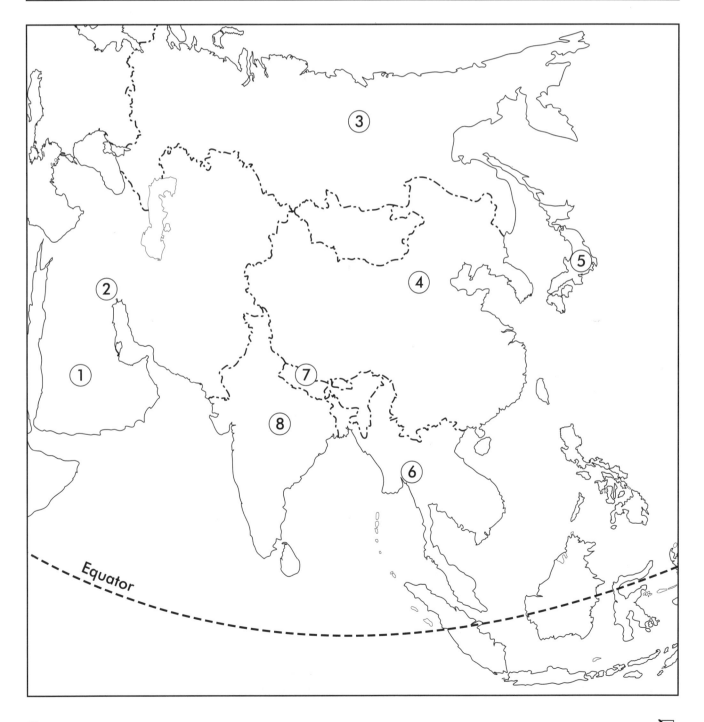

Equator

South America

Learning targets

On completion of this unit children should understand that:

1 ➡→ Brazil is a country with its own character and traditions
2 ➡→ the Amazon and Andes are key physical features of South America
3 ➡→ South America has many different weather conditions

Before you start

Focus

This unit provides an overview of South America and highlights Brazil, South America's largest country.

Background information

South America stretches southwards from North America to Antarctica. The Andes form the spine of the continent with snowy peaks over 6,000 metres high. The hot, steamy rainforests of the Amazon spread out to the east. Here, heavy convectional rain causes luxuriant plant growth and has created one of the world's most valuable habitats. On the other side of the Andes, offshore winds have produced desert conditions. The Atacama Desert in Chile is one of the driest places on Earth. It is also rich in minerals.

As well as forests, there are great areas of grassland in South America. These include the llanos of Venezuela and the pampas of Argentina. On the east coast, coffee, bananas and sugar cane are grown as cash crops. This is also the most populated area. Rio de Janeiro, São Paulo and Buenos Aires are some of the world's biggest cities and they are expanding rapidly.

Teaching points

This unit links with work on the Amazon rainforest and weather around the world.

Progression

The children may already have some rudimentary ideas about South America. This unit expands and develops them.

Vocabulary

Amazon, Andes, Brazil, carnival, cross-section, desert, Equator, hurricane, rainforest

Geographical skills

• Use of artefacts as sources of information
• Use of cross-sections
• Making of a geographical model

National Curriculum links

• Contrasting localities in Africa, Asia or South America
• Use secondary sources of information
• Weather conditions in different parts of the world

Assessment indicators

Children should be able to:
• identify Brazil on a map of the world
• name three features or places in South America
• describe some of the different weather conditions in South America

Personal application

These statements highlight the relevance of the children's learning:
• I can use artefacts as a source of information
• I understand that cross-sections are a way of conveying ideas
• I realise that continents are very large

Teaching the lessons

Lesson 1 ❶

Key question

What is Brazil like?

Introduction ⌷10min⌷

▦ Locate Brazil on a globe or atlas map and talk about it with the children. The following questions and answers are appropriate.

Which continent does Brazil belong to? (South America.)

How many countries surround it? (Ten – Brazil occupies half the land area of South America.)

What is the capital of Brazil? (Brasilia – São Paulo is the largest city.)

Does the Equator pass through Brazil? (Yes, it passes through the mouth of the Amazon.)

Using the information sheet ⌷30min⌷

▦ **Copymaster 79 Brazil** shows how artefacts can be used as geographical clues: coffee beans – Brazil has a tropical climate; football trophy – many Brazilians are avid football fans; carnival mask – Brazil has its own customs and ceremonies; Brazil nuts – Brazil has forest trees; map – Brazil occupies the eastern half of South America; postcard – Brazil has great cities; guitar – music is part of the culture of Brazil; cloth – Brazil has groups of tribal people.

Differentiate by talking about Question 1 with less-able children and write the answers on the board. Challenge more-able children to devise questions they would like to investigate about each artefact. For example, they might want to find out where the coffee beans grow or when carnivals are held.

Summary   `5min`

Ask the children, if they could choose only two artefacts to tell people about Brazil, which two would they choose and why?

Homework

Ask the children to make up a quiz with six questions about Brazil.

Lesson 2   ②

Key question

What are the main physical features of South America?

Introduction   `10min`

In this lesson, the children make a model showing an east–west cross-section of South America from the mouth of the Amazon to Lima in Peru. Discuss the idea of a cross-section before you begin. Practical examples include slicing through an apple or lump of Plasticine® or studying the growth rings on a log.

Using the activity sheet   `40min`

It is important that the children colour the drawings on **Copymaster 80 South America model** before they start to make the model. They need to fold and cut as accurately as possible.

Differentiate by enlarging the sheet to A3 size, where necessary, so it is easier to make the model. More-able children could write a description of a journey across South America to go with their models.

Summary   `5min`

Ask the children what they might see if they travelled across South America from the west coast to the east coast.

Lesson 3   ③

Key question

What different types of weather are found in South America?

Introduction   `10min`

Remind the children how weather varies from place to place.

Investigation   `45min`

Tell children that they are going to make a map of South America showing the following weather conditions: rain and strong winds at Cape Horn, snow on Aconcagua, thunderstorms on the Amazon, hot and dry weather in north-east Brazil, a hurricane in the Caribbean Sea, showers at Rio de Janeiro. Ask them to make symbols on small squares of paper and fix them to the correct places on a map.

Differentiate by providing less-able children with symbols to copy from the board. With more-able children, each group could adopt a city to study for a period of a week and find out actual weather conditions from daily reports in the broadsheet newspapers.

Summary   `5min`

Discuss why different places have different weather conditions. The heat of the sun at the Equator, the effect of altitude and the direction of the wind (onshore or offshore) should feature in the children's answers.

Extra activities

Locality study

Make a study of a specific place and family in South America. There are prepared teaching packs on Rio de Janeiro, Lima and villages in Peru as well as more thematic material on the Amazon.

Country study

Select a single South American country and find out more about it. Peru is an interesting choice because of its varied geography and its links with the Incas.

Brazil is the largest country in South America. In the north, the River Amazon flows for thousands of kilometres through thick rainforests. Further south, there are grasslands and low mountains. There are also big cities with lots of cars and factories.

Maria Santos works for the tourist office of Brazil. She visits schools in Britain to tell children about her country. She sets up displays for pupils to look at. Each item is a different clue to the way of life. At the end of her talk, she plays some music which is very exciting.

Things to do

1 Choose five things from Maria's display. What does each one tell you about Brazil?

2 Draw a table. Show all the items displayed on the table with labels.

3 What six things would you put in a display to tell children in Brazil about the UK?

A bag of coffee beans

A map of Brazil

A football trophy

A postcard of Rio de Janeiro

A carnival mask

A guitar

A box of Brazil nuts

A strip of cloth with traditional patterns

South America model

1. Colour the drawings of the Amazon, Andes and rocky desert.

2. Carefully cut out the model along the solid lines.

3. Fold carefully along the dotted lines.

4. Glue down the flaps.

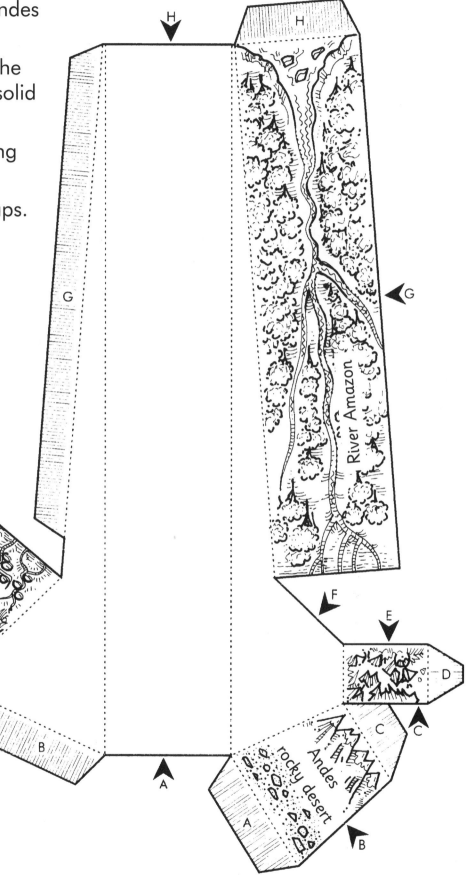

BIBLIOGRAPHY

Baldwin, H and M Opie 'Child's Eye View of Cities' in *Primary Geographer* No. 26 (1996), pp 16–17

Bartlett, D 'Using the school grounds' in *Primary Sources*, S Scoffham (Ed), Geographical Association (1998), pp 22–23

Bowles, R 'How well do you know your locality?' in *Primary Geographer* No. 23 (1995), pp16–18

Bridge, C 'The Way Ahead' in *Primary Sources*, S Scoffham (Ed), Geographical Association (1998)

Chambers, B 'Children's ideas about the environment' in *Primary Sources*, S Scoffham (Ed), Geographical Association (1998), pp 30–31

Fisher, S and D Hicks *World studies 8–13*, Oliver and Boyd (1985)

Green, J *Children's perceptions of gender stereotypes in the workplace*, unpublished student study, Canterbury Christ Church College (1994)

Halocha, J 'The European Dimension' in *Primary Sources*, S Scoffham (Ed), Geographical Association (1998)

Hart, R *Children's Experience of Place*, Irvington (1979)

Harwood, D and J McShane 'Young children's understanding of nested hierarchies of place relationship' in *International Research in Geographical and Environmental Education* 5, 1 (1996), pp 3–29

Mackintosh, M 'Learning from photographs' in *Primary Sources*, S Scoffham (Ed), Geographical Association (1998), pp 18–19

Matthews, M 'Environmental Cognition of Young Children', *Transactions of the Institute of British Geographers* 9 (1984), pp 89–105

Matthews, M *Making Sense of Place*, Harvester Wheatsheaf (1992)

May, T 'Children's Ideas about Rivers' in *Primary Geographer* No. 25 (1996), pp 12–13

Milburn, D 'Children's Vocabulary' in *New Movements in the Study and Teaching of Geography*, N Graves (Ed) Temple Smith (1974), pp 107–120

Moyle, R 'Weather' A working paper of the Learning in Science project, University of Waikato, New Zealand (1980)

Nussbaum, J 'The earth as a cosmic body' in *Children's Ideas in Science*, R Driver, E Guesne and A Tiberghein (Eds) Open University Press (1985), pp 170–192

Palmer, J 'Environmental cognition in young children' in *Primary Sources*, S Scoffham (Ed), Geographical Association (1998), pp 32–33

Piaget, J *The Child's Conception of the World*, Routledge & Kegan Paul (1929)

QCA *Maintaining breadth and balance at KS1 and KS2*, QCA (1998)

Qualter, A et al 'The greenhouse effect; what do primary children think? in *Education 3–13* No. 23, 2 (1995), pp 28–31

Scoffham, S *Using the school's surroundings*, Ward Lock Educational (1980)

Scoffham, S 'Children as young geographers' in *Primary Geography Handbook*, R Carter (Ed), Geographical Association (1998)

Smith, P 'Standards Achieved: a review of geography in primary schools in England, 1995/6' in *Primary Geographer* No. 31 (1997)

Wiegand, P 'Does travel Broaden the Mind?' in *Education 3–13* (1991), pp 54–58

Wiegand, P 'The known world of the primary school' in *Geography* 76 No. 2 (1991), pp 143–9

Wiegand, P *Children and Primary Geography*, Cassell (1993)